MEDIA STUDIES:
THE ESSENTIAL RESOURCE

Philip Rayner, Peter Wall and Stephen Kruger

Routledge
Taylor & Francis Group

LONDON AND NEW YORK

First published 2004
by Routledge
11 New Fetter Lane, London EC4P 4EE

Simultaneously published in the USA and Canada
by Routledge
29 West 35th Street, New York, NY 10001

Routledge is an imprint of the Taylor & Francis Group

Typeset in Bell Gothic and Novarese by
Keystroke, Jacaranda Lodge, Wolverhampton
Printed and bound in great Britain by
TJ International Ltd, Padstow, Cornwall

British Library Cataloguing in Publication Data
A catalogue record for this book is available from the British Library

Library of Congress Cataloging in Publication Data
A catalog record for this book has been requested

ISBN 0–415–29172–0 (hbk)
ISBN 0–415–29173–9 (pbk)

▼ CONTENTS

▼ ACKNOWLEDGEMENTS

We are grateful to copyright holders for permission to reproduce extracts from the following articles and publications:

Frith, S., 'The Value Problem in Cultural Studies', in S. Frith, *Performing Rites: On the Value of Popular Music* (Oxford: Oxford University Press, 1996), pp. 3–6. Reproduced by permission of Oxford University Press.

Gauntlett, D., from 'Web Studies: A User's Guide' in *Web Studies: Rewiring Media Studies for the Digital Age* (London: Arnold, 2000), pp. 31–2.

Seiter, E., from 'Semiotics, Structuralism and Television' in R. Allen (ed.), *Channels of Discourse Reassembled* (London: Routledge, 1992), pp. 126–8.

Monaco, J., 'The Language of Film: Signs and Syntax', in J. Monaco, *How to Read a Film: the Art, Technology, Language, History and Theory of Film and Media,* 3rd edn (New York: Oxford University Press), pp. 126–8. © 1977, 1981, 2000 James Monaco. Reproduced by permission of Oxford University Press Inc.

Fiske, J., *An Introduction to Communication Studies,* 2nd edn (London: Routledge, 1990), pp. 90–5.

Dyer, G., 'Semiotics and Ideology', in G. Dyer, *Advertising as Communication* (London: Routledge, 1982), pp. 124–6.

Scannell, P., 'Blind Date and the Phenomenology of Fun' in R. Lorimer and P. Scannell (eds), *Mass Communications: a Comparative Introduction.* (Manchester: Manchester University Press, 1994), pp. 284–6. © Paddy Scannell.

Davies, S., 'Semiotic Analysis of Teenage Magazine Covers', available online at www.aber.ac.uk/media/students/sid9901.html.

Tilley, A.C., 'Narrative', in D. Lusted (ed.), *Media Studies Book: A Guide for Teachers* (London: Routledge, 1991), pp. 61–6.

Bordwell, D. and Thompson, K., 'Narrative as a Formal System' in D. Bordwell and K. Thompson, *Film Art: An Introduction* (McGraw-Hill, 1990), pp. 58–9. Reproduced by permission of McGraw-Hill Education.

Hutchings, P., 'Genre Theory and Criticism', in J. Hollows and M. Jancovich (eds), *Approaches to Popular Film* (Manchester: Manchester University Press, 1995), pp. 68–71. Reproduced by permission of Manchester University Press.

'Television by Numbers', *Guardian*, 19 November 2001, p. 7, section G2. © *The Guardian*.

Glaessner, V., 'Gendered Fictions', in A. Goodwin and G. Whannel (eds), *Understanding Television* (London: Routledge, 1990), pp. 118–25.

Whitehorn, K., 'Same Old Story', *Guardian*, 1 December 2000. © *The Guardian*.

Blaikie, A., 'Altered Images', *Ageing and Popular Culture* (Cambridge: Cambridge University Press, 1998), pp. 98–100.

Abercrombie, N., 'Realism', in N. Abercrombie, *Television and Society* (Cambridge: Polity Press, 1996), pp. 26–30. Reproduced by permission of Blackwell Publishing.

Roscoe, J. and Hight, C., *Faking It: Mock-documentary and the Subversion of Factuality* (Manchester: Manchester University Press, 2001), pp. 36–40. Reproduced by permission of Manchester University Press.

www.Nickbroomfield.com webpage, featuring a still from *Behind the Rent Strike*, dir. Nick Broomfield, Lafayette Films, 1979.

London Metro newspaper front page, 21 March 2002.

Gibson, O., 'Channel 4 Takes Full Responsibility', *Guardian*, 20 March 2002 © *The Guardian*.

'The Look of Love', Peugeot advertisement. Reproduced by permission of Peugeot (please note that the offers in this advertisement are no longer valid).

Taylor, L. and Willis, A., *Media Studies: Texts, Institutions and Audiences* (Oxford: Blackwell, 1999), pp. 84–7. Reproduced by permission of Blackwell Publishing.

The Sun, London. © NI Syndication Limited, 5 May 2001.

50s Housewives advertisements courtesy of The Advertising Archives.

Fiske, J., 'Ideology and Meaning', in J. Fiske, *Introduction to Communication Studies* (London: Routledge, 2nd edn 1990), pp. 172–8.

Dyer, G., 'Conclusion', in G. Dyer, *Advertising as Communication* (London: Routledge, 1982), pp. 183–7.

Klein, N., *No Logo* (London: Flamingo, 2001), pp. 20–1. Reproduced by permission of HarperCollins Publishers Ltd. © Naomi Klein, 2001.

Hall, S., 'Encoding Decoding' in S. Hall *et al.* (eds), *Culture. Media. Language. Working Papers in Cultural Studies* (London: Hutchinson, 1980), p. 130.

Bell, A., Joyce, M. and Rivers, D., *Advanced Level Media Studies* (London: Hodder & Stoughton, 1999), p. 21.

Stevenson, N., 'Critical Perspectives within Audience Research' in T. O'Sullivan and Y. Jewkes (eds), *The Media Studies Reader* (London: Arnold, 1997), p. 235.

Extract from BARB website (www.barb.co.uk). Reproduced by permission of BARB.

Wakefield Express readership survey, JICREG website. Reproduced by permission of JICREG.

Lull, J., 'How Families Select Programs', in J. Lull, *Inside Television* (London: Routledge, 1990), pp. 88–9.

Moores, S., *Interpreting Audiences* (London: Sage, 1993), pp. 124–9. Reproduced by permission of Sage Publications.

TV & Satellite Week, 7–13 December 2002, p. 58. Reproduced by permission of the publishers, IPC Media.

Gauntlett D., 'Ten Things Wrong with the Effects Theory' available online at *www.theory.org.uk/effects.* Reproduced by permission of the author.

Barker, M., 'Critique: Audiences 'Я' Us', in R. Dickinson, R. Harindranath and O. Linné (eds), *Approaches to Audiences* (London: Arnold, 1998), pp. 184–7.

Rushdie, S., 'Reality TV: a Dearth of Talent and the Death of Morality', *Guardian,* 9 June 2001. © Salman Rushdie.

Greer, G., 'Watch with Brother', *The Observer,* 24 June 2001. Copyright © Germaine Greer.

Plunkett, J., 'Reality TV Shows Scoop Viewers' Choice Awards', *Guardian,* 16 October 2002. © *The Guardian.*

Bazalgette, P., 'It's Only a Gameshow', *Guardian,* 6 September 2000. © Peter Bazalgette.

Tasker, Y., 'Action Heroines in the 1980s', in Y. Tasker, *Spectacular Bodies: Gender, Genre and the Action Cinema* (London: Routledge, 1993), pp. 134–9.

Gabb, Jacqui, from 'Consuming the Garden: Locating a Feminine Narrative' in J. Stokes and A. Reading (eds), *The Media in Britain: Current Debates and Developments* (Macmillan, 1999).

Johnson, C., 'Buffy the Vampire Slayer' in G. Creeber (ed.), *The Television Genre Book* (London: BFI, 2001), p. 45.

Hanks, Robert, 'Deconstructing *Buffy',* *The Independent,* 1 July 2002. © *The Independent.*

Hill, A. and Calcutt, I., 'Vampire Hunters: The Scheduling and Reception of *Buffy the Vampire Slayer* and *Angel* in the UK' from www.cult-media.com. This material was originally published in *Intensities: the Journal of Cult Media.*

www.bbc.co.uk/cult/buffy/index.html

Dootson, W., 'I Will Remember You' from *www.immortalbliss.co.uk/lca/.*

Lister, D., 'Why We Should Be Worrying about the PCC', *Independent*, 5 February 2002. © *The Independent*.

HRH Prince Charles, Speech on the 300th Anniversary of the National Daily Press printed in *The Independent*, 12 March 2002. © *The Independent*.

Steve Bell cartoon in the *Guardian*, 12 March 2002. Reproduced by permission of the artist.

Allan, S., 'The Textuality of Television News', *News Culture* (Open University Press, 1999), pp. 991–1002.

Wells, M., 'TV Watchdog Attacks News Budget Cuts', *Guardian*, 6 March 2002. © *The Guardian*.

'"Quality" of News' table, reproduced in *Media Guardian*, 19 November 2001 (source data: University of Westminster).

Morrow, F., 'Dumb and Dumber?', *MediaWatch 2000* (London: BFI *Sight and Sound*, 2000), p. 22.

Harcup, T., 'What is News? Galtung & Ruge Revisited', *UK Press Gazette*, 4 May 2001. © Tony Harcup. Reproduced by permission of the author.

'Journalists at Work' from the Campaign for Press and Broadcasting Freedom website (www.cpbf.org.uk). Reproduced courtesy of the Campaign for Press and Broadcasting Freedom.

Michaels, K. and Mitchell, C., 'The Last Bastion: How Women Became Music Presenters in UK Radio', in C. Mitchell (ed.), *Women and Radio* (London: Routledge, 2000).

Van Zoonen, L., 'One of the Girls? The Changing Gender of Journalism', in C. Carter, G. Branston and S. Allen (eds), *News, Gender and Power* (London: Routledge, 2000), pp. 35–8.

O'Sullivan, T., Dutton, B. and Rayner, P. (eds), 'Professional Autonomy' from T. O'Sullivan, B. Dutton and P. Rayner (eds), *Studying the Media* (London: Arnold, 1998), pp. 168–9.

Murdoch, R., 'Freedom in Broadcasting', MacTaggart Memorial Lecture 1989. © Rupert Murdoch. Reproduced in B. Franklin (ed.), *British Television Policy: A Reader*, Routledge, pp. 38–40.

Potter, Dennis, 'Defending Public Service Broadcasting from "Occupying Powers"' MacTaggart Memorial Lecture 1993. © Dennis Potter. Reproduced in B. Franklin (ed.), *British Television Policy: A Reader*, Routledge, pp. 41–2

Dyke, G., 'Maintaining the Gold Standard', MacTaggart Memorial Lecture, 2000. © Greg Dyke. Reproduced in B. Franklin (ed.), *British Television Policy: A Reader*, Routledge, pp. 109–10.

BBC4 leaflet, reproduced courtesy of Mind the Gap Marketing Communications Ltd.

'What's in the Freeview Package?', *Radio Times*, 26 October–1 November 2002, p. 14.

'What Makes Auntie's New Digital TV Channel, BBC Three, So Different?', *London Metro*, 10 February 2003, p. 23.

Lister, M., Dovey, J., Giddings, S. and Grant, I., *New Media: Critical Introduction* (London: Routledge, 2003), pp. 30–1.

Winston, B., 'Why Picture Messaging Won't Take Off', *The New Humanist*, Winter 2003. Reproduced courtesy of the author and *The New Humanist* (www.newhumanist.org.uk).

'Sound & Vision, Digital Equipment', *Satellite TV Europe*, January 2003, p. 214.

Cox, A., 'Why We Should Join in an Attack on the Digital Clones Debate', *Guardian*, 27 May 2002, p. 22. © *The Guardian*.

Sullivan, C., 'Robbie's £80m Deal Puts EMI on New Path', *Guardian*, 5 October 2002. © *The Guardian*.

Cope, N., 'Metal and Rap put Vivendi Universal at Top of the Pops', *Independent*, 19 February 2002. © *The Independent*.

'Piracy Blamed for CD Slide', BBC Online News, 27 August 2002. Reproduced courtesy of the BBC.

Redmond, S., *Interpreting Institutions* (London: Auteur, 2001).

Barker, C., *Television, Globalization and Cultural Identities* (Buckingham: Open University Press, 1999), pp. 45–51. Reproduced by permission of the Open University Press.

Hebdige, D., *Hiding in the Light: On Images and Things* (London: Comedia, 1988), pp. 181–2.

Strinati, D., 'Postmodernism and Popular Culture', *Introduction to Theories of Popular Culture* (London: Routledge, 1995), pp. 223–8.

Channel 4, 'Who Are You?' publicity flyer.

▼ INTRODUCTION: WHY MEDIA STUDIES?

Media Studies is a relatively young academic discipline when it is compared to English, Modern Languages, Classics or History. Despite, or perhaps because of, its rapid development throughout the education system, both in schools and in higher education, it still finds the need to justify itself in a way in which more established disciplines do not.

In addition to the relatively late arrival of Media Studies on the academic scene, we also need to bear in mind that media are readily accessible to and consumed by all of us, unlike for example classic novels and Renaissance drama. This very familiarity, and some would say mundanity, of the subject matter that constitutes a study of the media may well militate against its being taken seriously. Famously dismissed by one Secretary for Education as a 'cultural Disneyland', Media Studies feels obliged to spend some time justifying itself as a viable part of the academic establishment.

Another important issue confronting a student of the media is that the discipline itself is in a state of flux. Although a relative newcomer on the academic scene, many of the ideas and theories that have been used to underpin Media Studies during its rapid growth are themselves being questioned. The following extracts provide an interesting contrast which may help illustrate some of the issues that are under debate.

In the first extract, Simon Frith, Professor of Film and Media at the University of Stirling, writes about the significance of popular culture and identifies for us some of the ways in which he feels studying it can be a valuable and worthwhile experience. One of the things you may find interesting about the extract is the accessible way in which it is written. Other than the word 'dialectic', there is little terminology that is not readily understood by a well-informed lay reader. Indeed ,the style is in many ways quite conversational and journalistic in contrast to the rather more serious approach common in academic essays.

At the centre of Frith's argument is the key issue of how values are transmitted through popular culture. Media Studies, and related disciplines such as Film and Cultural Studies, provide us with an important insight into the value system of our society. Frith was one of the first academics to underscore the importance of studying mass cultural forms such as popular music as a way of gaining this insight.

Before you read the extract, write down a short paragraph explaining why you think a study of the media is important.

It was my third night in Stockholm, a very cold February night, and I'd gone to have supper with old friends, people I see maybe every two years, usually at conferences. There was one other guest, the professor in the department in which I was a visiting scholar, a man I hadn't met before. A few years older than I am, I'd guess . . . We talked, we ate, and about halfway through the main course, Johan said, 'Let me play it to you!' and jumped over to the CD player.

The rest of the evening was driven by the dialectic of liking things. We ate, we talked, and at least some of the time (this wasn't an obsessive boys' night in, rock critics pouring over the runes) we argued about music. As hosts, Johan Fornäs and Hillevi Ganetz had the advantage – they could illustrate their claims (why someone could or couldn't sing; why the Flesh Quartet were Sweden's most amusing band; why Eva Dahlgren's latest album was more interesting than it first sounded). I could only respond – 'Yeah that's really good' 'No, I don't like that at all' – and write down titles, and ask occasionally, 'Have you heard . . .? I must tape it for you.

A mundane and enjoyable evening, in short, not unlike Sunday evening suppers happening all over this and many other cities; and if the conversations elsewhere weren't necessarily about music they would almost certainly have been, at some point, about books or films or TV programs, about footballers or models or magazines. Such conversations are the common currency of friendship, and the essence of popular culture. We may have been a group of intellectuals, used to talking, to arguing publicly for our prejudices, but similar talk can be heard every day in bars and on buses, on football terraces and in school yards, as people wait at the hairdresser or take lunch in the office cafeteria, and have conversations about last night's TV, Take That's hit record, the new Clint Eastwood film, the latest headline in the *Sun*.

Part of the pleasure of popular culture is talking about it; part of its meaning is this talk, talk which is run though with value judgments. To be engaged with popular culture is to be discriminating, whether judging the merits of a football team's backs or an afternoon soap's plots. 'Good' and 'bad' or their vernacular versions ('brilliant,' 'crap') are the most frequent terms in everyday cultural conversation. To return to that Stockholm evening for a moment, two further features of our talk need noting. First, though all of us knew well enough that what was at issue was personal taste, subjective response, we also believed, passionately at times, that we were describing something objectively *in the music*, if only other people could hear it. Value arguments, in other words, aren't simply rituals of 'I like/you like' (which would quickly become tedious, even in *Metal Mania*); they are based in reason, evidence, persuasion. Every music fan knows that moment of frustration when one can only sit the person down and say (or, rather, shout) despairingly, 'But just listen to her! Isn't she fantastic!'

But if value judgments in popular culture make their own claims to objectivity (to being rooted, that is, in the quality of objects) their subjectivity can't be denied either – not, however, by banal reference to people having their own (essentially irrational) likes and dislikes, but because such judgments are taken to tell us something about the person making them. I was struck that evening in Sweden by how little the professor contributed to the talk about music (he talked engagingly about everything else), not, I think, because he was uninterested (I discovered later that he was a great jazz fan, a gifted amateur jazz pianist), nor because he didn't have things to say, but because he didn't really know me: he could not yet judge how an argument about music might affect the evening's good will.

In his pioneering sociological study of literary taste, Levin Schücking comments on the importance of books for the shifts in courtship rituals in late nineteenth-century Germany: 'Here, in reading together, the opportunity was gained of securing from the other's judgement of men and things an insight into thoughts and feelings; an insight likely to become the first bond between kindred souls.' And nowadays listening to music, watching television, and going to movies together serve similar functions. We assume that we can get to know someone through their tastes (eyeing someone's book and record shelves the first time we visit them, waiting nervously to see what a date says as we come out of a movie or a concert). Cultural judgments, in other words, aren't just subjective, they are self-revealing, and to become another person, to fake ourselves for whatever reason, means having to pretend to like things in which we find nothing valuable at all – a problem, as Pierre Bourdieu points out, for people attempting to *buy* cultural capital, and a secret shame, as Frank Kogan suggests, for those of us who have ever tried to impress new friends.

The point is not that we want friends or lovers just like us; but we do need to know that conversation, argument, is possible. In the pop world this is most obvious to musicians, who have to get along well enough to play together, who have to balance the creative/destructive effects of shared and different tastes, and who conduct the delicate business of coming together (and falling apart) almost entirely through stated pop judgments:

> Me and Graham thought that King was terrible but The Three Johns were great; we go down the pub and Malc and Chris thought King was great and hated The Three Johns – that said it all really so we split up.

> We were into bands like Bryan Adams and King, whilst Clint and Ad were into The Three Johns and The Shop Assistants. It was just no good.

As Pat Kane (from Hue and Cry) concludes:

> Everybody has a theory of pop – not least those who make it. Even the least self-conscious of artists can be jolted into an extended analysis of 'what's

good about rock'n'roll,' if you trade the wrong reference with them. There is a real evaluative disdain when two musicians react opposingly to the same source. 'How can you love/hate Van Morrison/Lou Reed/Springsteen/Stevie Wonder/Kraftwerk? These people are/are not "great popular music." How can you say otherwise?' I have suffered (and inflicted) the worst aesthetic hauteur, as my opponent and I push each other to our fundamentalist positions. You are a rocker, I am a soulboy; you find solace in raw-throated guitar release, I am consoled by the bubbling symmetry of a Muscle Shoals rhythm section. Different planets, Kiddo.

For fans, whose musical values don't matter so much, or, rather, matter in different ways, with different consequences, trading pop judgments is a way to 'flirt and fight.' As Frank Kogan suggests, this means that for the pop listener (if not for the pop player) the stability of our judgments matters less than their constant deployment: as pop fans we continually change our minds about what is good or bad, relevant or irrelevant, 'awesome' or 'trivial' (our judgment in part determined by what happens to a sound in the marketplace, how successful it becomes, what other listeners it involves), but we never cease to believe that such distinctions are necessary 'social pressure points, gathering spots for a brawl over how we use our terms. If our comparisons stood still, how could we have our brawl?'

As I was leaving that supper party I got involved in a dispute about the Pet Shop Boys, which delayed me in the hall for another twenty minutes. 'But *you* like disco!' said Hillevi, in mock dismissal, as I left. I got back to my room and put on *Very*.

S. Frith, 'The Value Problem in Cultural Studies', in Performing Rites,
Evaluating Popular Music, Oxford University Press, 1996 pp. 3–6

ACTIVITIES

➤ Frith's main focus is on popular music. Make a list of the other sorts of 'cultural judgements' that people make. You might like to think about television, cinema, and the press to get you started.

➤ What do you think is meant by the phrase 'trading pop judgements is a way to "flirt and fight"'?

➤ Do you think we should take popular culture seriously?

In David Gauntlett's influential book, *Web Studies* (2000), the value of Media Studies as it exists as an academic discipline is put under close scrutiny. In his User's Guide to the book, Gauntlett argues that Media Studies at the end of the twentieth century had entered 'a middle-aged, stodgy period and wasn't sure what it should say about things any more'. For him Media Studies has arrived at a dead end in which its contribution to academic debates has become of doubtful value because it is starting to question what its function might be.

He makes a list a seven major points that he feels represent where Media Studies stood at the end of the last century. Each of these points covers a major concern of Media Studies, in such fields as textual analysis and audience studies. Gauntlett goes on to suggest that the media have become so sophisticated in analysing themselves that this makes academic study unnecessary. His argument is clearly a contentious and provocative one, but all is not doom and gloom.

'Thank goodness the Web came along.' For Gauntlett the Internet and New Media represent a new focus from Media Studies because it is 'exploding, vibrant and developing'. The Internet also allows academics to 'participate in the new media, not just watch from the sidelines'. But in Gauntlett's phrase, let's rewind to see what it is about contemporary Media Studies that he objects to.

MEDIA STUDIES WAS NEARLY DEAD: LONG LIVE NEW MEDIA STUDIES

By the end of the twentieth century, media studies research within developed western societies had entered a middle-aged, stodgy period and wasn't really sure what it could say about things any more. Thank goodness the Web came along. See where media studies had got to . . .

- Studies of media texts, such as a 'critical reading' of a film which identified a bunch of 'meanings' the director hadn't intended and which nobody else had noticed, were clearly a waste of time.
- Similarly, people had noticed that semiotic analysis and psychoanalytic approaches were all about saying that something had a hidden cause or meaning, but you couldn't prove it, so it became embarrassing.
- Audience studies had run out of steam. Unable to show that the media had a clear and identifiable impact upon people's behaviour, audience researchers had been trying to make some descriptions of how people *use* the media look interesting, with little success.
- The 1990s theoretical view that we had to consider media usage within the very broad context of everyday life had actually ruptured the impetus for research, since nobody could afford, or be bothered, to do such wide-scale, in-depth, qualitative research. And even if anyone did get all that data, it wasn't clear what they would have to do with it.
- Studies of media effects and influences had shown that the mass media do not have predictable effects on audiences. Nevertheless, the right-wing psychologists who argued (for reasons best known to themselves) that the mass media were responsible for the decline of western civilization seemed

CONTINUED

to be winning the argument (within the public sphere, anyway). Cue despair, resignation and boredom amongst researchers in this area.

- Historical studies of the mass media justified themselves by saying that we could learn from history when planning the future. But nobody ever did.

- Most importantly, media products and the organized use of communications technologies had become so knowing, clever and sophisticated that academic critics were looking increasingly redundant. In other words, media products, and their producers, had themselves become self-analysing and multilayered. It is difficult to say something about Tony Blair's clever use of political communications, for example, which is *more* clever, as a theory, than the actual practice. To make an intelligent film like *The Matrix* (Wachowski Brothers, 1999) or *Fight Club* (Fincher, 1999) is a substantial achievement, whereas writing a typical academic article about it is, in comparison, pathetic. Even mainstream TV shows like *Who Wants to be a Millionaire* (a UK format sold to numerous other countries) were already, in themselves, super-analysed dissections of the style and culture of populist TV. All academics could do was write obvious explanations of what the producers were up to (boring and ultimately sycophantic), or make predictable critiques of what such shows tell us about capitalist or postmodern society (which you could do in your sleep).

Media studies, then, needed something interesting to do, and fast. Happily, the area of new media is vibrant, exploding and developing, and nobody is certain of the best way to do things. There is change (look at how the Web was just three years ago) and there is conflict (look at the Microsoft trial and the impassioned feelings it provoked). New good ideas and new bad ideas appear every week, and we don't know how it's going to pan out. Even better, academics and students can *participate* in the new media explosion, not just watch from the sidelines – and we can argue that they have a responsibility to do so. So it's an exciting time again.

D. Gauntlett, 'Web Studies: A User's Guide', *Web Studies: Rewiring Media Studies for the Digital Age*, Arnold, 2000, pp. 31–2

ACTIVITY

➤ Consider each of the seven points made in the Gauntlett extract. For each one, decide precisely what he is attacking or dismissing. Do you think there is a counter-argument?

6

FURTHER READING

Frith, Simon (1988) *Music for Pleasure: Essays in the Sociology of Pop,* Routledge.
An interesting and stimulating book that explores popular music as a cultural form.

David Gauntlett's website: www.NewMediaStudies.com.
An opportunity to get up-to-date information and ideas about this approach to Media Studies.

PART 1: READING THE MEDIA

▼ 1 INTRODUCTION

Textual analysis is one of the cornerstones of Media Studies. But no matter how great the virtuosity demonstrated in analysing texts, this is rarely an end in itself. Textual analysis is a process by which we can both reveal the inner workings of a text and identify its significance in terms of the wider social and cultural issues to which it relates. For example, the analysis of an advertisement for a beauty product is rarely an end in itself. Its significance is more likely to lie in the way in which it reveals to us the underlying nature of gender relations within our culture. This significance may become more evident when we consider the cumulative effect of the many similar advertisements alongside which a particular text is situated. In fact, it is likely to be the cumulative impact of a group of related texts that reveals the ideological forces that are at play within each one individually.

In order to carry out a textual analysis, it is important to equip yourself with an effective toolkit. In this first part of the book we explore some of the tools that form this toolkit. Although we look at these individually, it is important to bear in mind that they are intended to be used in combination in order to unpack the meanings and functions that may be latent within a text. Nor should the impression be taken that any one tool may be more valuable than the others. The title of this part is 'Reading the Media'. The word 'reading' carries with it the connotation that texts are polysemic, or open to a range of interpretations. Part of the richness of textual analysis is that it allows the individual reader to interpret a text in light of their own experiences and cultural perspective.

In consequence, individual texts may require different approaches. Some text may best be tackled initially using genre theory, while others may reveal themselves by starting off with the application of image analysis. In an exam situation particularly, students should develop confidence in adopting their own individual approach, selecting the individual tools at their disposal according to the specific job in hand.

In organising this part of the book there is, however, an underlying logic. Image analysis is placed first because, given the visual nature of many media texts, it does provide a crucial insight into the working of sign systems which are essential to an understanding of the functioning of such texts. Ideology is placed last because it can be seen as the logical outcome of textual analysis. The ideological work of a media text helps reveal to us the

functioning of that text within broader social and cultural contexts. This is a key role played by textual analysis: to open our eyes to the value systems within our culture, signified by popular cultural forms such as media texts.

▼ 2 IMAGE ANALYSIS

A key item in a student's analytical toolkit is a grasp of semiotics. In order to explore the many visual signs that constitute media texts, it is important to have a grasp of semiotic analysis as well as a functional vocabulary of semiotic terms. However, it should be borne in mind that knowing the principles and the terminology is in itself of no great value. It is necessary to develop an awareness of the way in which semiotic analysis shows us how meaning is created. In other words, semiotics is a means of focusing on the underlying structure of sign systems enabling us to talk about how texts are constructed in order to make meaning. This underlying structure is concerned with how a sign can be seen as a combination of a *signifier*, the physical representation of a sign (such as a spoken or written word, or a symbol), and a *signified*, which is the mental concept or meaning conveyed by the signifier.

HOW IMAGE ANALYSIS WORKS

In the following extract, Ellen Seiter explains the significance of semiotics and structuralism in relation to television. She also provides a useful insight into the way in which semiotics has developed into the field of Cultural Studies.

Contemporary television criticism derives much of its vocabulary from semiotics and structuralism. This chapter will introduce the basic terminology of these methods, offer a case study of structuralist methods applied to children's television, and introduce some of the concepts the so-called post-structuralists have used to critique and expand upon semiotics and structuralism. The late Paddy Whannel used to joke, 'Semiotics tells us things we already know in a language we will never understand.' Learning the vocabulary of semiotics is certainly one of its most trying aspects. This vocabulary makes it possible, however, to identify and describe what makes TV distinctive as a communication medium, as well as how it relies on other sign systems to communicate. Both questions are vital to the practice of television criticism, and these terms will be encountered in a broad range of critical methods from psychoanalysis to cultural studies.

Semiotics is the study of everything that can be used for communication: words, images, traffic signs, flowers, music, medical symptoms, and much more. Semiotics studies the way such 'signs' communicate and the rules that govern their use. As a tool for the study of culture, semiotics represents a radical break from traditional criticism, in which the first order of business is the interpretation of an aesthetic object or text in terms of its immanent meaning. Semiotics first asks *how* meaning is created, rather than *what* the meaning is. In order to do this, semiotics uses a specialized vocabulary to describe signs and how they function. Often this vocabulary smacks of scientism to the newcomer and clashes with our assumptions about what criticism and the humanities are. But the special terminology of semiotics and its attempt to compare the production of meaning in a diverse set of mediums – aesthetic signs being only one of many objects of study – have allowed us to describe the workings of cultural communication with greater accuracy and enlarged our recognition of the conventions that characterize our culture.

The term *semiotics* was coined by Charles S. Peirce (1889–1914), an American philosopher, although his work on semiotics did not become widely known until the 1930s. The field was also 'invented' by Swiss linguist Ferdinand de Saussure. The term he used to describe the new science he advocated in *Course in General Linguistics*, published posthumously in 1959, was *semiology*. Structuralism is most closely associated with anthropologist Claude Lévi-Strauss, whose studies of the logic and worldview of 'primitive' cultures were first published in the 1950s. Although it relies on many of the principles of semiotics, structuralism engages larger questions of cultural meaning and ideology and thus has been widely used in literary and media criticism. Semiotics and structuralism are so closely related they may be said to overlap – semiotics being a field of study in itself, whereas structuralism is a method of analysis often used in semiotics.

Structuralism stresses that each element within a cultural system derives its meaning from its relationship to every other element in the system: there are no independent meanings, but rather many meanings produced by their difference from other elements in the system. Beginning in the 1960s, some leading European intellectuals applied semiotics and structuralism to many different sign systems. Roland Barthes carefully analyzed fashion, French popular culture from wrestling to wine drinking, and a novella by Balzac. Umberto Eco turned his attention to Superman comic strips and James Bond novels. Christian Metz set out to describe the style of Hollywood cinema as a semiotic system. By addressing the symbolic and communicative capacity of humans in general, semiotics and structuralism help us see connections between fields of study that are normally divided among different academic departments in the university. Thus they are specially suited to the study of television.

E. Seiter, 'Semiotics, Structuralism and Television', in R. Allen (ed.), *Channels of Discourse Reassembled*, Routledge, 1992, pp. 126–8

One of the important aspects of semiotics is the way in which it considers all sign systems rather than focusing solely on the use of written and spoken language. One of the reasons why the analysis of media texts is such a complex business is that they often combine both 'language' and an elaborate system of visual signs. The two then work together to create complex meanings which the television viewer or movie-goer is able to decode. It is of little surprise therefore that semiotics was rapidly appropriated by students of film in order to help with the analysis of their texts.

In his seminal book, *How to Read a Film*, James Monaco explores the relationship between 'language', in terms of written or spoken communication, and the way a film communicates its meaning to an audience. In the extract that follows, he explores the relationship between signifier and signified and makes the important point that whilst in language these two bear little relation to each other, in film they are almost identical. Film works by presenting us with a series of iconic signs which closely mimic the reality they represent.

The irony is that we know very well that we must learn to read before we can attempt to enjoy or understand literature, but we tend to believe, mistakenly, that anyone can read a film. Anyone can see a film, it's true, even cats. But some people have learned to comprehend visual images – physiologically, ethno-graphically, and psychologically – with far more sophistication than have others. This evidence confirms the validity of the triangle of perception uniting author, work, and observer. The observer is not simply a consumer, but an active – or potentially active – participant in the process.

Film is not a language, but is like a language, and since it is like language, some of the methods that we use to study language might profitably be applied to a study of film. In fact, during the last ten years this approach to film – essentially linguistic – has grown considerably in importance. Since film is not a language, strictly linguistic concepts are misleading. Ever since the beginning of film history, theorists have been fond of comparing film with verbal language (this was partly to justify the serious study of film), but it wasn't until a larger category of thought developed in the fifties and early sixties – one that saw written and spoken language as just two among many systems of communication – that the real study of film as a language could proceed. This inclusive category is semiology, the study of systems of signs. Semiologists justified the study of film as language by redefining the concept of written and spoken language. Any system of communication is a 'language'; English, French, or Chinese is a 'language system.' Cinema, therefore, may be a language of a sort, but it is not clearly a language system. As Christian Metz, the well-known film semiologist, pointed out: we understand a film not because we have a knowledge of its system, rather, we achieve an understanding of its system because we understand the film. Put another way, 'It is not because the cinema is language that it can tell such fine stories, but rather it has become language because it has told such fine stories' (Metz, *Film Language*, p. 47).

THE PONZO ILLUSION. The horizontal lines are of equal length, yet the line at the top appears to be longer than the line at the bottom. The diagonals suggest perspective, so that we interpret the picture in depth and conclude, therefore, that since the 'top' line must be 'behind' the 'bottom' line, further away, it must then be longer.

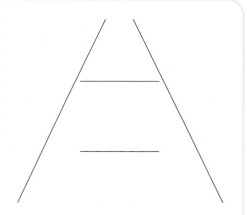

For semiologists, a sign must consist of two parts: the signifier and the signified. The word 'word,' for example – the collection of letters or sounds – is a signifier; what it represents is something else again – the 'signified.' In literature, the relationship between signifier and signified is a main locus of art: the poet is building constructions that, on the one hand, are composed of sounds (signifiers) and, on the other, of meanings (signifieds), and the relationship between the two can be fascinating. In fact, much of the pleasure of poetry lies just here: in the dance between sound and meaning.

But in film, the signifier and the signified are almost identical: the sign of cinema is a short-circuit sign. A picture of a book is much closer to a book, conceptually, than the word 'book' is. It's true that we may have to learn in infancy or early childhood to interpret the picture of a book as meaning a book, but this is a great deal easier than learning to interpret the letters or sounds of the word 'book' as what it signifies. A picture bears some direct relationship with what it signifies, a word seldom does.

It is the fact of this short-circuit sign that makes the language of film so difficult to discuss. As Metz put it, in a memorable phrase: 'A film is difficult to explain because it is easy to understand.' It also makes 'doing' film quite different from 'doing' English (either writing or speaking). We can't modify the signs of cinema the way we can modify the words of language systems. In cinema, an image of a rose is an image of a rose is an image of a rose – nothing more, nothing less. In English, a rose can be a rose, simply, but it can also be modified or confused with similar words: rose, rosy, rosier, rosiest, rise, risen, rows (ruse), arose, roselike, and so forth. The power of language systems is that there is a very great difference between the signifier and the signified; the power of film is that there is not.

Nevertheless film is *like* a language. How, then, does it do what is does? Clearly, one person's image of a certain object is not another's. If we both read the word

CONTINUED

'rose', you may perhaps think of a Peace rose you picked last summer, while I am thinking of the one Laura Westphal gave to me in December 1968. In cinema, however, we both see the same rose, while the filmmaker can choose from an infinite variety of roses and then photograph the one chosen in another infinite variety of ways. The artist's choice in cinema is without limit; the artist's choice in literature is circumscribed, while the reverse is true for the observer. Film does not suggest, in this context: it states. And therein lies its power and the danger it poses to the observer: the reason why it is useful, even vital, to learn to read images well so that the observer can seize some of the power of the medium. The better one reads an image, the more one understands it, the more power one has over it. The reader of a page invents the image, the reader of a film does not, yet both readers must work to interpret the signs they perceive in order to complete the process of intellection. The more work they do, the better the balance between observer and creator in the process; the better the balance, the more vital and resonant the work of art.

J. Monaco, *How to Read a Film: the Art, Technology, Language, History and Theory of Film and Media*, 1970, 3rd edn, Oxford University Press, pp. 126–8

At the core of much semiotic theory is the idea that the meaning generated by a text is not some fixed entity common to all of us. Texts are by their very nature polysemic or capable of multiple interpretations. How a text is interpreted is largely determined by the cultural experiences that a reader bring sto it. A key figure in the development of this concept was Roland Barthes. Barthes wrote about the orders of signification. In his book *Introduction to Communication Studies,* John Fiske explains these orders of signification by exploring the way in which denotation and connotation are central to the way in which we interpret or read a text.

DENOTATION

The first order of signification is the one on which Saussure worked. It describes the relationship between the signifier and signified within the sign, and of the sign with its referent in external reality. Barthes refers to this order as denotation. This refers to the commonsense, obvious meaning of the sign. A photograph of a street scene denotes that particular street; the word 'street' denotes an urban road lined with buildings. But I can photograph this same street in significantly different ways. I can use a colour film, pick a day of pale sunshine, use a soft focus and make the street appear a happy, warm, humane community for the children playing in it. Or I can use black and white film, hard focus, strong contrasts and make this same street appear cold, inhuman, inhospitable and a destructive environment for the children playing in it. Those two photographs could have been taken at an identical moment with the cameras held with their lenses only centimetres apart. Their denotative meanings would be the same. The difference would be in their connotation.

CONNOTATION

Basic concept

Connotation is the term Barthes uses to describe one of the three ways in which signs work on the second order of signification. It describes the interaction that occurs when the sign meets the feelings or emotions of the user and the values of his culture. This is when meanings move towards the subjective, or at least the intersubjective: it is when the interpretant is influenced as much by the interpreter as by the object or the sign.

For Barthes, the critical factor in connotation is the signifier in the first order. The first-order signifier is the sign of the connotation. Our imaginary photographs are both of the same street: the difference between them lies in the form, the appearance of the photograph, that is, in the signifier. Barthes (1977) argues that in photography at least, the difference between connotation and denotation is clear. Denotation is the mechanical reproduction on film of the object at which the camera is pointed. Connotation is the human part of the process, it is the selection of what to include in the frame, of focus, aperture, camera angle, quality of film and so on. Denotation is *what* is photographed, connotation is *how* it is photographed.

Further implications

We can extend this idea further. Our tone of voice, *how* we speak, connotes the feelings or values about *what* we say; in music, the Italian directions *allegro ma non troppo* are the composer's instructions about how to play the notes, about what connotative or emotional values to convey. The choice of words is often a choice of connotation – 'dispute' or 'strike', 'oiling the wheels of commerce' or 'bribery'. These examples show emotional or subjective connotations, although we have to assume that others in our culture share at least a large part of them, that they are intersubjective.

Other connotations may be much more social, less personal. A frequently used example is the signs of a high ranking officer's uniform. In a hierarchical society, one that emphasizes distinctions between classes or ranks and that consequently puts a high value on a high social position, these signs of rank are designed to connote high values. They are usually of gold, models of crowns or of laurel wreaths and the more there are, the higher the rank they denote. In a society that does not value class distinction or hierarchy, officers' uniforms are rarely distinguished from their men's by signs that connote the high value of rank. The uniforms of Fidel Castro or Chairman Mao differed hardly at all from those of the men they led. Yet they were denoted as of high rank just as clearly as was a nineteenth-century Prussian officer who could hardly move under his signs of rank.

Connotation is largely arbitrary, specific to one culture, though it frequently has an iconic dimension. The way that a photograph of a child in soft focus connotes nostalgia is partly iconic. The soft focus is a motivated sign of the imprecise nature of memory, it is also a motivated sign for sentiment; soft focus = soft hearted! But we need the conventional element to decode it in this way, to know that soft focus is a significant choice made by the photographer and not a limitation of his equipment. If all photographs were in soft focus, then it could not connote nostalgia.

Because connotation works on the subjective level, we are frequently not made consciously aware of it. The hard focus, black and white, inhuman view of the street can all too often be read as the denotative meaning: that streets *are* like this. It is often easy to read connotative values as denotative facts; one of the main aims of semiotic analysis is to provide us with the analytical method and the frame of mind to guard against this sort of misreading.

MYTH

Basic concept

The second of Barthes's three ways in which signs work in the second order is through *myth*. I wish Barthes (1973) had not used this term because normally it refers to ideas that are false, 'it is a myth that . . .' or 'the myth that Britain is still a major world power'. This normal use is the unbeliever's use of the word. Barthes uses it as a believer, in its original sense. A myth is a story by which a culture explains or understands some aspect of reality or nature. Primitive myths are about life and death, men and gods, good and evil. Our sophisticated myths are about masculinity and femininity, about the family, about success, about the British policeman, about science. A myth, for Barthes, is a culture's way of thinking about something, a way of conceptualizing or understanding it. Barthes thinks of a myth as a chain of related concepts. Thus the traditional myth of the British policeman includes concepts of friendliness, reassurance, solidity, non-aggressiveness, lack of firearms. The photographic cliché of a corpulent, jolly bobby patting a little girl on the head relies for its second-order meaning on the fact that this *myth* of the police is common in the culture, it exists before the photograph, and the photograph activates the chains of concepts that constitute the myth. If connotation is the second-order meaning of the signifier, myth is the second-order meaning of the signified.

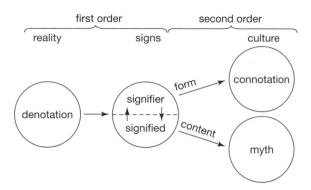

Barthes's two orders of signification. In the second order, the sign system of the first is inserted into the value system of the culture.

Further implications

Let us return to our example of the street scene with which we illustrated connotation. If I asked a dozen photographers to photograph this scene of children playing in the street, I would predict that most would produce the black and white, hard focus, inhumane type of photograph. This is because these connotations fit better with the commonest myths by which we conceptualize children playing in the street. Our dominant myth of childhood is that it is, or ideally should be, a period of naturalness and freedom. Growing up means adapting to the demands of society, which means losing naturalness and freedom. Towns are normally seen as unnatural, artificial creations that provide a restricted environment for children. There is a widespread belief in our culture that the countryside is the proper place for childhood. We can contrast these myths with those of other periods. For instance the Elizabethans saw a child as an incomplete adult; the Augustans saw the countryside as uncivilized – the human values were to be found in the civilized cities and the country had to be seen as pastoral, that is made suitable for urban understanding.

But no myths are universal in a culture. There are dominant myths, but there are also counter-myths. There are subcultures within our society which have contradictory myths of the British bobby to the dominant one outlined above. So, too, there is a myth of the urban street as a self-supporting community, a sort of extended family that provides a very good social environment for children. This would be the sort of myth to fit with the connotations of our alternative photograph of the street.

Science is a good example where the counter-myths are strongly challenging the dominant. We are a science-based culture. The dominant myth of science presents it as man's ability to adapt his nature to his needs, to improve his

CONTINUED

security and standard of living, to celebrate his achievement. Science is seen as objective, true and good. But the counter-myth is also very strong. This sees science as evil, as evidence of man's distance from and lack of understanding of nature. Science is man at his most selfish, short-sighted, in pursuit of his own material ends. It is interesting to note that in popular culture both myths of science are well represented. The factual side of television, news, current affairs, documentaries, tends to show more of the dominant than of the counter-myth: fictional television and cinema, on the other hand, reverse the proportions. There are more evil scientists than good ones, and science causes more problems than it solves.

For example, Gerbner (1973) shows that scientists portrayed on American fictional television were rated as the most 'deceitful', 'cruel' and 'unfair' of all professional types. He also cites a study in 1963 by Gusfield and Schwartz which again describes the fictional image of the scientist as 'cool', 'tough', 'anti-social', 'irreligious' and 'foreign'. Gerbner also found that scientific research leads to murder in nearly half of the twenty-five films which portrayed it. One example was a psychologist who hypnotized gorillas to murder girls who rejected him. A typical plot is an obsessive scientist whose invention gets out of control and kills him to the obvious relief of the rest of society and the audience.

The other aspect of myths that Barthes stresses is their dynamism. They change, and some can change rapidly in order to meet the changing needs and values of the culture of which they are a part. For instance, the myth of the British bobby to which I referred earlier is now growing old-fashioned and out of date. Its last major fictional presentation on television was in *Dixon of Dock Green*.

Connotation and myth are the main ways in which signs work on the second order of signification, that is the order in which the interaction between the sign and the user/culture is most active.

SYMBOLS

But Barthes (1977) does refer to a third way of signifying in this order. This he terms the *symbolic*. An object becomes a symbol when it acquires through convention and use a meaning that enables it to stand for something else. A Rolls Royce is a symbol of wealth, and a scene in a play in which a man is forced to sell his Rolls can be symbolic of the failure of his business and the loss of his fortune. Barthes uses the example of the young Tsar in *Ivan the Terrible* being baptized in gold coins as a symbolic scene in which gold is a symbol of wealth, power and status.

Barthes's ideas of the symbolic are less systematically developed than those of connotation and myth, and are therefore less satisfactory. We might prefer

Peirce's terms. The Rolls Royce is an index of wealth, but a symbol (Peirce's use not Barthes's) of the owner's social status. Gold is an index of wealth but a symbol of power.

J. Fiske, An *Introduction to Communication Studies*, 1990 2nd edn, Routledge, pp 91–5

One particularly rich seam for semiologists to explore is the world of advertising. By its very nature, advertising uses signs in a complex way in order to create responses in the reader. Often these responses are about awakening or even creating desire at a deep level in a way that the reader may not even be aware of. Some important pioneering work was done in the early 1980s by Gillian Dyer in her book *Advertising as Communication*.

In the extract that follows, she looks at the different nature of signs and explores further the nature of iconic and indexical signs, particularly as they are used by advertisers to convey ideas.

ICONIC, INDEXICAL AND SYMBOLIC SIGNS

It is worth digressing here to explain in a bit more detail the nature and form of signs, since they are the bedrock of communication. It is easy to be misled by advertisements, which consist mainly of photographic representations.

Photographic images look like the thing, place or person being represented. This makes them *iconic* signs, and the signifier–signified relationship one of resemblance or likeness. A portrait of a person is an obvious example of an iconic sign, because the picture resembles that person. Some signs go beyond the mere depiction of a person or thing and are used *indexically* to indicate a further or additional meaning to the one immediately and obviously signified. For example, the idea of Paris or Parisian holidays can be indicated by a picture of the Eiffel Tower, a landmark in the city which is frequently associated with it. The costume a person is wearing may denote iconically the mode of dress worn by a person or character in an ad, but at the same time stand *indexically* for a social position or profession. A character's movements may simultaneously represent some (dramatic) piece of action and indicate his or her frame of mind, habits or livelihood. For example a man who walks with a rolling gait is probably a sailor and one who has a swagger might be a cowboy. A woman in ads is often represented indexically by bits of her body – hips, eyes, head, hands or legs – which signify not only in themselves but also her whole being. They can also signify a commodity – lipstick, eye make-up, shampoo, nail polish, tights, etc. – thus suggesting that women are commodities also.

If an advertiser wants to convey the idea of heat, he or she could show a picture of a thermometer rising, beads of sweat on a person's brow, hot, shimmering

colours, etc. As with all indexical signs, there is a sequential or causal connection between signifier and signified – the mercury in a thermometer rising, sweat, or shimmer, and the idea, concept or feeling of heat.

The relationship between signifier and signified in some signs is arbitrary, based neither on resemblance nor on any existential link. In other words, the signifier does not resemble or cause the signified, but is related to it only by convention or 'contract'. This kind of sign is called a symbol. A rose is a symbol of love or passion not because a rose looks like love or passion or even because the flower causes it. It is just that members of some cultures have over the years used the rose in certain circumstances to mean love; just as in the ad campaign for gold we are invited to connect gold with love; and in cigarette ads, cool, refreshing things like mountain streams or fresh-looking and tasting foods, are made to symbolize (very unhealthy) cigarettes. In some ads, people like judges, policemen or nurses are used to mobilize feelings associated with the job or profession. In many cases the symbols used to convey meanings or ideas are not entirely arbitrary: the symbol for justice, a pair of scales, for instance, could not be replaced by any other symbol. In other words there are the rudiments of a 'natural' bond between signifier and signified in many symbols. An example of a pure symbol, with no such bond, would be that of the white horse used by White Horse Whisky, where the horse standing in a bar or on top of a mountain or at a building site stands for the bottle of whisky itself, although there is no 'logical' connection between the bottle and the sign horse. The sign and its referent co-exist in the brand name. The function of presenting a horse in these ads is to make more real the meaning the brand name gives the drink and is backed up by the slogan 'You can take a White Horse anywhere'. Brand images generally act as symbols for their products, but it is perhaps important to note that in most ad campaigns iconic, indexical and symbolic signs invariably overlap and are co-present.

Advertisements may look 'real' and 'natural' and the connections they make between dissimilar things may have the appearance of a system that is 'logical', and belongs to a 'real' or 'natural' order, but such connections are not inevitable. Even in the incongruous and illogical case of placing a white horse in a bar or living room or an enormous bottle of whisky on top of a mountain, the 'system' of the ad makes more 'real' the natural signification that the brand name gives to the drink, which is never out of place in a bar, as a horse never is on a mountain side, and vice versa. The whisky becomes a natural object through the white horse. In the end we come to accept the 'logic' of the system without question. The signs of other meaning systems, which have certain images, feelings or ideas attached to them, are transferred to the products rather than springing from them and are given the status of 'facts'. We are of course meant to see the meaning of the product as already there in its image on the screen as it unfolds. We rarely notice the inherent dissimilarity of objects and products placed together. As

Judith Williamson has pointed out, 'a product and image/emotion become linked in our minds, while the process of this linking is unconscious' (1978:30).

This linking of thoughts, emotions or feelings with something 'objective' and external is not a new phenomenon; it forms the basis of much art and many myths and rituals. However, advertising has a particular function in evoking emotions and feelings through promises of pleasure connected to the purchase or possession of a product. A product can even go from being the signified of a correlating thing, person or lifestyle which acts as a signifier, to generating or being that feeling, e.g. 'Happiness is a cigar called Hamlet', 'Bacardi and friends'. The act of consuming the product sign releases or creates the feelings it represents. As Williamson reminds us, when the product precedes the feeling we can end up not only speaking but feeling clichés: 'The connection of a "thing" and an abstraction can lead them to seem the same, in real life'.

G. Dyer, 'Semiotics and Ideology', Advertising as Communication, 1982, Routledge, pp. 124–6

To end this section we look at two examples of textual analysis. The first is an extract from Paddy Scannell's essay, '*Blind Date* and the Phenomenology of Fun'. As he explains: 'Fun is a human, social phenomenon. It shows up, is manifest, as one aspect of ordinary life. To study it is to examine what it is, and how it is achieved.' He points out that *Blind Date* is an important programme in the schedules as it is strategically placed on a Saturday night to win viewers to ITV. Although the programme is pre-recorded, it must be made to appear spontaneous, just like fun itself.

The social organization of *Blind Date* is [. . .] an invitation to enter the social space of the television studio. It is not much fun watching other people having a good time if we ourselves feel excluded from what's going on. How are viewers included in the programme? Consider the role of the studio audience. Clearly the programme is performed before 'live' audiences, but this does not necessarily mean that it is performed *for* them. In fact the studio audience is there for us, the viewers. How so? Well, consider the well-known fact that studio audiences, in shows like this, are always rehearsed. They are advised when to applaud and cheer, and join in. Their behaviour is treated by the producers as part of the overall effect of the show, as something to be managed and controlled with viewers in mind. But does a show like *Blind Date* need a studio audience? If the show is for an absent audience of viewers, why not perform directly to them and do without a studio audience? Would anything be lost? The answer is, surely, obvious. The studio audience is vital to creating the atmosphere of the show, its 'mood'. Mood is a fundamental concern of any phenomenological analysis. The

CONTINUED

studio audience in B*lind Date* is essential to the creation of a specific public mood – a collective willingness to have a good time, a shared disposition to laughter and fun.

Fun is a spontaneous thing. But the conditions in which fun can spontaneously be had have themselves to be created. Mood is something you have actually to get into, and there are ways of doing this and aids to getting there. In television shows the studio audience is always 'warmed up' to get it in the right mood for the show. This warm-up helps to prevent the show from starting 'cold' and so having to work to get into its desired and appropriate mood. For viewers the effect of a live and present studio audience, when unobtrusively managed and controlled, is to produce the essential sense of the show as a public, sociable occasion, of which they themselves are a part.

How are viewers made part of the show? It all depends on the programme host or presenter, whose key role in the management of the occasion we must now consider. The interactive organization of B*lind Date* – its template or fore-structure – is reducible to a format that goes back to the beginnings of broadcast entertainment. In essence the show is a set of interactions between:

■ host and participants (who play the game)
■ host and studio audience
■ host and viewers or listeners.

These three different circuits of interaction are 'in play' throughout the show and what holds them together, at all times, is the performative skill of its presenter, Cilla Black. The people who play the game and the studio audience all contribute to the performance, but it is the host – and she alone – who has overall responsibility for the management, control and direction of the show from the moment it starts to the moment it finishes. Cilla Black is a highly paid, professional entertainer. No one else is. All the other participants in the studio are 'ordinary people' for whom being in the television studio is a rare and unusual experience. How do you get an appropriate performance, in the very public space of a television studio, from people who are not paid and professional performers in public? Remember, this is 'live' television. Those who play the game are out there in front of a real 'live' studio audience. What if they get stage fright and dry up? The demonic problem of live broadcasting is the ever-present possibility of the whole thing suddenly going wrong. Part of the programme's care-structure is a concern to avoid technical failure and ensure performative success. This responsibility is vested in the whole invisible production apparatus of television. But what is highly visible from start to finish is the programme presenter. The production team delivers the show technically. Cilla Black delivers the show as 'the real thing', the thing that makes millions watch, week in week out. How does she do it?

It is worth recording an episode of B*lind Date* and going back and he watching the beginning. If you can do this, pay careful attention to how Cilla Black makes her entrance. Note especially her 'body language', how she uses her hands and arms for instance. Characteristically as she comes in she raises both arms, a gesture that acknowledges the cheers from the studio audience and the start of a complex interweaving of the three sets of interactions that she must keep going throughout the show. Cilla comes downstage to a prearranged position in front of the studio audience and a studio camera. She has begun to speak to the studio audience as she walks to her camera spot. Now she addresses her talk direct to camera, to absent viewers 'out there somewhere' watching.

The direct address to camera produces a look and discourse which is peculiar to television and essential to the interactive regime that it routinely establishes between institutions and audiences. In narrative cinema, and in fictional television, the actors in the story never look directly to camera. The regime of oblique looks and glances in film and television drama creates a self-sustaining world whose fictional 'reality' would be destroyed if ever the actors went 'out of character' and looked or spoke directly to the audience. To sustain their imagined worlds fictional narratives rigorously exclude any aknowledgment of the real world in which viewers (or readers) are situated. It is an essential aspect of the ordinary everyday worldliness of radio and television that they are in continuous dialogue with their audiences, thereby acknowledging that both – institutions and audiences – are part of the same 'world' with the same basic assumptions about and attitudes towards this world-in-common that broadcasting creates. [. . .]

Cilla Black ensures that viewers are part of what's going on by talking to them directly and thereby bringing them into the picture and into the show. We effortlessly understand her talk and body language as a complex weave of interactions between herself as host, the studio audience, those who play the game each week and ourselves as viewers. The play of these interactions folds us into the show as it unfolds We, the viewers, are not detached observers of Blind Date. We are active participants, part of the action. We are made so by the performative skills of Cilla Black.

P. Scannell, 'Blind Date and the Phenomenology of Fun'
in R. Lorimer with P. Scannell (eds), Mass Communications: a Comparative
Introduction, Manchester University Press, 1994, pp. 284–6

ACTIVITY

Take another popular television prime-time television programme that relies on the notion of 'fun' and subject it to a similar analysis, especially in relation to how 'spontaneity' is constructed.

Teenage magazine covers provide an interesting example of how a semiotic analysis can offer a meaningful ideological insight into the most everyday media texts.

In the following extract, which appears on the Media and Communications tudies website hosted by the University of Wales, Sian Davies analyses the front cover of two teenage magazines:

SEMIOTIC ANALYSIS OF TEENAGE MAGAZINE FRONT COVERS

[. . .] Firstly, the titles anchor the texts to the genre of teenage magazines. *19* seems to be directed at a person who is 19, or at least who thinks she is as mature as a 19 year old. As the title stands boldly in the top left-hand corner of the page, this is the image that the eye is initially drawn towards. If we are to adopt Kress and Leeuwen's theory of layout, this will also give the magazine a sense of idealism, suggesting that the reader should aspire to attain the life and image referred to within the pages . . . The title *More!* also acquires this quality of idealism, but as the word stretches across the width of the page, it could be suggested that the *More!* reader is more sassy and larger than life in comparison to the more mature or sophisticated reader of *19* (this is further substantiated by the exclamation mark – *More!* – and by the girlish pink colour of the *19* logo).

The taglines reinforce these ideas as they are placed directly underneath the titles in a contrasting black font. *19* states that the magazine is 'Barefaced Cheek!' which implies that all is bared in the magazine, the reader is given extensive coverage of the issues of sex, love and fashion. However this tagline could also be interpreted (perhaps to a non-teenager reader) as implying that the reader of *19* is cheeky and impertinent. It is only the exclamation mark after the words and the positioning underneath the well-known and recognisable logo of 19 that anchor the preferred reading for the reader – as the reader will presumably be familiar with the content of the magazine, the polysemic nature of the tagline will not be apparent to them. This familiarity with content is also needed to fully appreciate the tagline on the cover of *More!* – 'Smart Girls Get More!' On the one hand, it is suggested that smart girls buy the magazine as they know it will provide pleasure and information for them, and on the other hand it is suggested that smart girls (the attractive *More!* reader) get more out of life, love, and, most importantly, sex. Reading *More!* will improve your life on many levels, if you listen to the advice offered within the magazine. The tagline adopted by *More!* is therefore effective as the modern British teenage girl will construe an appropriate interpretation that will give [her] the urge to buy the product.

Both *19* and *More!* also attempt to attract their readers by placing a female character in the centre of the cover. This is a particularly interesting characteristic if we are to consider that corresponding male magazines similarly adopt central female models, either posing seductively or like the typical 'girl-next-door', on their covers. It could indeed be argued that one could successfully (and with minimal disruption) take the models from the covers of More! and 19 and place them on a magazine such as FHM that adheres to its own set of generic codes and conventions and encourages very different interpretations from its reader. According to Bignell (1997: 69), the images of beautiful women on the covers of female magazines are 'iconic signs which represent the better self which every woman desires to become . . .' The figure thus represents the self for the reader, a future image that is attainable for her if she continues reading and learning from the magazine. On a male magazine, however, the same figure would represent a sexual image, an object to be attained by the male reader. It becomes evident therefore that 'men look at women. Women watch themselves being looked at . . . Thus she turns herself into an object – and most particularly, an object of vision: a sight' (Berger in Vestergaard & Schrøder 1992: 81). This is a somewhat negative interpretation of the centrality of women on the covers of magazines. However, Bignell sees that 'while the cover image is for a woman to look at, it is constructed with reference to a wider social code in which being feminine means *taking pleasure in looking at oneself*, and taking pleasure in being looked at by men' (my italics, Bignell 1997: 71). Bignell therefore seems to empower the woman in his analysis of cover models, noting that women simultaneously enjoy looking and being looked at. The genre (or textual code) in which the image appears is therefore a fundamental contributor to the construed interpretations made by the reader.

As stated above, the model on the cover of a female teenage magazine represents the self for the reader. The models seen on the given issues of 19 and More! therefore seem to illustrate the characteristics of their targeted readers. The model seen on the cover of 19 is the typical blonde-haired, tanned, tall and slim girl with perfect complexion and perfect features. But the reader is not led to feel envious of the model – on the contrary, she is encouraged to believe that this is an ordinary 19 reader (on the inside cover she is identified simply as 'Emily'), and is the beautiful woman inside each of us, waiting to be unleashed (and reading 19 will unleash this beauty from within the reader). The diamanté necklace connotes luxury and sophistication, and the sequined boob tube connotes a fun, bubbly nature and draws attention to her slim body (her sex appeal). With her long blonde hair flowing gently away from her face to reveal dazzling green eyes (ironically in this context, green traditionally being associated with the colour of envy), she can be seen as iconic for the reader (in the non-semiotic sense), and as seductive for the male reader. She embodies the message that 19 habitually transcribes to the reader – look innocent and beautiful and yet be in control of your own sexuality and your relationships.

On the cover of More! the character again embodies the self for the reader. She represents the More! 'ethos of youthful, cheeky impertinence'. Her red, low-cut dress suggests that she is sassy; a vixen that has sexual needs and is not afraid to fulfil them. Again, the clear skin and perfect features encourage the reader to believe that there is an inner beauty within everyone that will shine through. However, the *More!* model does not appear as innocent as the *19* model. Her hair is swept more vigorously from her face and therefore creates a more disrupted, chaotic image than the previous. The innocence depicted by the clear complexion of the *19* model is challenged here as the *More!* model raises her eyebrow into an arch; she has a glint in her eye and pouts her lips proudly. As we notice the presence of a man in the left-hand side of the front cover, we therefore interpret this facial expression as sexual prowess – this girl knows what she wants and she knows exactly how to get it. The male figure is not personalised; indeed we only see a leg, an arm and a crotch and yet we are fully aware of the masculinity of the character. This could suggest that, in subversion to the representation offered within male magazines, the man is the sexual object here. It is also significant that the male is wearing a kilt as it could suggest that the female is metaphorically wearing the trousers in the relationship. This interpretation would only become apparent if the reader was accustomed with the relevant social codes and textual codes of gendered magazines. If the reader is familiar with popular culture however, they could assume the man in the kilt to be the actor James Redmond who portrays Finn in *Hollyoaks* (a half-Scottish lord) and therefore presume that there is an in-depth interview with him in the magazine – this is suggested by the text at the top of the magazine cover – 'Finn-tastic! We Check out James Redmond's Morning Glory'.

By analysing the title, tagline, and central images of the magazine cover, we have therefore deduced the readership and content of the magazines effectively. As McRobbie notes, sex now fills the space of the magazines' pages. It 'provides the frame for women's magazines in the 1990's' and 'marks a new moment in the construction of female sexual identities' (McRobbie 1996: 177). It is worrying to think that the explicit sexual representations within the magazines (such as *More!*'s 'Raunchy resolutions to spice up your sex life') are being read by underage teenagers; sex has been packaged as a 'commodity' by these magazines in recent years and the young readers have eagerly jumped at the chance to buy such (what was previously) censored material.

Indeed, fifty years ago the teenage magazine industry differed greatly to that of today. According to Vestergaard, we have seen a shift from 'motherhood and childcare to the maintenance of physical appearance' (Vestergaard & Schrøder 1992: 81) (in the discussed examples, we see 'Be your own stylist – steal insider know-how from the women who dress the stars' on the cover of *19*, and on *More!* 'Happy New Gear – what every glam girl will be wearing this season'). Dr Nancy Signiorelli of the University of Delaware undertook a study on 'A Focus on Appearance' in the media in November 1996, and she found that one in three (37 per cent) articles in leading teen girl magazines included a focus on appearance, one in three (35 per cent) focused on dating and less than 2 per cent discussed either school or careers. This is certainly reflected on the front covers analysed above – every feature on the covers refer to beauty, fashion, dating, sex and celebrities. Kimberley Phillips argues that these magazines therefore 'reinforce the cultural expectations that an adolescent woman should be more concerned with her appearance, her relations with other people, and her ability to win approval from men than with her own ideas or expectations for herself'.

It can also be argued however that young women are encouraged to develop independence by these magazines. In recent years the magazine industry has therefore successfully extended the notion of what it is to be a woman. A teenage girl will see hunting boyfriends and beautifying as a norm; it is argued indeed that these are transcribed as their sole purposes in life. The magazines do not seem to cater for minority interests such as politics, environmental issues, or any kind of music that ventures beyond Westlife or Britney Spears. The teenage girl has therefore been heavily stereotyped by the teenage magazine industry, and her interpretation of the codes and conventions used in the magazine will depend on her personal knowledge of this culture and society. Indeed, some of the readers of these magazines are male (e.g. the brothers or boyfriends of the female readers – Bignell refers to these as 'non-ideal readers') and they will interpret the codes differently to their female counterparts as they arguably do not share their interests in beauty products and fashion. Their interpretations of the sex issues may also differ, as they will gaze at the images of women as sex objects as opposed to icons and role models. Chandler sees that 'social semiotics alerts us to how the same text may generate different meanings for different readers', and this is certainly true of the gendered readings of teenage magazines. Chandler further notes that the signs (or codes) within the text 'do not just "convey" meanings, but constitute a medium in which meanings are constructed'. Through reading a magazine aimed at her demographic group, a teenage girl will therefore come to learn that society expects her to be interested in boys, sex, fashion, beauty and fame. The magazine is therefore a 'powerful ideological force' in society; the image and behavioural ideologies presented within the magazine covers become the stereotypical norm for the teenage girl.

Applying semiotic analysis to the magazine text therefore allows us to identify social ideologies of the teenage girl. One could analyse the front covers of magazine extensively, decoding the codes of colour, font, layout and spatial arrangements as well as the titles, taglines, language and central images to show the construction of the teenage girl in the media. Teenage magazines may not provide an altogether accurate representation of all teenage girls today, but it is certainly a medium that provides escapism and enjoyment for the reader whilst subliminally educating and informing at the same time.

Magazines analysed: *More!*, Issue 359,
27 December 2001–8 January 2002; *19*, January 2002 edition

➤ How would you respond to Paddy Scannell's assertion that 'Semiotics tells us things we already know in a language we will never understand'?

➤ Select an advertisement from a glossy magazine. In what ways does it make use of iconic and indexical signs? What do you think is the impact on the reader of these signs?

➤ Choose the covers of two magazines that are aimed at a market other than teenage girls. Produce your own semiotic analysis of the covers.

FURTHER READING

Selby, K. and Cowdery, R. (1995) *How to Study Television*. Macmillan.
Detailed analysis of a Royal Mail advertisement.

Taylor, L. and WillIs, A. (1999) *Media Studies. Texts, Institutions and Audiences*, Blackwell.
Useful chapter on 'Reading Media Images'.

Communication and Media website: www.aber.ac.uk/media/index.html.
Some useful material to help develop skills in textual analysis.

▼ 3 NARRATIVE AS AN ANALYTICAL TOOL

Narrative is another valuable tool in our textual analysis toolkit. Unfortunately its literary associations often mean that we are inclined to link it exclusively to fictional texts. Narrative therefore tends to be associated with the way a fictional story is told in terms of how events unfold and are revealed to the audience. However, it is important to realise that in Media Studies, narrative is an equally important element in the construction of both fiction and non-fiction texts. Although it is a logical tool to reach for when we undertake the analysis of moving image texts, its use is by no means limited to this. In Media Studies, looking at narrative structure implies that we explore the way in which the information contained within a text is revealed to us. Consequently it has implications for the way in which print texts, images on computer screens and sound texts are constructed.

Clearly, one important aspect of the narrative is how the flow of this information is controlled. A tabloid newspaper story contains information. The flow of this information to the reader is controlled through such devices as the headline, the opening paragraph, or intro, the illustration and the final outcome or conclusion of the narrative.

A key narrative device is identified by Roland Barthes as the enigma code. In the control of the flow of information we are often teased by a riddle that requires us to guess the next piece of information to be revealed. Think of trailers at the cinema or the cliffhangers in television serial dramas. The enigma is a useful narrative device to keep the reader interested by whetting his/her appetite to find out more. Magazine front covers are another example of the enigma code. They sit on shelves of newsagents and tease the reader with snippets of information in an effort to persuade him or her to buy a copy to find out more.

Equally, narrative analysis need not be limited to texts that set out specifically to tell a 'story'. A magazine advertisement, although relying on a static image, works as narrative, in the sense of offering a frozen moment of an implicitly ongoing narrative. We are invited to complete in our minds what happened before and after the frozen moment. Perhaps more importantly, narrative can be said to organise the flow of information on the page, determining how we 'read' the text before us.

The first extract below by Adrian Tilley is aimed at teachers of Media Studies to suggest ways of introducing narrative as a concept in the classroom. Tilley argues that although storytelling often appears invisible, it is in fact a complex process. Narrative, he points out, is an important part of our socialisation as it moderates our behaviour.

'The nature of media narratives and their relations to our social situations is the object of narrative study.' He offers three main reasons for studying media narratives:

1   It shifts the focus of attention from content to the structure and process of storytelling.
2   It allows us to investigate the similarities and differences in narrative across media forms.
3   It can reveal how 'the meanings and pleasures of these narrative forms relate to the wider disposition of social power'. Such narrative discourses offer us 'powerful ways of understanding the social world and our place in it'.

NARRATIVE CODES

The narrative models of Todorov and Propp offer valuable textual analyses of narrative but they are not much concerned with the reader. We need to look elsewhere than these *formalist* models for a mode of analysis disposed towards the reader.

One way of understanding the text/reader relation is to see a story as a set of intended meanings expressed by the narrator in particular ways that are interpreted by the reader. The intended meanings and the interpreted meanings will differ unless the mode of expression is commonly understood by sender and receiver. To guarantee that agreement, the mode of expression takes the form of *codes* working to make meanings and reproduce those meanings. In other words, meanings will be *en*coded by the narrator, transmitted through a medium and *de*coded by the narratee. This 'ideal' model rather mechanistically expresses the social nature of reading, however. Rather than a model of an active text and a passive 'receiver' of its meanings, the idea of *cultural codes* can make claims for *active* reading. In this more sophisticated model, the reader *produces* meaning from a text, whether intended or not, from their own cultural experience and identity. Thus, the pleasures of *Minder*, for instance, can be activated by a reader who recognizes the subtleties of a subterranean world suggested by a Ford Capri, a pork pie hat and a fast line in street slang; pleasure comes then from the meanings made by readers as they interact with the pleasures offered by the text.

Work on the *codes* of narrative and the *activity* of reading is provided by Roland Barthes in a model which offers an account of how the reader is enticed by and transported through the narrative. Barthes proposes five codes of meaning or signification. Three (the Semic, Referential and Symbolic) refer to the form and style of a narrative, cutting 'vertically' through a narrative. Two (the Proiaretic and the Hermeneutic) are concerned with the sequencing of a narrative and therefore function 'horizontally'. The Proiaretic is the Action code and the Hermeneutic the Enigma code; both are concerned with narrative *development*. They determine the other three codes which organize the 'texture' of the narrative. The Semic code is the descriptive code especially applied to characters. The Referential code refers outwards from the word/image to the 'real world'. The Symbolic code embodies the metaphoric – the substitution of one small or concrete thing for a larger, abstract one.

Barthes' analysis was applied to the literary text of Balzac's short story *Sarrasine*, so care needs to be taken in applying it to visual texts like films and television programmes. However, the action and enigma codes, because they deal with the linear structure of stories, are clearly transferable.

Enigma codes generate and control what and how much we know in a narrative. They also engage and hold the interest of the reader. The tap of Blind Pugh's stick along the street in *Treasure Island*; Mr Bingley's arrival as a single, marriageable man at Netherfield Park in *Pride and Prejudice*; Marnie's long walk along the station platform in the film *Marnie*; a news headline announcing an economic crisis – all are presented as enticing enigmas, puzzles which demand to be solved. Answers to the questions posed by the enigmas are provided in a sequence according to their narrative significance. In the course of the story, the enigmas will multiply and interweave. The less important will be forgotten or readily solved while central ones will be held over to the end of the story before they are resolved; Blind Pugh will soon be forgotten in favour of Long John Silver, Mr Bingley's initial importance will recede as Darcy becomes the heroine's favourite, and Marnie's importance will grow as she becomes the film's central enigma.

The enigma code is discernible in a wide range of media: the tantalizing build-up to a new TV series through previews, the TV *Times* and *Radio Times*, and in newspaper articles; the release of a major film with a campaign of posters, trailers and television appearances by its star; the birth of a new daily newspaper; the publication of a devastating exposé novel; an advertisement for a new car with a new braking system; the release of a government report on nuclear waste. All use enigma codes to stimulate maximum public interest and, at the same time, contain and limit what we are to know. . . .

Action codes makes complex ideas and feelings immediately recognizable, at the same time ordering their significance in the narrative. In a western, the buckling on of a gun belt signifies a set of possible intentions of character – decisiveness and determination – and action – to solve a problem through violence. In other situations, the simple action of packing a suitcase can connote determination, despair or duplicity. In both examples, the action, however coded, will forward the narrative. If enigma codes build a story through (lack of) knowledge, action codes explain the significance of moments in the story. We know (because we have learned from other stories) that the gun belt being buckled on heralds a showdown, and we know (from other stories, but also, perhaps, from our social experience) that the packed suitcase will lead to a confrontation or escape.

How puzzles arise within a story – how they can be delayed, extended, and resolved – can be made into open-ended discovery activities for students. Central enigmas can be charted through a story and distinguished from delays, complications and minor resolutions.

The following diagram charts in this way the story of *Coma*, a film about a doctor's investigation of a series of unexplained deaths at her hospital:

Central enigma resolution	Delay event/ sequence	Minor event/ sequence	Complication event/ sequence	Final resolution
Why are there so many coma cases in the Boston Hospital?	Doctor is reassured by the Head of the hospital.	Doctor takes an enforced holiday.	Doctor discovers where coma patients are taken.	Head of the hospital revealed as villain.

The enigmas of any narrative can be charted like this. Comparing three or four formally different texts can reveal some suggestive similarities and differences between genres and between fictions and non-fictions; list action codes in a narrative, relate each to similar examples in other texts, predict their possible narrative effect (i.e. what *might* happen as a result) and compare their actual narrative effect.

This form of narrative analysis considers the nature of the pleasures of the text and how they 'call up' its audiences. It may be the pleasure of being 'in the know', recognizing, understanding and re-experiencing the familiar. To be able to predict what will happen is as pleasurable as having those predictions and expectations confounded by a new twist or shock in the narrative. Ultimately, it is that desire for knowledge and the drive to know which is stimulated by the narrative form.

A. C. Tilley, 'Narrative' in D. Lusted (ed.), *Media Studies Book: a Guide for Teachers*, Routledge, 1991, pp. 61–6

While it is necessary to recognise the importance of narrative across a range of media forms, we should also remember that narrative remains an important dimension in cinema. As David Bordwell and Kristin Thompson point out, 'When we speak of "going to the movies" we almost always mean we are going to see a narrative film.'

Part of the pleasure of going to the cinema is the opportunity to suspend disbelief and to become engrossed in the 'invisible' process of storytelling.

In their essay, Bordwell and Thompson define narrative as 'a chain of events in cause effect relationship in time and space'. They then proceed to examine each of these elements in detail.

The following extract from the essay looks at cause and effect as narrative elements. The authors seek to identify for the reader one of the prime agents of cause in film narrative as the characters themselves. Although the essay is illustrated by some films that you may not have seen, this does not matter. One useful activity you can undertake is to find your own contemporary equivalents to the examples given.

CAUSE AND EFFECT

If narrative depends so heavily on cause and effect, what kinds of things can and effect are function as causes in a narrative? Usually the agents of cause and effect are *characters*. Characters in narratives are *not* real people (even when the characters are based on historical personages, like Napoleon in *War and Peace*). Characters are constructed in a narrative; they are collections of character *traits*. When we say that a character in a film was 'complex' or 'well developed,' we really mean that the character was a collection of several or varying traits. A rich character such as Sherlock Holmes is a mass of traits (his love of music, his addiction to cocaine, his skill in disguise, and so on). On the other hand, a minor character may have only one or two traits.

In general, a character will have the number and kind of traits needed to function causally in the narrative. The second scene of Alfred Hitchcock's *The Man Who*

Knew Too Much (1934) shows that the heroine, Jill, possesses the trait of being an excellent shot with a rifle. For much of the film this trait seems irrelevant to the narrative, but in the last scene Jill is able to shoot one of the villains when a police marksman cannot do it. This skill with a rifle is not a natural part of a person named Jill; it is a trait that helps make up a character named Jill, and it serves a specific narrative function. Character traits can involve attitudes, skills, preferences, psychological drives, details of dress and appearances and any other specific quality the film creates for a character.

But some causes and effects in narratives do not originate with characters. Causes may be supernatural. In the book of Genesis, God causes the earth to form; in Greek plays, gods bring about events. Causes may also be natural. In the so-called disaster movies, an earthquake or tidal wave may be the cause that precipitates a series of actions on the parts of the characters. The same principle holds when wild animals, like the shark in *Jaws*, terrorize a community. (The film may tend to anthropomorphize these natural causes by assigning human traits, for example, malevolence, to them. Indeed, this is what happens in *Jaws*: the shark becomes personified as vengeful and cunning.) But once these natural occurrences set the situation up, human desires and goals usually enter the action to develop the narrative. For example, a man escaping from a flood may be placed in the situation of having to decide whether to rescue his worst enemy.

In general, the spectator actively seeks to connect events by means of cause and effect. Given an incident, we tend to hypothesize what might have caused it, or what it might on turn cause. That is, we look for causal motivation. . . . In the scene from *My Man Godfrey*, a scavenger hunt serves as a cause that justifies the presence of a beggar at a society ball. Casual motivation often involves the 'planting' of information in advance of a scene. In John Ford's *Stagecoach*, there is a last-minute rescue from Indians by a cavalry troop. If these soldiers appeared from nowhere, we would most likely find the rescue a weak resolution, of the battle scene. But *Stagecoach* begins with a scene of the cavalry discovering that Geronimo is on the warpath. Several later scenes involve the cavalry, and at one of their stops the passengers on the coach learn that the soldiers have had a skirmish with the Indians. These previous scenes of cavalry troops causally motivate their appearance in the final rescue scene.

Most of what we have said about causality pertains to the plot's direct presentation of causes and effects. In *The Man Who Knew Too Much*, Jill is shown to be a good shot, and because of this she can save her daughter. The townsfolk in *Jaws* respond to the shark attack that is shown at the start of the film. But the plot can lead us to *infer* causes and effects and thus build up a total story. The detective film furnishes the best example of how this active construction of the story may work.

A murder has been committed; that is, we know an effect but not the causal factors – the killer, the motive, perhaps also the method. The mystery tale thus depends strongly on curiosity, our desire to know events that have occurred before the plot action begins. It is the detective's job to disclose, at the end, the missing causes – to name the killer, explain the motive, and reveal the method. That is, in the detective film the climax of the plot (the action that we see) is a revelation of the earliest incidents in the story (events which we did not see). We can diagram this.

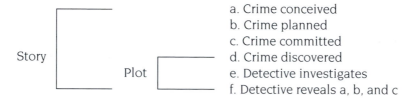

Story
Plot

a. Crime conceived
b. Crime planned
c. Crime committed
d. Crime discovered
e. Detective investigates
f. Detective reveals a, b, and c

Although this pattern is most common in detective narratives, any film's plot can withhold causes and thus arouse our curiosity. Horror and science-fiction films often leave us in the dark about what forces are behind certain events. The plot of *Citizen Kane* delays revealing what causes the hero to say 'Rosebud' on his deathbed. In general, whenever any film creates a mystery, it does so by suppressing certain story causes and by presenting only effects in the plot.

The plot may also present causes but withhold story effects, prompting the viewer to imagine them. During the final battle in *Jaws*, the young scientist, Hooper, is last seen hiding on the ocean bottom after the shark has smashed his protective cage open. Although we are not shown the outcome, we might assume that Hooper is dead. Later, after Brody has destroyed the shark, Hooper surfaces: he has escaped after all. A plot's withholding of effects is most noticeable at the end of the film. A famous example occurs in the final moments of François Truffaut's *The 400 Blows*. The boy Antoine Doinel has escaped from a reformatory and runs along the seashore. The camera zooms in on his face and the frame freezes. The plot does not reveal whether he is captured and brought back, leaving us to speculate on what might happen next.

D. Bordwell and K. Thompson, 'Narrative as a Formal System',
Film Art: An Introduction, McGraw-Hill, 1990, pp. 58–9

➤ Explain the ways in which a television news report uses narrative to organise the flow of information.

➤ Choose a still photograph from a newspaper or magazine and explain how it uses narrative.

➤ Look at the diagram for a detective film in the extract above. Choose another genre of film and see if you can create a similar diagram demonstrating how cause and effect operate.

➤ Find another example of a film or television programme in which the outcome of some part of the narrative is withheld from the audience. What do you think is the impact of this?

➤ Bordwell and Thompson argue that 'narrative is a fundamental way that humans make sense of the world'. Consider some of the ways that media texts can be said to help people 'make sense of the world'.

FURTHER READING

Bell, A., Joyce, M., Rivers, D. (1999) *Advanced Media Studies*, Hodder & Stoughton
Contains a chapter on the narrative of news production.

Branston, G. and Stafford, R. (1996) *The Media Student's Book*, Routledge.
Includes a chapter that looks at the role of narrative across fictional and non-fictional forms together with a case study of narrative in *Psycho*.

Stokes, J. (2003) *How to Do Media and Cultural Studies*, Sage.
Has a useful and accessible section on how to carry out various forms of narrative analysis.

▼ 4 THE ROLE OF GENRE

Genre is a concept that is usually associated with classifying media texts into different categories. This process of classification is, however, not necessarily a useful end in itself. To understand the function of genre as a tool to support our reading of media texts, we need to understand how it can help to develop our understanding of these texts and the ways in which they function. One aspect of genre that we need to recognise is how it works on audience expectations. As Taylor and Willis (1999) argue:

> The pleasure and enjoyment audiences derive from the media often depend upon text broadly fitting into certain generic groupings. Their judgements as to how successful

a text is are formed by generic expectations based on their experiences as media consumers.

It is not only audiences that can be seen to utilise the concept of genre. It is also an important concept in relation to media production. In the high-stakes game of predicting audience tastes, media producers often rely on established genre formulas in order to reduce the risk of producing products that audiences will not wish to consume. *Big Brother*, for example, has spawned a myriad of reality TV programmes on the back of its initial success.

Genre study has its origins in film criticism, prevalent in this country in the late 1960s and 1970s. Film lends itself especially to the genre criticism approach, not least because the massive budgets necessary for film production mean that working with an established and successful genre is very much the norm in the film industry. However, it is important to acknowledge that not the entire output of an institution like Hollywood relies on reworking genre formulas. Indeed, it is important that as a counterpoise to genre theory, we acknowledge the significance of auteur theory, which privileges films in terms of their individual style or the artistic 'signature' that a director brings to them. For example, the work of a director such as Alfred Hitchcock or Martin Scorsese, it is argued, is more recognisable as that of an individual director than it is of a genre formula.

In an essay entitled 'Genre Theory and Criticism', Peter Hutchings takes stock of the pioneering theoretical work on genre, most of which had revolved around the western. In the extract that follows, he focuses on the iconographic study of genre. The iconography or recurring images, such as props, within a film is a key means of giving a genre its identity.

[The iconographic approach] can and has been criticized for its unquestioning acceptance of a form/content distinction . . . . However, inasmuch as it focuses on the ways in which films can be meaningful without the presence of an auteur figure, there are many useful insights to be gleaned from this material. That most of these accounts eventually turn back to a form of auteurism and away from some of the other avenues they have opened up – most notably, the ways in which audiences might relate to this site of meaning – should not detract unduly from their significance.

If for 1970s critics iconography provided the outer form of a genre, the underlying thematic preoccupations constituted its inner form. One important example of thematic genre analysis is provided in *Horizons West*, Jim Kitses's book on the western. Kitses argues that the idea of the West within American culture is 'an ambiguous, mercurial concept' which held together a number of ambivalent feelings and ideas about the progress of white American civilization. In order to illustrate this 'philosophical dialectic', Kitses sets out in tabular form a series of opposed values and ideas which, for him, identify the essential focus of thematic concerns for the western.

THE WILDERNESS	CIVILIZATION
The Individual	*The Community*
freedom	restriction
honour	institutions
self-knowledge	illusion
integrity	compromise
self-interest	social responsibility
solipsism	democracy
Nature	*Culture*
purity	corruption
experience	knowledge
empiricism	legalism
pragmatism	idealism
brutalization	refinement
savagery	humanity
The West	*The East*
America	Europe
the frontier	America
equality	class
agrarianism	industrialism
tradition	change
the past	the future

The deliberate looseness of Kitses's defining thematic parameters enables him to describe the western as 'a loose, shifting and variegated genre with many roots and branches' and to chastise those critics who 'have ever tried to freeze the genre once and for all in a definitive model of the "classical" Western' (although in Kitses's reading of the genre, most of this variety and vitality is seen to be provided by auteurs such as John Ford, Anthony Mann and Sam Peckinpah). Of course, whether a comparable table of polarities could be drawn up for other genres is another matter entirely, and this problem in turn raises the question of the applicability of Kitses's approach to genre definition in general.

Unlike Kitses, Will Wright's *Sixguns and Society: A Structural Study of the Western* will have no truck with auteurs, but, as with Kitses, one is left wondering about the effectiveness of the proposed methodology outside the relatively limited confines of the western. In his account, and in a manner strikingly reminiscent of André Bazin's account of different types of western, Wright seeks to identify particular structural formats and types within the historical progression of the western form and then attempts to relate these to broader shifts in American society. Wright argues that the western is a myth (although his notion of myth, which draws

CONTINUED

heavily upon the work of anthropologist Claude Lévi-Strauss, is very different from that proposed by Bazin) or rather a set of myths which bind the viewer/audience to a particular social order: 'the structure of the myth corresponds to the conceptual needs of social and self-understanding required by the dominant social institutions of that period; the historical changes in the structure of the myth correspond to the changes in the structure of those dominant institutions'. Wright's four principal western types – the classical plot, the vengeance variation, the transition theme and the professional plot – are identified through a listing of narrative functions which, according to Wright, each film of a particular type must by definition share.

Wright's book is certainly detailed (and, in parts, dense to the point of laboriousness) and probably represents the most ambitious attempt to define once and for all a particular genre. Despite its exhaustiveness, however, this account of the western often feels rather sketchy, as if, even with all the details given here, further variants and more functions are required. In many ways, Wright's approach lives up to Tom Ryall's claim that genre studies should be about the defining of limits. However, it seems that in reality such an ambitious project finds it very difficult, if not impossible, to incorporate all the variations available within a particular genre into anything more than a provisional critical model. It is the combination of this approach with his mechanistic notion of how cultural production relates to dominant social institutions that finally makes Will Wright's *Sixguns and Society* an intriguing, but decidedly problematic, intervention in the field of genre criticism.

Some of the difficulties that dogged 1970s genre studies in its attempts to pin down the identity and meaning of genres can also be seen to have derived from an overinvestment in the western, which to a certain extent was figured at this time as the 'typical' genre, an understanding of which would eventually lead to an understanding of all genres. With its very specific historical and geographical setting (which in turn delimited the iconographic and thematic resources available to film-makers), the western offered an apparently hospitable terrain for 1970s genre critics to start their work. However, as it turned out, even with the western the whole business of definition was not at all straighforward; and this was even more the case with genres which did not figure prominently in this debate. For example, both horror and melodrama lacked the visual and iconographic unity of the western. It might be argued that many of the ideas and models developed within genre criticism at this time really only worked for the western (and then only to a limited extent), and when it came to constructing a broader understanding of other genres and genre in general, genre studies as it stood was relatively ill-equipped for the task.

P. Hutchings, 'Genre Theory and Critisism', in J. Hollows and M. Jancovich, (eds), *Approaches to Popular Film*, Manchester University Press, 1995, pp. 69–71

➤ The western obviously provides good examples of how iconography can be identified within the genre. Try choosing a different film or television genre and make a list of the icons that are representative of it. Consider also the themes of the genre.

It is important to recognise that genre as a concept can be applied across most media forms, including television, magazines and even websites. A problem does emerge, however, in that not all media texts are easily categorised and with the increasing saturation of the marketplace with media texts, many draw upon several different genres. This latter phenomenon is called hybridity. An example of a hybrid genre is the docu-soap, which as its name suggests draws on both documentary and soap opera conventions for its impact.

➤ Look at the chart below, taken from *The Guardian* (November 2001). It shows the output of BBC1 and BBC2 over the past 30 years broken down according to genre. Consider how useful are the genre categories used in the chart. Do you think there might be an argument for splitting them down into smaller categories? How would you account for the change in the BBC's output as signalled in the charts?

In the final extract for this section we consider the issue of genre and gender. Clearly, certain genres are associated with male and female audiences although we are again not dealing with watertight categories. Although television sport can be identified as a predominantly male genre, that does not mean that a significant female audience does not tune in. Similarly with soap operas, which are generally seen as appealing primarily to a female audience, a significant number of men may well be 'in the room' when these are transmitted.

In her essay, 'Gendered Fictions', Verina Glaessner challenges the notion of soaps as low-status programmes and points to the fact that soaps 'open up a space for women characters and for an examination of the concerns of women and representation of the texture of women's lives'. She then goes on to explore the nature of soaps and the pleasures that they offer a female audience.

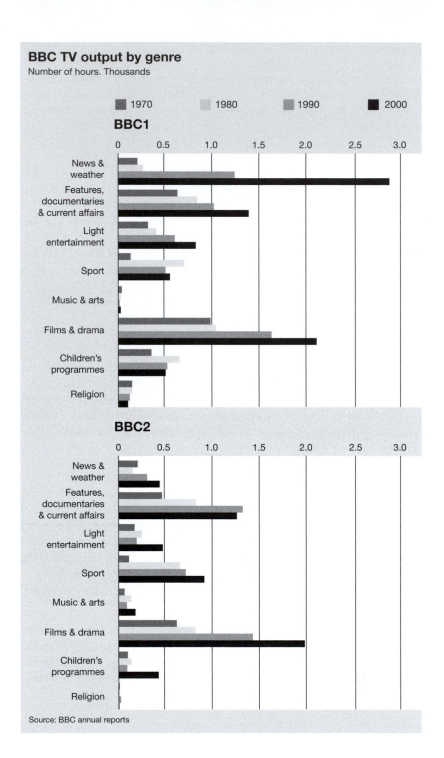

BBC TV output by genre

Number of hours. Thousands

■ 1970   ■ 1980   ■ 1990   ■ 2000

BBC1

	0	0.5	1.0	1.5	2.0	2.5	3.0

News & weather

Features, documentaries & current affairs

Light entertainment

Sport

Music & arts

Films & drama

Children's programmes

Religion

BBC2

	0	0.5	1.0	1.5	2.0	2.5	3.0

News & weather

Features, documentaries & current affairs

Light entertainment

Sport

Music & arts

Films & drama

Children's programmes

Religion

Source: BBC annual reports

MEDIA STUDIES: THE ESSENTIAL RESOURCE

Soap opera as a form is more popular than ever. At least five different programmes are regularly listed amongst the top ten audience ratings. The popular
press both celebrates and exploits soap operas for their news value – witness
the manner in which the personal lives of the stars become mixed almost
inextricably with those if the characters they play.

Yet serious critical opinion derides soaps, and their position within the institution of television has traditionally been low. Soaps rarely win BAFTA awards.
Jean Alexander was nominated for best actress in 1988 after years in the role of
Coronation Street's Hilda Ogden – but didn't win. *Eastenders* producer Julia Smith
did get an award – but for her whole career in television, rather than for being a
soap opera producer.

Daytime soap operas in America and local ones like *Coronation Street* are
television's bread and butter, and their budgets, casting, and scheduling reflect
this. They are regularly lambasted for the fact that both 'nothing' and 'too much'
happens in them.

It is typically assumed that their audience consists of those whose lives are so
deprived as to need spurious enrichment. It is portrayed as an aesthetically naive
audience, unable to tell fiction from reality. This critical disdain must be related
to the structure of the audience which, especially in the case of the daytime and
early-evening soap operas, is assumed by programme makers, advertisers,
and those producing the attendant publicity material, to be a largely female one.
Forms of popular culture comsumed mainly by women, such as soap opera,
romantic fiction, or bingo have rarely been accorded a high cultural status in the
public domain.

Over the past decade or so this low status has been challenged. The soaps have
been claimed by some feminists as one of the few areas of television to open up
a space for women characters and for an examination of the concerns of women
and a representation of the texture of women's lives. The soaps are seen to allow
a focus on the area of relationships outside of waged labour, the area that has
conventionally been seen as woman's sphere of activity.

Within the genre it is possible to suggest a broad typology. British soap operas,
such as ITV's *Coronation Street*, *Crossroads*, *Brookside* (Channel 4) and the BBC's
EastEnders, are broadly within the tradition of social realism, featuring everyday
characters, plots, and language, often located within working-class communities.
At the other end of the scale is the romantic and melodramatic world of the
United States' exports: *Dallas*, with its offshoots *Knots Landing* and *The Colbys*, and
Dynasty. In these the 'social' background disappears beneath the expressive
excesses of *nouveau riche* wealth, thereby throwing the struggles for power, identity,
and family control into relief. Some American commentators make a further
distinction between these prime-time programmes and the lower-budget
daytime and early-evening soaps, whose titles suggest the world of romantic

fiction – *Guiding Light*, *All My Children*, *Search for Tomorrow*. Their preoccupations are, again, with family and identity, rather than the representation of a certain particular social reality.

HISTORY

The daytime soap opera had its origins in American radio with serials during the 1930s often sponsored by major soap manufacturers. Both the serials themselves and the commercials that introduced and punctuated them were directed almost exclusively at a female audience, assumed to be housebound and engaged in domestic chores between 9 a.m. and 3 p.m. These programmes concentrated on female characters, often shown within a professional setting, such as the medical and legal worlds, but with the emphasis on the emotional aspects of the narrative. The same applied in Australia through the late 1940s and 1950s. Many soaps, such as *Dr Paul*, and *Portia Faces Life* (featuring a female lawyer), were broadcast both in the USA and Australia. Other Australian soaps were produced by companies, such as Crawfords, who later went on to produce television series. . . .

PLEASURE AND GENDER

The pleasures of soap opera hinge on the particular relationship established between narrative and character. According to the expectations brought to an action series or an adventure serial, 'nothing' seems to happen in a soap like *Coronation Street* or *Brookside* because the satisfactions gained reside elsewhere than in a fast-flowing sequence of narrative events. The repercussions events will have on the lives of the characters are brought to the fore. This is registered largely through talk – through gossip, confessions, speculations, and exchanges of confidence.

Conventionally the world of gossip is seen as a woman's world, existing as part of the realm of the domestic and personal. Within this context the world of work becomes another arena for exhibiting a concern for people and their problems – it is humanized. Typically work within realist soaps is within the service industries – pubs, shops, and launderettes (although see below with reference to *Coronation Street*), which produce naturalized settings for the exchange of gossip.

Soaps also tend to focus on female characters not as the mysterious or peripheral figures of crime and action series but as everyday people coping with the problems of life. . . .

While audiences consist of both men and women, some writers have argued that the soap opera genre speaks specifically to women – the gender of the viewer is inscribed in the text. This is because they draw upon and speak to the specific skills attendant upon finding the mainspring of one's existence within the world of the personal and private and within the knowledge of the conventions of personal life that this brings. Charlotte Brunsdon argues that it is in gossip, the repeated mulling over of actions and possibilities, that the moral and ideological frameworks adhere. Modes of behaviour are tested and explored through talk: will she marry or not? Will she tell or not? It is not a crime that is being investigated but possible modes of behaviour. . . .

While critics argue that nothing happens in the British social realist soaps, they frequently level the very opposite criticism at the more melodramatic American soaps, in which 'too much happens'. In such programmes there is indeed typically an over-plenitude, derived from the location of a multiplicity of narratives around a permanent family of characters.

In *Dallas*, which some prefer to label a melodramatic serial, J.R.'s business deals are important, not in the way they might be within a dynastic chronicle or an exposé of capitalism, but as indices of his character – examples of his power and deviousness and expressions of his relationship with other characters. As the core of the genre is the private world, attendant rituals of family life, births, marriages, divorces, and romances come to the fore, and because of the nature of the genre these rituals become a source of uncertainty, worry, confusion, doubt, and threat rather than resolution, reassurance, or closure. If a classically socially-oriented British soap opera like *Coronation Street* can be seen to be about the 'settling of people in life' a prime-time American soap like *Dallas* could be understood as being precisely about the unsettling of its characters, its realism coming not through documentation of ordinary life, but through scrutinizing the emotional urgency that underpins all family life.

The pleasures available from any generic text depend in part upon one's familiarity with its conventions – to what extent are they adhered to, stretched, or contravened? The pleasures available from the soap opera also by definition depend upon a certain amount of knowledge of that specific programme. To catch the full implications of certain scenes in *EastEnders* we have to know who the father of Michelle's baby is. We must also have an interest as well as a competence in handling the conventions of personal life, and competence within this area belongs, it is argued, especially to women. . . .

SOAP: AUDIENCE AND REALISM

[. . .] *Brookside* producer, Phil Redmond . . . declared that Brookside would 'tell the truth and show society as it really is', recalling realism to its social base in 'issues' and 'problems'.

Like *Coronation Street*, *Brookside* has a northern location, in a newly built housing estate on the fringes of Liverpool. The serial's much discussed authenticity is there to underscore the veracity of its characters and the pointedness of its social

critique, the topicality of which Redmond sees as the peculiar province of the soap. Redundancy, union organization, the legal system, gambling, prostitution by housewives, infertility, the Church, have all fallen within the broad net of the serial's scripts. . . .

Realism has always been seen as a trap for its female characters. Christine Geraghty argues that the setting, the separate houses of the close, function to push the female characters out of the community and into the home. The women have then to be brought into contact with each other through the deliberate action of the narrative. . . .

Geraghty also argues that the weight of dramatic interest in this serial is deflected from its female characters in a way that renders it akin to 'drama proper', which elbows aside the particular pleasures to be gained from the intricate plotting and charting of action and reaction that allows space for domestic concerns.

EastEnders was also launched on the claim of greater realism. Julia Smith, the producer, in an interview in *Television Weekly* (30 November 1984) emphasized that *EastEnders* was to be about 'today', about 'everyday life', and that it was to be as topical and documentary as possible. It had to be, she argued, as real in today's terms as *Coronation Street* was when it started.

The initial episodes were bleakly shocking, offering a fairly relentlessly dark, lower-depths study of a post-industrial Britain of unremitting sourness. It struck chords familiar from the best days of the BBC's *Play for Today* and certainly in its gritty realism went beyond anything previously attempted for mass-market viewing.

The similarities with *Coronation Street* are there but to an extent the tables have been turned. Young characters are given far greater prominence and are drawn with some vigour. They are also frequently given the role of recalling their elders to the path of conventional morality (a role familiar from melodrama). *EastEnders* has learnt from American soaps the value of family dramas, and questions of paternity, adoption, fidelity, and so on are played to the hilt. Through its attempts to mobilize the 'real' and the 'topical' alongside the drama of the family, it has a sharper edge, while still staying within the constraints of social realism.

SOAP AS MELODRAMA

The byzantine relationships that are played out among the super-elite of *Dallas*, *The Colbys*, or *Dynasty* would seem to have little in common with the familiar drabness of the everyday world of British soaps. You have to look hard to find traces of the geographical Dallas within the serial. These soaps, too, are about family relationships and it is no accident that two of the three choose titles that directly reference the family, used as the basis for epic melodrama.

Dallas focuses on the oil-rich Ewing family and their rivalry with the Barnes family. There are a number of interpenetrations of the two families which, as Dave Kehr points out in *Film Comment* (July-August 1979), poses a constant threat to their integrity. These conflicts are played out against a whole series of oppositions of country/city, industrial/rural, domestic/commercial, with, in the background and in the titles, a sense of the vanished West and its codes. This already fissured environment serves as a means of magnifying the drama of family life.

Ien Ang (1985) argues that

> Women in soap operas never rise above their problematic positions. On the contrary they completely identify with them. In spite of all their miseries they continue to believe in the ideals of patriarchal ideology . . . the patriarchal status quo is non-viable but remains intact.

What melodrama and the melodramatic soaps explore is the struggle that takes place within them. It is a struggle to which the family is central. This is why it is no more relevant to complain that *Dallas* is only about the wealthy than it would be to grumble that *King Lear* is only about royalty.

Jane Feuer traces the origin of prime-time soaps to film melodramas like Douglas Sirk's *Written on the Wind*, which also uses what she calls a process of intensification by which the subject of the film becomes not the events themselves but the emotions these events arouse. These emotions are expressed through opulent sets and costumes and a rhetorical shooting style which forces the characters constantly away from 'ordinariness' and the 'everyday' and towards an emblematic goodness or evil. *Dynasty* interestingly focuses on a female villain but lacks the intensity of writing and sense of multi-layered meanings that characterize *Dallas*. One notable feature of *EastEnders*, at least while Dirty Den and Angie provided the central focus, was the attempt to emulate the emotional flamboyance of *Dallas* while remaining true to its social realist roots.

The emotions that, in this analysis, become the subject of the serial are grounded within the family. Identity becomes something fought for, and over, in relation to the constraints of family life, and motherhood, marriage, and sexuality become dangerous counters in the game rather than issues within a social setting.

Discussion of the soap opera as a genre has come primarily from two different areas: that of film study which has tended towards a theoretical study of the text itself and the possibilities the genre might offer for a progressive reading, and that of television studies which has placed more emphasis on the institutional context. This latter frequently involves taking the empirical existence of a female audience as a starting point. A more theoretically oriented study could involve locating a position inscribed within the text itself, which would apply regardless of the gender of the particular viewer.

The soap opera could be seen as embodying a distinctively 'feminine' way of seeing or being. A key statement in the debate around gender and pleasure in relation to visual texts is Laura Mulvey's 'Visual pleasure and narrative cinema' (1975). This looks at the way in which a narrative positions the viewer, regardless of sexual identity, within a system of visual pleasure set up according to a particular masculine point of view. Mulvey is discussing mainstream Hollywood narrative cinema, but, in extending this direction of analysis, Tania Modleski (1982) argues that soaps are not only 'made for' women but that, through the closeness with which they reproduce the world of the private and the domestic, they construct a position for the viewer that accords with feminine rather than patriarchal desire.

For the implications of a genre like soap opera, made for and watched by women, to be explored, it is necessary to look at the ways in which the conventions of social realism and melodrama are articulated. In Britain the form is currently more popular than ever and a full understanding of the ways in which it structures popular consciousness can reveal much about the relation between televisual representation and broader social processes.

V. Glaessner, 'Gendered Fictions' in A. Goodwin and G. Whannel (eds),
Understanding Television, Routledge, 1990, pp. 118–25

ACTIVITIES

➤ Choose a genre that interests you and make a list of the expectations that you think an audience is likely to have in relation to texts of that genre. Now choose a specific text within the genre and examine how you feel it fulfils these expectations.

➤ It has been argued that audiences soon tire of predictable genre formulas. Taking an example such as reality TV or docu-soaps, consider some of the ways in which producers have sought to modify the formulas in order to maintain audience interest. How far do you think they have succeeded?

➤ What film genres do you think can be seen to have a specific gender appeal? Make three lists:

■ Genres that you think appeal predominantly to women
■ Those that appeal mostly to men
■ Those that you believe appeal to both genders

What conclusions can you draw about the appeal of genres and the pleasures they offer? How useful do you feel this exploration of the relationship between genre and gender has been?

FURTHER READING

Branston, G. and Stafford, R.(1996) *The Media Student's Book*, Routledge.
Contains a useful chapter on genres.

Livingstone, S. (1990) *Making Sense of Television*, Routledge.
Includes an informative chapter examining the appeal of soap operas as a genre.

O'Sullivan, T. Dutton, B. and Rayner, P. (1994) S*tudying the Media*, Arnold.
Features a short section exploring the nature of genre across a range of media forms.

▼ 5 REPRESENTATION AND AGEISM

Television, radio, newspapers and magazines all mediate real events and conditions. To mediate means to come between, change or re-present. Although they attempt to produce a factual account of the way the world is, the constraints of the different media and the selection of words and images mean that it is impossible to reproduce exactly the world 'the way it is'.

In identifying the beliefs and attitudes involved in the selection of words and images that attempt to show real life, many questions arise about the way in which the media re-presents to the world back to us. Whose version of reality is being presented or re-presented to us? Who is doing the presenting? Who or what is being re-presented? How is it being re-presented? To whom is it addressed? Why is it being re-presented in this way? Who makes the decisions in selecting/constructing/editing on our behalf, and what makes them qualified to make these decisions? What view of the world are we given? How familiar does it look?

Representation is one of the key concepts in the study of the media. The media, and particularly television, are often described as a 'window on the world' although in fact media are highly selective in the way in which they construct and represent the world back to us. The various media forms mediate between us and the 'real world'. Representation has largely dealt with how particular social groups are, or have been represented in the media, focusing on women, ethnic minorities, young people and particular subcultures.

Representation examines the content of media texts, their signs, etc., as well as examining how these signs are interpreted and given meaning by their audiences. In many cases, analysis of representations or particular social groups can identify how they are *mis*-represented by the media.

> ➤ 'The mass media do not simply reflect social reality, they represent it.' Discuss with selected examples.
> ➤ Choose one group that you believe is positively represented in the media. Evaluate how and why this particular group is represented positively. (AQA Unit 4 January 2002).

AGE

Old age and the aging process in general have limited coverage in the media. Positive representations of the elderly tend to be even more limited. This is therefore a potentially fruitful area of study and offers an alternative to the studies of representations of gender, race and class that might be considered more established areas of the media syllabus.

Katharine Whitehorn is an agony aunt for *Saga* magazine. In the article below she discusses the results of a report published by the ITC and Age Concern. She asks why advertising agencies and television production companies offer a very limited and largely negative representation of people over 50, and why a 'grandmother' is usually represented as a 'white-haired old thing'. She argues that the over-50s of today came of age in the 1960s and have a wide range of interests. She is particularly critical of media portrayals of women over 50.

SAME OLD STORY

If you accuse the bright young sparks in TV or ad agencies of being behind the times, they think you're accusing them of still liking Duran Duran or wearing the wrong sort of scarf (*so* last year). What's really out of date is their notion of what older people look like, do, talk about and want to see on TV, and the only surprising thing about the current fuss is that it's apparently taken a survey commissioned by the ITC and Age Concern to make them even dimly aware of it. For the over-50s are truly fed up with the way they are shown – or not shown – on television.

We know, of course, that TV people rate themselves on how they impress other TV people, most of whom are under 40 or feel the need to pretend they are. (Jane Root, new controller of BBC2, and herself 43, is quoted as saying that all people think they're under 40, which is nonsense.) But the ads that support these programmes, you'd have thought, would be more concerned with the sheer marketing idiocy of aiming everything at the young – the young who, in any case, are much more likely to be out or bonking in front of the box than actually watching it.

There are, after all, 19 million over-50s, who will outnumber the others in a few years' time, and already spend £145 billion a year. Half of them, maybe, are the penniless pensioners who appear on the news every single time 'pensions' are mentioned, but the other half – with mortgages paid, children (with luck) off their hands – are free to spend money – more so than they've ever been – and they're not spending it on Ovaltine and corn plasters.

I wouldn't be unkind enough to suggest that the programme-makers simply can't count, but I can't understand why, whenever they want to show the over-50s, they usually show the over-80s, preferably in an old folks' home or crouching over a single-bar fire in their mouldering bedroom slippers. Nobody makes programmes for 10-year-olds on the assumption they're the same as 40-year-olds, after all, but it's the same age gap in either case.

Why does the word 'grandmother' instantly throw up a white-haired old thing who's either going goofy or rotting up her descendants' lives, instead of the harried, working, busy factotums that actually do the job – the ones who are running charities, starting pressure groups, gardening, working, and looking after their grandchildren half the time (one consequence of family break-up)? Or going on holidays – and no, I don't just mean cruises. I mean mountaineering expeditions, dog-sledding with Eskimos, camel trekking across the Australian outback – just three well-subscribed senior holidays.

I am, I should maybe say, currently Agony Aunt for *Saga* magazine for the over-50s. People hearing this usually laugh till their gums bleed and then ask if I get questions about Zimmer frames and false-teeth fixative. When I mention the man who, at her request, wears his lover's nightdress when he goes to visit her (should he wear it in front of her sister?), or the ones who don't know how to handle the surges of desire brought on by aromatherapy, or the 70-year-old woman asking about reliable computer courses – she must have heard that the biggest users of email in the States are grans and grandchildren – they are amazed. Why? Because they haven't noticed – and TV hasn't helped them notice – that today's over-50s aren't like the parents and grandparents they remember. These are the kids of the swinging 60s, and they're not about to take up knitting and the inglenook.

The people who are complaining most, according to the Age Concern survey, are the people in their 50s and 60s, most of whom don't want special golden-oldie programmes – they are mainstream, they just want to be let off things aimed only at the young. They are possibly bored with programmes that are entirely full of violence and swearing or programmes aimed at the notional 'younger viewer' who is thought to want everything jazzed up, jokey, instant – who wouldn't watch a first-class programme like *Local Hero*, it says here, without Adam Hart-Davis wearing that foul pink bicycle helmet, or switch on to anything unless the girl seems to be having an orgasm as she announces a programme about global warming or the NHS.

CONTINUED

Older women feel especially poorly treated by TV. They are mostly allowed on the box only if they're guyed up like Clarissa Dickson-Wright on her silly scooter, or preceded, like Victor Meldrew's wife, by 200-year-old tortoises and the grim little dirge of *One Foot In The Grave*. There are exceptions – there was Hetty Wainwright, we get occasional bouts of Claire Rayner, there are grown-up dramas like *Sins* and *Middlemarch*; but the idea of showing, say, a senior female presenter with her white hair superbly blow-dried like Michael Aspel would be unthinkable.

All right, we all like to think that we're a bit younger than we are, but not ludicrously so, and certainly we prefer handsome to plain people. But those in their 60s, according to the survey, are choosier than their elders. They watch more television than they did – at the moment, but this may not continue. And how will TV fare if half its audience drops away?

K. Whitehorn, 'Same Old Story', *Guardian*, 1 December 2000

In the following extract, Andrew Blaikie undertakes a review of magazines aimed at the 'grey market', their evolution and the representations that they offer. He suggests that some of the earliest of these magazines were aimed at 'pensioners' and those either in or about to start 'retirement'. In 1974, he suggests, there was a shift in the attitude of these magazines, with more of a focus on how pensioners would spend their new-found free time.

As long ago as 1984, Featherstone and Hepworth published a study of images of ageing in the magazine *Choice*. The main points they noted are worth reiterating. Tellingly, the periodical starts out as a vehicle for the Pre-Retirement Association, in October 1972, with the title *Retirement Choice*. The visual emphasis is on the masthead RETIREMENT, in block capitals, superseding 'Choice' in lower-case.

The cover shows a black-and-white shot of a large crowd of men, with speech-bubbles pasted on, rather in the vein of *Private Eye*, only this is serious. The message is not vigorous or glamorous but worthy and rather drab, reflecting the concerns of male retirees as a mass, along the lines of 'What about our rights?' Yet, even this first issue carries a section on women's fashions, lambasting the 'dull uniform' of retirement and praising modern grandmothers for their modish outlook. By the next year, a fresh, individualised focus becomes evident. Instead of the great mass of undifferentiated 'pensioners', the cover image is of the married couple – further acknowledgement of the importance of older women as the numerical majority, if not the majority voice. In late 1974, the magazine was taken over by a commercial organisation and the format became more bookstall-friendly, filled with colour photographs. There are the beginnings of a discourse on what people might do with their leisure time. There are articles about how to fill two and a half thousand hours, and about travel and DIY. Shifts in the magazine's title reflect this transformation: first the emphasis switches from 'RETIREMENT Choice' to 'Pre-retirement CHOICE'; then the wording becomes 'CHOICE – the only magazine for retirement planning' and another magazine, *Life Begins at 50*, gets incorporated. Eventually, the subtitle becomes '*leisure* and retirement planning'. We see a move from what might be considered a retirement broadsheet for those immediately contemplating their pension, to agenda-setting about self-help and change management (note the word 'planning' in the subtitle) for the over-50s. The glossy visual appeal is altogether more bright-eyed and bushy-tailed.

As the 1970s run into the 1980s, *Choice* comes to reflect a broader cultural reorientation. All the resonances are there: financial awareness, 'heritage' holidays, Prime Minister Thatcher on the cover, a role model of careful grooming, juxtaposed with an inset shot of her from the 'milk snatcher' years, looking older, staider, out-of-fashion, when in fact she was decades younger. (Ironically enough the same cover advertises the lure of a free redundancy booklet within.) A 1984 issue carries a feature by Miriam Stoppard inviting readers to 'put the sparkle back into your sex life'. By now, the publisher's house style makes it difficult, in places, to distinguish *Choice* from *Cosmopolitan*. Sexuality would never have been openly discussed in a retirement magazine twenty, or even ten, years previously. The perceived 'naturalness' of sex in later life renders clichés like 'dirty old man' and 'mutton dressed as lamb' increasingly obsolete. 'Sexagenarian . . . it comes after sex in the dictionary' noted a cover story by famous popular writer Jilly Cooper in the summer 1997 issue of *World of Retirement*.

A number of magazines from the 1980s and 1990s very much echo this reworking. The titles themselves are indicative of pro-active Third Age awareness. Take, for example, *Retirement Planning and Living*, whose message lies in getting readers to ask of themselves a series of questions about time management: what are we going to do with these twenty, twenty-five, thirty years? We cannot go on that cruise of a lifetime forever, so what happens when we get home? Finance, fitness, fashion, travel – the remit is beginning to widen – and it is very much about self-help, planning one's own lifestyle. The Association of Retired Persons' *050* magazine promotes consumerism through attractive discounts but also considers second careers and educational opportunities. *Saga* is renowned for its golf-buggies and high-living style of package-travel selling. Meanwhile, in the United States, *Grandparents Today* illustrates the increased youthfulness of the modern grandparent and *Lear's* filled an important lacuna in the women s magazine market as 'the magazine for the woman who wasn't born yesterday'. Along with the fresh *Choice* subtitle – 'Britain's magazine for successful retirement – comes *Good Times* – 'changing attitudes to age', later 'for those old enough to know better' – *Yours* – 'for the young at heart' – *Active Life* – 'the lively magazine for the years ahead', and *World of Retirement* – 'for people who enjoy life'. Research is only beginning to map the field of older people's magazines in ways similar to that done for, say, those directed at teenage girls. Parallels are none the less obvious in the broadening of the range of titles and themes on offer to both audiences, in the foregrounding of topics such as sex, and – *People's Friend* excepted – a shift from romance narratives dependent on heroic others to 'a new, more confident, focus on the self'.

Undoubtedly, the leading edge has come from the United States, where the American Association of Retired Persons makes great play on its 30 million plus and growing membership. In the UK, although the political culture of Thatcherism – certainly the emphasis on consumerism – helped to break the mould, numerous contradictory messages can also be found: neither sexual sparkle, nor older postwomen, for instance, rest comfortably with Victorian values. But the point is that nowadays much of what is marketed at mid-lifers is indistinguishable from the interests of younger adults. The inculcation of 'lifestyle' covers a vast domain that embraces all ages.

A. Blaikie, *Ageing and Popular Culture*, Cambridge University Press, 1998, pp. 98–102

According to Blaikie, a 'cultural reorientation' took place during the 1980s, particularly in relation to sexual activity amongst the over-50s, when clichés of the 'dirty old man' and 'mutton dressed up a lamb' began to be challenged. By the 1990s, he suggests, public figures like Mick Jagger, David Bowie, Joan Collins, Jane Fonda and Raquel Welch were promoting positive images for the over-50s, especially in terms of their continued sex appeal.

Although there is now a range of magazines aimed at this readership, *Choice, Good Times, Saga, Yours, Active Life* and so on, Blaikie notes that researchers are now beginning to look at these publications in the same ways they might look at those aimed at teenage girls. Blaikie argues that this shift is a reflection of 'post-modern times', where older people are no longer constrained by rules governing how their lives should be, but are encouraged to choose their own lifestyles, just as people a generation younger are doing.

ACTIVITY

➤ These two extracts by Whitehorn and Blaikie seem to offer contradictory statements about the way in which the over-50s are represented. One addresses television and suggests that representations of the over-50s are largely negative. The other discusses magazines and finds more positive representations. Do you think that one of these two views is more correct than the other? Might they both be correct? How do you account for these differences?

THANKS TO the right oil she still goes like the clappers.

Rosanna knows that the right oil will help keep you in perfect working order for years. That's why Olivio use Bertolli Olive Oil, one of Italy's best loved oils. First produced in Lucca in 1865 it's been running smoothly ever since.

OLIVIO. MADE WITH OLIVE OIL.

Blaikie places this attitude within the context of a 'consumer culture' and the way in which media producers are increasingly aware of the 'grey market' as a potential source of revenue and advertising income. He also identifies the growth of an ideology of Third Age 'personal fulfilment', where leisure is achieved through effort, both physical (keeping fit) and financial (dressing well, taking holidays).

It is interesting to consider what the defining characteristics might be of media texts aimed at the grey market and how they might be considered 'positive'. This could be contrasted with a piece of research looking at how over-50s are represented in popular television programmes and to what extent these might be considered 'negative'.

As Blaikie notes, there is a potentially fruitful area of research in terms of these magazines, perhaps using models taken from studies such as McRobbie's work on *Jackie* and *More!* (McRobbie 1996, 2000). (See also the section on teenage magazines in Part 2 of *Media Studies: The Essential Introduction* by Rayner, Wall and Kruger 2001).

A semiotic analysis of the Olivio advert will help in identifying the humour it uses. This advert could be considered along with a range of other media representations of over-50s to identify the context, activities, clothing and body language that they are most often associated with.

ACTIVITIES

> ➤ How useful a concept do you think representation is to understanding the nature of media messages?
> ➤ What representations can you find in the media that might be considered stereotypes? In which media do stereotypes most commonly appear?
> ➤ Undertake a survey of a range of popular television programmes. What are the main features in the reporting and representation of youth and old age?

FURTHER READING

Barker, C. (1999) *Television, Globalization and Cultural Identities,* Open University Press.
Particular chapters focus on the construction and representation of race and nation and sex and gender.

Cottle, S. (1999) 'Ethnic Minorities and the British News Media: Explaining (mis)Representation', in J. Stokes and A. Reading (eds) *The Media in Britain: Current Debates and Developments,* MacMillan.
This offers a look at the way in which ethnic minorities are represented in the news media with a specific focus on the institutional practices that determine particular representations.

Hall, S. (ed.) (1997) *Representation: Cultural Representations and Signifying Practices,* Sage.
One of the key texts in relation to the concept of representation.

O'Sullivan, T., Dutton, B. and Rayner, P. (1998) 'Representations and Realism', in *Studying the Media*, Arnold.
An accessible introduction to the concept with particular emphasise on the British nation as an ideological construct as well as exploring the relationship between ethnic and gender stereotypes and ideology.

▼   6 REALISM AND DOCUMENTARY

Realism is an important and complex concept in the analysis of media texts. Discussions about realism are usually based around the extent to which the media are able to represent the world as it really is.

REALISM

Television seems to be describing the world as it is. This is most obvious with news and current affairs programmes. These clearly make a claim to be telling the truth; they are describing the world as it really is. This claim is enhanced by the feeling that television is operating in the present, unlike any other medium. Not only is it describing reality, it is giving us the events as they happen. As Feuer puts it, television has the quality of 'liveness'. Contemporary satellite technology has enhanced these qualities, with often dramatic and bizarre results. For example, during the Gulf War, there were television reports of American bombing of Baghdad which described missiles as they passed the reporter's hotel window.

Realism, however, is not only a characteristic of factual programming. Perhaps more importantly, fictional output can be described in this way. Television drama of all kinds usually tries very hard to give the *feel* of reality. An historical drama, *The Buccaneers* for example, creates a period setting in loving detail and, even if the speech may be modern, a great deal of care goes into trying to persuade the audience that it is actually present in the Victorian period. Similarly, soap operas like *EastEnders* aim to be realistic. Trouble is taken to make the characters and sets authentic so that the illusion is created that these are real people in a real east London setting.

Although this attempt at creating reality may seem be an obvious feature of television, the concept of realism itself is very difficult to define. Abercrombie et al. (1992) argue that there are three features that distinguish realist texts. First, realism offers a 'window on the world'. In the case of television, there is no mediation between the viewer and what he or she is watching. It is as if the

television set were a sheet of clear glass which offered the viewer an uninter-rupted vision of what lay beyond. Television is, or *seems* to be, like direct sight. Second, realism employs a narrative which has rationally ordered connections between events and characters. Realist cultural forms, certainly those involving fictional presentations at any rate, consist of a caused, logical flow of events, often structured into a beginning, a middle and a closed conclusion. Events and characters, therefore, do not have a random or arbitrary nature, but are organized by rational principles. In these respects, realist forms may be contrasted with those texts that are essentially 'spectacular'. The pleasure of texts that involve 'spectacle' lies in the images themselves; it is a visual, not a narrative pleasure. It is important to note that static images can also be narrative. Many photographs and paintings often have a 'before' and 'after' outside the specific moment captured in the frame. They are episodes in a story and imply the rest of the narrative; the meaning of the picture is given by its place in an implied narrative. Non-realist forms do not imply such a narrative. They do not so much tell a story as invite contemplation.

The third aspect of realism is the concealment of the production process. Most television is realist in this sense in that the audience is not made aware, during the programmes themselves, that there is a process of production lying behind the programmes. The illusion of transparency is preserved. It is as if there were no author. The form conspires to convince us that we are not viewing something that has been constructed in a particular fashion by a determinate producer or producers. This concealment of the production process, this hiding of the author's hand, is best seen when the occasional television programme does not follow the convention. When in the 1995 series of A B*it of Fry and Laurie* the camera moves from filming the set to following one of the characters out of the set and into the studio with its plain brick walls, other cameras, and a maze of cables and other equipment, the audience feels a shock as the illusion of realism is disrupted.

However powerful its effects, realism is only a *convention*. Television may appear to be a window on the world but it is not really *transparent*. What it offers is essentially a *construction* of the world, a version of reality. This is not a conspiracy to mislead the audience. It is simply that there is no way in which any description of reality can be the only, pure and correct one, just as people will give very different descriptions of what they see out of their kitchen window. As soon as television producers start to film, they are necessarily selecting and interpreting; they *must* do so in order to present a coherent programme of whatever kind. As a result, of course, all sorts of thing can be excluded by realist conventions. For example, Jordan (1981) argues that:

> *Coronation Street* conventionally excludes everything which cannot be seen to be physically present . . . This means, in effect, that most social explanations,

and all openly political ones, are omitted. The differing situations, the troubles or successes, of the various characters are explained largely in terms of their (innate) psychological make-up, occasionally attributed to luck.

The critical question raised by the convention of realism is then: is there a systematic exclusion of particular features of the world from television? A number of writers argue that there is and the effect on audiences is particularly powerful because the realist convention does *seem* to be a correct description of the world. Television presents one reality and audiences are persuaded to accept it as the only reality. MacCabe (1981a, 1981b) argues for this position. He suggests that a variety of points of view may be articulated in a television text, but one reality is still preferred; there is a dominant point of view, that of the narrator, which is presented as the natural, transparent one, There is therefore a *hierarchy of discourses* or points of view in which one discourse controls the others.

It might be replied, however, that MacCabe's is too simplified a view. Jordan (1981), for example, argues that there is not a single realism in television, but rather a number of realisms. She therefore describes *Coronation Street* as a version of realism which she calls soap opera realism. This is a combination of the social realism of films of the 1960s with the realism of soap opera. The former demands that:

> life be presented in the form of a narrative of personal events, each with a beginning, a middle and an end, important to the central characters concerned but affecting others in only minor ways; that though these events are ostensibly about *social* problems they should have as one of their central concerns the settling of people in life; that the resolution of these events should always be in terms of the effect of personal interventions; that characters should be either working-class or of the classes immediately visible to the working classes (shopkeepers, say . . .) and should be credibly accounted for in terms of the 'ordinariness' of their homes, families, friends; that the locale should be urban and provincial (preferably in the industrial north); that the settings should be commonplace and recognisable (the pub, the street, the factory, the home and more particularly the kitchen); that the time should be 'the present'; that the style should be such as to suggest an unmediated, unprejudiced and complete view of reality; to give, in summary, the impression that the reader, or viewer, has some time at the expense of the characters depicted. (p. 28)

The latter, on the other hand, requires that:

> though events must carry their own minor conclusions they must not be seen as finally resolving; that there should be an intertwining of plots so deployed as to imply a multiplicity of experience whilst effectively covering only a narrow

range of directly 'personal' events; that these personal events should be largely domestic; that there should be substantial roles for women; that all roles should involve a serious degree of stereotyping; that the most plausible setting, in view of these later requirements, would be the home; and that the long-term passage of fictional time should mirror fairly accurately the actual passage of time. (p. 28)

Although this form of realism does exclude certain features it also does allow alternative realities to emerge. Furthermore, as Jordan notes, the pleasure of a soap opera like *Coronation Street* may partly lie in the perception by the audience that it *is* a construction. The programme, in other words, breaks with the third feature of the definition of realism put forward at the beginning of this section. It may, indeed, be doing this quite deliberately in a number of ways. For example, some of the characters are caricatures rather than realist depictions. Reg Holdsworth in *Coronation Street* is a good example. Again, the programme uses the self-conscious linking technique of shifting to a scene involving characters who have been the subject of a conversation in the previous scene. As Jordan argues:

> My argument then is that *Coronation Street*, though deploying the devices of the Soap Opera Realism upon which it is based, far from attempting to hide the artifice of these devices (other than by the generic imperative to hide) rather asks us to take pleasure in its artistry, much as a stage magician will not show us how his tricks are done yet never claims . . . that he has actually sawn a woman in half. (p. 39)

Jordan's view of *Coronation Street* suggests that there can be a substantial dislocation of realism's effects. Such dislocation may, of course, be even more noticeable in other sorts of programme which set out to *play* with reality (*The Singing Detective*, for example).

N. Abercrombie, *Television and Society*, Polity Press, 1996, pp. 26–30

The extract by Nicholas Abercrombie considers various different theories about the nature of realism on television. As Abercrombie notes, this debate is complicated by the fact that 'realism' itself is associated with a set of codes and conventions that we recognise as 'real' or 'realistic' but are in fact as artificial and constructed as any other media text. Abercrombie suggests that for most viewers the news on television appears to be realistic, an impression enhanced by its sense of 'liveness': 'not only is it describing reality, it is giving us the events as they happen'. However, we also recognise that it is not real but a highly mediated version of events. Abercrombie argues that what television realism offers is essentially a 'construction of reality which is not deliberately misleading, but which cannot hope to speak for everyone's experience and understanding of the world.

It is probably easiest if we accept that realism is itself a system of codes and conventions that represent world events in a particular manner which we accept as 'true to life', in so far as this is possible. Abercrombie suggests that current affairs, news and documentary programmes are regarded as the most realistic television genres. However, the way in which the subject is selected and framed by the camera, the use of narration or voice-over and the very choice of subject matter, all lead to a certain construction or representation of reality. Abercrombie refers to the ideas of Colin MacCabe (1981a, 1981b) who argues that 'Television presents one reality and audiences are persuaded to accept it as the only reality . . . a dominant point of view, that of the narrator, which is presented as the natural, transparent one'. Some might argue that different audiences will interpret programmes in different ways, making judgements about the degree of realism contained in particular texts. A documentary programme suggesting that there is a high level of alcohol abuse amongst university students may seem realistic to someone who has no direct experience of university life, but may seem artificial and biased to someone who is a university student.

ACTIVITIES

➤ 'Documentaries, like plays, novels and poems, are fictional forms' (Frederick Wiseman, American film-maker).
What do you think Wiseman meant by this statement? Do you agree with Wiseman's view? Discuss with reference to a range of documentary material. (NEAB Paper, 2 June 1997)

➤ 'Documentary makers attempt to do more than just entertain their audiences.' Do you agree? Refer to specific examples in your answer. (AQA Unit,2 June 2001)

NEW HYBRIDS

As we have argued, 'documentary' is a term that is used by broadcasters and audiences alike to refer to an ever-expanding body of texts. In the last ten years there have been numerous documentary spin-offs, rips-offs and cast-offs. These have extended the documentary genre in a number of ways which have collectively served to blur the boundaries between fact and fiction, and to complicate what we might consider to be the documentary project. Unlike the reflexive and performative modes, docu-soap and Reality TV, which we consider next, blur boundaries in less reflexive or critical ways. Their popularity has had an impact on the shape of contemporary television documentary and there is now considerable international trade of such formats. These forms have also opened up debates concerning documentary's access and representation of the real. As with the texts above, such discussions have provided viewers with opportunities to reflect critically on the documentary project.

Docu-soap

As the name suggests, this particular spin-off combines aspects of documentary with those of soap opera, and to date appears to have developed most success-fully in the United Kingdom. Docu-soap producer Andrew Bethell has argued that the 'docu-soap has been the most significant development in recent British television'. The success of the British versions of this form has in turn spawned numerous copies in New Zealand, Australia and the United States.

These hybrid texts tend to take shape around an 'exposé' or 'behind the scenes' look at large institutions – especially those that have day-to-day contact with 'the public' Their documentariness lies in their claim to present real people, places and events. Utilising the observational mode, or 'fly-on-the-wall' tech-niques, these programmes present a slice of 'naturally' occurring everyday life. This visual mode of spontaneous reality is undercut slightly by an often-used authoritative voice-over which guides viewers through the narrative. Unlike the documentaries of Wiseman, for example *Hospital* (1970) in which intimate portrayals of institutions are used to raise broader ideological questions, docu-soap merely makes a spectacle out of the ordinary.

These programmes gain their credibility through their association with the documentary form, but their appeal lies in the way in which their narratives are constructed along the lines of soap opera. Like the fictional serial form, these programmes usually have several narrative strands which are on-going, and although such programmes are limited to series lengths of six to twelve weeks, narrative closure is deferred as long as possible. Individual episodes usually contain a summary of the various narrative strands, allowing new viewers to catch up and regular viewers to re-visit major themes and characters. Here, an argu-ment is only indirectly constructed, with instead a main narrative drive coming from the personal experiences of the central personalities. These programmes explicitly make 'stars' out of ordinary people, with their experiences rendered worthy of our scrutiny, an agenda which also has the interesting effect of foregrounding the performance of identity itself.

These programmes make good use of the recent lighter, smaller cameras which make observational filming less intrusive and cumbersome. Yet we are typically made acutely aware of the presence of both the camera and the crew. Very often the 'stars' of the programme will talk directly to the camera in a quasi-confessional style. Although sometimes their comments are directed more widely towards the imagined viewer, often we as viewers feel as though we are being given direct access to a private interaction between an individual and the crew.

Many of these programmes have been criticised for staging sequences, most famously scenes from UK *Driving School*. Interestingly, the realisation that the presence of the camera and crew are having an impact on the social actors and action, while implicitly pointing to the constructed nature of these texts, seems to do little to challenge the 'reality' or the 'documentariness' of the form. Having said this, it is possible to argue that through such a foregrounding of the constructed nature or 'performed' nature of such representations, a space is opened up for viewers to engage more critically and reflexively with the form. In this sense, although docu-soap does not seem to reflect the questioning stance toward documentary of either the reflexive or performative mode, it can still be grouped with those developments which work to challenge documentary proper.

Reality TV

Another hybrid documentary form is reality TV, which is distinctive because it pairs documentary traits with fictional aesthetic devices. By this we mean that it maintains the claims for access to the real, while presenting this reality in a highly popularised and stylised manner. Reality TV, with its characteristically shaky hand-held camera, gives the impression of unmediated, spontaneous action, captured as it happens. Yet these are also the aspects which alert us to the presence of the camera and thus the constructed nature of the representations on offer. Such programming seems both to extend a particular mode of documentary (the observational mode) and to reinforce its claims to give direct access to the real, yet it potentially also contains a critique of such modes and their truth claims. These new hybrid reality formats make careful attempts to establish their public service credentials by claiming an educative role, and by arguing that such programmes encourage viewers to help solve crimes. However, they owe more to tabloid sensationalism and similarly reflect the need to entertain and retain large audiences. In ideological terms, it is significant that their investigative potential is muted and they do little to challenge the dominant order.

Docu-soap and Reality TV are connected to mock-documentary because they too have developed in the spaces between fact and fiction. These formats can be regarded as a response to both changing economic and broadcasting contexts, but their most interesting aspect is their apparent relation to some of the critiques offered by postmodern theorising. While docu-soap and reality TV seem to offer very little in the way of a critique of documentary, they can be seen as representing a popularisation of a postmodern scepticism toward the expert and the professional. Both of these formats are built around lay experiences and perspectives, rather than that of the experts so central to certain documentary modes. They both reject professionalism for a more general amateurism which is seen as being more truthful or 'authentic'.

'Faking it' has never been so easy

Finally, within this discussion of recent transformations of the genre, we need to mention recent technological developments that have also impacted upon documentary in a number of ways. Advances in image construction and manipulation have allowed filmmakers a much greater latitude to mediate representations of the social-historical world. Such technological advancements can be seen as presenting the potential to capture new audiences through new formats, while also posing a direct threat to the integrity of documentary's claims to truth.

Digital technologies perhaps present the most potent challenge to documentary's privileged truth status. These advancements in photographic and computer technology have already had an impact on journalism. Computer programs such as Adobe Photoshop allow even the relatively unskilled to manipulate photographic stills. Extend this to the general post-production process and the implications are clear. Although documentaries are always 'constructed' to some extent, because of the need to select and structure information into textual form, these new technologies allow the referent itself to be manipulated – in other words, the basic integrity of the camera as a *recording* instrument is fundamentally undermined.

In this way, it has never been easier to 'fake it' and to be able to go as far as producing evidence, in the form of stills or film, of events, people and objects that really have no referent in the 'real world'. Feminist filmmakers have used particular stylistic strategies in order to break the direct relationship between the image and the referent, yet this was done in the knowledge that the process was highly constructed and was not necessarily meant to look natural or real. With these particular texts, we were not supposed to believe that such presentations were to replace such images of the real. However, technology now allows us to make the same breaks, to manipulate stills and film footage, without anyone being the wiser. This, more than any other development, challenges documentary's reliance on the power of referentiality.

This developing capability to play with the referential quality of documentary representation is obviously most 'dangerous' when combined with an intent to hoax. Popular documentary formats in Britain have recently been the target of media witch-hunts and of various official inquiries over fears of this very tendency. . . . [H]eadlines in British newspapers such as 'Can We Believe Anything We See on TV?' [are] typical of the panic over fakes. Documentary originally secured its privileged status as a representational form by promoting its trustworthiness. Recently, that trust has been eroded. Although it is widely acknowledged that documentary is inevitably 'constructed' to a certain extent, viewers nevertheless have trouble accepting that it may deliver images of the social world that are not true. Hence the public outcry when it was revealed that a major producer of documentaries in the UK, Carlton TV, had set subjects up and lied to audiences.

Documentary is undergoing a number of quite complex transformations in the light of recent challenges to its status and public role. As a consequence the genre has been extended and developed in new and innovative ways. This process of transformation has always been an inherent, if not always openly acknowledged, aspect of documentary and in recent years has opened up space for hybrid formats such as docu-soap and Reality TV. Mock-documentary needs to be discussed in relation to these hybrid forms because it also partly derives from and reveals a weakening of the bond between factual discourse and the codes and conventions typically associated with documentary.

J. Roscoe and C. Hight, *Faking It: Mock Documentary and the Subversion of Facuality*, Manchester University Press, 2001, pp. 36–40

Many contemporary documentary makers have moved away from the codes and conventions of realism. The extract by Roscoe and Hight (2001) examines the way in which the documentary genre on television is being reinvented through a 'borrowing' of the codes and conventions of other genres (particularly soap opera) but also as a result of technological changes that have resulted in the miniaturisation of camera and sound equipment.

In the article 'The egos have landed', Jon Ronson looks at a new style of documentary film-makers like Nick Broomfield and Michael Moore. He describes them as film-makers who question and draw attention to the process of film-making itself. In their films we see the film-maker take prime position both in the narrative and in front of the camera. Rather than the anonymity of 'fly-on-the-wall', these film-makers address the camera directly, are shown being refused access to particular people or organisations, and in the case of *Biggie and Tupac*, reflecting on air about the dangerous nature of the documentary investigations.

Below is the dialogue from the opening scene of the film *Behind the Rent Strike* made in 1974 by Nick Broomfield when a student at the National Film School. The visual is a shot of a woman who lives on the local council estate talking to the camera in response to questions asked by Nick Broomfield.

Woman: Maybe it's just me, that I am so sceptical. I am so sceptical that the working-class position will ever change. I know it could change in actual fact, the working-class position could change, but it won't change through the media. And that's why I am so sceptical about the media. It won't change by films, television, newspapers. It will not change because as you have just said

NickBroomfield.com

HOME · E-MAIL

BEHIND THE RENT STRIKE

NOTES: **REVIEWS**

Made with Phillip Jones Griffith, Diana Ruston, and Graham Berry; and a special thanks to the Singletons who were the inspiration for the film.

Running Time: 50 minutes

DIRECTOR'S COMMENTS:

"My graduating film from the National Film School. Colin Young the head of the N.F.S., helped me a great deal to structure the film, as did Brian Winston."

STILLS

news · bio · filmography · store · links · awards

---

yourself it's middle-class views, it's controlled and owned by the middle class who put across what is in their own best interest. In actual fact I am very sceptical about them ever changing the working-class position. They just cannot. The only people who change the working-class position are the working class themselves.

Broomfield: So what do you think of me making a film down here?

Woman: Well I don't think anything about it, you can come in, you can make it and it will have no effect like I've just said. It will make people think for a few minutes and that's all, but the position of the working class won't change. It won't change by you making a film nor for that matter any other film-maker coming in, it just won't make any difference. There've been dozens of film-makers we've seen on local estates and . . .

Broomfield: Why do you think I am making it then?

Woman: I'm asking you that, why are you making it? It's only personal self-satisfaction that's all, it is, it must be. How can you get the interest to sort it all out unless you feel deeply enough about it? And the only way to feel deeply about it is for it to be bloody well happening to you and it is not happening to you, because at the end of the three months you know you can go back home.

(*Behind the Rent Strike*, Director Nick Broomfield, Lafayette Films, 1974)

In the spring of 2003 there was some controversy over the television programme *Living with Michael Jackson* made by Martin Bashir and broadcast on ITV1. Michael Jackson accused Martin Bashir of using film and interview extracts out of context and later broadcast his own version of the interviews using footage filmed by his own staff. Jackson claimed that Martin Bashir had been manipulative and had misrepresented Michael Jackson and Neverland.

ACTIVITIES

- ➤ Consider the questions that the Bloomfield extract raises about the role of the documentary film-maker. There is an assumption that films like this have the power to alter circumstances or that film-makers may wish to make films that alter circumstances or improve the lives of their subjects. Do you think that this is true?
- ➤ What do you consider to be the motivation of documentary film-makers like Nick Broomfield and Martin Bashir? What do you think is the motivation behind Nick Broomfield's latest film *Biggie and Tupac*?
- ➤ Using websites such as *www.guardian.co.uk/Archive* or www.pamediapoint. press.net research the controversy surrounding *Living with Michael Jackson*. Do you think that it is possible to provide a 'truthful' and fair account of someone's life in a television documentary?
- ➤ What are the motivations for making docu-soaps or reality tv programmes? Do you think the motivation for making documentary films has changed over the years? If so, why is this?
- ➤ Consider a range of documentary films and try and identify those that might have led to some kind of positive change in the circumstances of those featured in the film.
- ➤ Are the criticisms made in the film about middle-class film makers who can go home after three months justified? If so, does this mean that all documentary film-makers must come from within the situation that they are reporting on? What might the problems be with this idea?

Roscoe and Hight call these new hybrid forms of documentary 'mock-documentary' because they reflect a 'post-modern scepticism towards the expert and the professional' and instead offer a 'more general amateurism which is seen as being more truthful or 'authentic' (2001: 39). It is perhaps because these types of programmes are seen to use 'real' people and 'real' situations that they appear to give a heightened sense of realism. Roscoe and Hight suggest that the increasing sophistication of digital editing and post-production facilities means that the makers of these types of programmes are (at best) manipulating or (at worst) faking much of their content.

> ➤ In recent years docu-soaps have been particularly popular with both television producers and television audiences. What reasons can you suggest for the popularity of docu-soaps with (a) television producers and (b) television audiences?
> ➤ Consider the range of documentaries that regularly appear on British television and consider the argument that market forces and the drive for ratings have undermined the standards of professional documentary film-making.

The current vogue for various types of docu-soaps and fly-on-the-wall documentaries has resulted in a series of scandals about faked scenes and other types of hoaxes (see, for example, the reference to the BBC programme *Driving School* in *AS Media Studies: The Essential Introduction*.) In 1996 Carlton was fined 2 million pounds by the ITC for its documentary *The Connection*. The programme was supposed to be a 'gritty' documentary about the drugs trade and included a scene where a courier swallowed heroin. However, it turned out that the whole programme was a fake and the heroin was in fact sweets. Other programmes exposed as fakes included several made for Channel 4, including *Too Much Too Young: Chickens* (1997) about rent boys in Glasgow and *Daddy's Girl* (1998) about an incestuous relationship between a father and daughter. This was pulled when it was discovered that the father and daughter were not related but rather were a couple, trying to cheat the television production company.

TV SCHOOLBOY WAS REALLY 30

CHANNEL 4 has been forced to scrap a £400,000 documentary after conning a school into thinking a 30-year-old TV producer was a teenage student.

The network claimed it was filming a 'fly-on-the-wall' series about a 16-year-old drop-out Howard Simmons, who wanted to return to sixth-form studies. 'Howard' attended classes for two months and socialised with other pupils – even throwing a rowdy joint '17th birthday' party with a girl classmate.

But the staff of Kingdown Community School in Warminster, Wiltshire, were outraged to discover the student with teeth braces was in fact Oxford graduate Sheridan Simove.

Head Sheelagh Brown halted filming after confronting Channel 4's Head of Entertainment.

She wrote to parents saying she was 'shocked and stunned'. Ms Brown added: 'The whole school, and especially the sixth form, had taken this man into their confidence and their lives.

'Our trust has been totally abused and many staff and pupils are upset and disappointed.

'It is now clear that all members of the production team and Channel 4 Television had planned their deceit from the outset in order to pass Howard off as a teenager.'

Channel 4 said it intended to reveal Howard's identity before filming ended. But, as the school had withdrawn permission, the project would now be scrapped.

The channel has been in trouble before. It was fined £150,000 for the 1997 documentary Too Much Too Young, where members of the production team posed as clients asking rent boys for sex. A year later, it was forced to pull a programme about a father and daughter's relationship after they turned out to be unrelated lovers.

F. Davern, 'TV Schoolboy was Really 30', *Metro*, 21 March 2002

The *Metro* front page relates to a more recent example where the producer of a fly-on-the-wall documentary based around a school pretended to be a 17-year-old student.

In a statement, Channel 4 said it accepted full responsibility for the undercover operation, declaring it had aimed to show what life was like for A-level students in a successful sixth form. The following public acknowlwdgement was published in *The Guardian* (20/03/2002):

The school was told that at the heart of the programme there was a unique experiment involving the introduction of an extra 17-year-old student, Howard, for a fixed period of one term only. At the time of the placement the school was not made aware that he was in fact a 30-year-old member of the production team.

From the outset it was always the channel's intention that his real identity would be explained to the school and its students, long before the completion of the experiment, and that the school would have the final say on whether it wished to continue to collaborate on the project.

It was always accepted that the completed programme would not be broadcast without the school's express consent . . . The school is entirely blameless and Channel 4 accepts full responsibility.

(O. Gibson, 'Channel 4 Takes Full Responsibility', *The Guardian*, 20 March 2002)

Channel 4 argued that it had always planned to tell the school of Howard's true identity and to give it the final say on whether it wished to continue with the project.

'There was no intention by the channel or the production team to compromise or hurt staff or students. Everyone knew they were being filmed and nothing would have been broadcast unless consent had been obtained,' added the Channel 4 statement.

Channel 4 insisted that it had complied with its regulatory code at all times and that full police checks and an independent psychological assessment were obtained to ensure Howard did not pose any physical or moral threat to students.

The station said the idea was 'unusual' but that it had allowed programme-makers to gauge teachers' and students' reactions to Howard (www.media.guardian.co.uk/broadcast/story/0,7493,670959,00).

ACTIVITIES

➤ Imagine a television company wants to do a documentary on your school or college. Consider what might be some of the main advantages and disadvantages from the institution's point of view. Could you suggest any safeguards that the institution could put in place to ensure that it is not misrepresented? Suggest some particular 'angles' or narrative strands that the film-makers might wish to include. To what extent do you think that people's behaviour would change when the cameras were present? How could this be minimised?

➤ Consider how audiences distinguish between 'reality' and fiction on television.

➤ Undertake a survey of documentaries across a range of channels over a short period of time. Consider how many of these documentaries present their subjects in a positive light and how many in a negative light. Are there particular difficulties in showing subjects in a positive light? What might be the advantages of showing the subjects of documentaries in a more negative light? If your research shows that there is a bias towards one particular approach, suggest reasons to explain this.

➤ Record and analyse the first few minutes of a recent television documentary. Consider the way in which the producers have used photography, sound, music, editing and narrative devices. To what extent do you feel that the producers have manipulated their subjects to present a particular 'version' of reality?

➤ The advert on p. 136 appeared in the *Guardian* in the summer of 2002. How do you think the producers might present the girls who reply to this advert? How might their stories be presented? Write a description of the type of programme that might result from this advert, consider the type of audience targeted and where in the television schedules this programme might eventually appear.

FURTHER READING

Burton, G. (2000) 'Television and Realism', *Talking Television. An Introduction to the Study of Television*. Arnold.
Accessible discussion of realism, its modes and categories and the relationship between realism and ideology. Contains a brief history of documentary on British television.

Casey, B., Casey, N., Calvert, B., French, L., and Lewis, J. (2002) '*Realism', in Television Studies. The Key Concepts*. Routledge.
A short but comprehensive overview of the main issues in relation to television realism.

Winston, B. (1995) *Claiming the Real: The Documentary Film Revisited*, British Film Institute.
One of the key texts on the development of documentary film-making.

Nick Broomfield's website: *www.nickbroomfield.com/home.html*
Contains much information on his films and awards as well as an opportunity to buy videos and posters.

▼ 7 INTERTEXTUALITY

Intertextuality is an increasingly significant concept in Media Studies. Its primary importance is that it encourages us to look at texts not in isolation, but to identify the key links through which they relate to one another.

Recognition is an important factor in the way in which we consume and approach media texts. For example, advertisers love to share a joke with their audience by making allusions in their advertisements to other media texts. In doing so they cleverly engage an audience with the text by allowing them to feel pleased that they have understood the allusion and can become party to the cleverness of it. In an article on 'Intertextuality' on the Media and Communication Studies website (*www.aber.ac,uk/media/index.html*), Daniel Chandler pinpoints how intertextuality is often used in media texts in order to appeal to audiences in this way:

> The debts of a text to other texts are seldom acknowledged (other than in the scholarly apparatus of academic writing). This serves to further the mythology of authorial 'originality'. However, some texts allude directly to each other – as in 'remakes' of films, extra-diegetic references to the media in the animated cartoon *The Simpsons*, and many amusing contemporary TV ads (in the UK, perhaps most notably in the ads for Boddington's beer). This is a particularly self-conscious form of intertextuality: it credits its audience with the necessary experience to make sense of such allusions and offers them the pleasure of recognition. By alluding to other texts and other media, this practice reminds us that we are in a mediated

reality, so it can also be seen as an 'alienatory' mode which runs counter to the dominant 'realist' tradition which focuses on persuading the audience to believe in the ongoing reality of the narrative. It appeals to the pleasures of critical detachment rather than of emotional involvement.

'Diegetic' refers to those things that are on the screen in a film and can be accounted for by what occurs visually. For example, diegetic sounds include the dialogue spoken by the actors. 'Extra-diegetic' or 'non-diegetic' refers to those things that cannot be accounted for by what is on the screen. This might include such phenomena as voice-overs or music added to create atmosphere.

Look at the example above. It is an advertisement for the Peugeot 206 car. It works on a number of different levels by making references to other texts that we may be familiar with. The first is the obvious link to a Bollywood film poster. At first glance it is easy to mistake this for a poster for a typical Bollywood film. This is because it relies heavily on the conventions, style and content that we would expect to see in a Bollywood poster.

> ➤ Make a list of the conventions used in the Peugeot advertisement that you would expect to find in a Bollywood film poster.

There is also an important secondary element of intertextuality about the advertisement. It refers directly to a series of television advertisements that themselves play upon the conventions of Bollywood cinema in which the hero is seen to 'modify' an old unfashionable car by crashing and hammering it to give it the shape of the Peugeot 206. So the audience is being asked to identify at least two ways in which the advertisement makes references to other texts. In each case audiences will identify both similarities and differences between the text and those to which it relates.

The two different ways in which the Peugeot advertisement links to other texts are referred to by John Fiske as 'horizontal' and 'vertical'. Horizontal links broadly relate to genre. Texts that share elements with others of the same genre can be said to be horizontally linked. Of course, in this case genres exist across media forms.

The vertical dimension relates primarily to the promotion or marketing of a media texts through other media. For example, soap operas are often promoted through tabloid newspaper stories, celebrity appearances on other television programmes and even studio tours.

Advertising is a particularly rich field through which to explore intertextuality. Advertisers are constantly looking for ways of gaining the attention of audiences through clever, thought-provoking advertisements. One way to do this is through reference to other media texts. There are several benefits to the advertiser from adopting this strategy. First, it situates the audience 'inside' the joke, feeling pleased and included because they 'get' what is happening. Second, by association it imbues the advertised product with the often powerful connotations of the original text.

However, intertextuality is not limited to advertising. It plays a key role in our understanding of many media forms. In their book *Media Studies: Texts, Institutions and Audiences*, Lisa Taylor and Andrew Willis explore how intertextuality functions in popular music and film. They relate intertextuality specifically to postmodernism and suggest that one way to look at media images is the ways they relate to each other, rather than subjecting individual texts to semiotic analysis. This inward-looking relationship between media texts, exclusive of the outer world, is described by the postmodern thinker Jean Baudrillard as 'implosion'.

Perhaps the ultimate outcome of this is a world consisting only of media surfaces reflecting back on each other. This is an idea that will be explored further in the conclusion to this book, when we look in more detail at postmodernism.

In the extract that follows, Taylor and Willis explore the concept of intertextuality further within the contexts of popular music and film genre.

INTERTEXTUALITY AND ADVERTISING

Some of the clearest examples of intertextuality within the media can be found within advertising. For example, many high-profile advertising campaigns clearly make reference to films and other forms of popular culture such as music and television. This can often be at the level of imagery. The post-apocalyptic world of the *Mad Max* series of films (*Mad Max*, 1979; *Mad Max 2*, 1981; *Mad Max Beyond Thunderdome*, 1985) is used as the setting for the series of promotional adverts for Foster's lager that follow the adventures of two survivors as they seek out the remaining 'amber nectar'. These advertisements clearly draw on the search for gasoline present in the *Mad Max* films. This example is also useful when considering Fredric Jameson's idea that all this process of textual refer-encing of other texts does is create what he calls a pastiche. Jameson argues that pastiche is a 'stylistic mask' which he says is often confused with parody, but which in fact lacks the latter's mocking criticism. He argues that pastiche exists in a world where 'stylistic innovation is no longer possible', and that 'all that is left is to imitate dead styles, to speak through the masks and with the voices of the styles in an imaginary museum'. Arguably, there is no deeper meaning to the Foster's *Mad Max* adverts, apart from selling the product, than the fact that they seek to entertain in an intertextual way, and do so by using imagery and ideas in an empty, surface way. They are clearly referring to other popular texts, but not in a way that seeks to 'comment' upon them, or the society that produced them. The sole purpose of the campaign, it may be argued, is to deliver con-sumers for the product and increase the profits of the company producing the alcoholic drink.

However, the intertextuality of advertising campaigns such as this one may also offer audiences enormous pleasure because they allow them to celebrate and share their cultural knowledge. This point may be extended, since the intertextuality of advertising not only involves an audience's recognition of references drawn from popular culture, but also what may be labelled high culture, as some campaigns use images from fine art, opera and classical theatre.

These may be moments of classical music, references to artwork such as the Mona Lisa, or characters from Shakespeare's plays. Whatever the cultural source of the intertextuality present in many advertisements, it undoubtedly offers audiences a range of pleasures, and in doing so creates meaning in a number of ways. It may be argued, therefore, that the intertextual referencing in so much contemporary advertising potentially empowers consumers, as it allows them to exchange their knowledge of other cultural references in a social context such as the workplace, when discussing the previous evening's television viewing.

Referencing other texts is not the only way in which contemporary advertisements may be thought of as intertextual. Certainly, in the mid-1990s there were a number of advertising campaigns that built upon and used audience knowledge, not only of the product being advertised but also the past campaigns employed to promote it. In these campaigns characters reappeared and events unfolded across a number of linked adverts. For example, the characters of Papa and Nicole were successfully used to promote the Renault Clio car on a number of occasions. In each case the audience built upon its knowledge of the characters and brought this knowledge to bear upon its reading of each new advert. Another example is Gold Blend coffee, which was successfully promoted through an ongoing series of advertisements that developed a romantic love triangle in the style of a mini soap opera, each one employing a cliff-hanger ending to ensure that audiences sought out the next instalment. Other products have been promoted in the same successful way over an even longer period of time. The best example of this form of advertising intertextuality is the PG Tips chimpanzees, which have appeared in a number of promotional campaigns for tea since the I960s. In all these cases the prior and ongoing knowledge and awareness of the consumer is central to the construction and success of each advertisement and the campaign as a whole. It is also possible to argue that the ability of an audience to read intertextually is a prerequisite to their understanding of these types of campaign, and pays testament to the sophistication of the contemporary consumer's ability to operate across Fiske's horizontal dimension when reading advertisements.

INTERTEXTUALITY, POLITICS AND POPULAR MUSIC

As we have argued, postmodern media images may be considered intertextual because they continually reference other texts and images. Using this definition of intertextuality, we now wish to turn our attention to popular music. Meaning does not simply reside within the sound of a piece of popular music. It creates meaning through the forms in which recorded music is distributed (LP, CD or MC), the television and magazine images that help promote it, and the references to other music and media that performers include in their work. It is the

increasing level of reference to other performers and texts, its intertextuality, that has led some critics to the conclusion that the contemporary music scene is postmodern. This is supported by the fact that so much of the promotional work undertaken in the music industry continually talks about, or pays homage to, earlier popular cultural images. For example, the arrival of 'Brit Pop' in the mid-1990s was accompanied by a great number of journalistic articles that claimed Blur were the new Kinks or that Oasis were the new Beatles. This reference to the past was not just present in the music press; it seemed to be something that was consciously being promoted by the bands themselves. For example, Blur included pastiches of the early 1970s film A *Clockwork Orange* (1971) in their videos.

Such popular cultural references can be found in many other pop videos by artists not associated with Brit Pop. Rapper 2Pac, for example, accompanied his single *California Love* (1996) with a promotional video that, in a similar way to the Foster's adverts discussed earlier, was clearly modelled on the *Mad Max* series of films. The settings, props, lighting, costume and make-up for the video are all clearly drawn from the *mise-en-scène* of the Australian films. This brings us back to Jameson's argument 'that all postmodern texts do is superficially reproduce earlier images and ideas. His general criticism seems particularly suited to the case of Blur and their aping of A *Clockwork Orange*, which carries none of the attempts to grapple with issues of social violence that are present, however unsuccessfully, in Stanley Kubrick's film. Blur merely celebrate the images of A *Clockwork Orange*, whilst steadfastly ignoring the film's attempts at social commentary. The case of the 2Pac's *California Love* video, however, offers a more complex set of issues. Whilst clearly referencing the *Mad Max* films, as we have observed, it also invites the viewer to identify the performers as outsiders. Like the film's characters, they are presented as survivors in a post-apocalyptic world. Given the oppressed position many African-Americans occupy in contemporary US society, it becomes possible to read the appropriation of such images of survival as significant, and potentially carrying a political message. The *California Love* video becomes more than simply a jokey, empty pastiche as it offers images of survival for the young African-American audience consuming it. The fictional world created by the video is exclusively inhabited by black characters, and this works to heighten the possibilities that the video might be read as a political statement which consciously chooses to use particular popular cultural references as part of its vocabulary. The choice of images from popular cinema is important, because they are likely to constitute a significant part of the cultural knowledge of contemporary black American urban youth.

INTERTEXTUALITY AND FILM GENRE

Jim Collins, writing about genre and film in the 1990s, identifies that there are two co-existent but divergent manifestations of genre within contemporary Hollywood film-making: what he calls an 'eclectic irony' and a 'new sincerity'. Films that fall into the former category, he argues, combine very traditional elements of genre within a context where they would not normally be found. He cites as an example of this trend *Back to the Future* III (1990), which he argues is a hybrid of the traditional western and the science-fiction film. In this case the manifestation of genre is shot through with a strong sense of irony, which is reflected by such knowing moments as Marty McFly citing contemporary western icons such as Clint Eastwood in his dialogue, and his time-machine being chased in the same way as the stagecoach in Ford's 1939 eponymous film. The second trend identified by Collins is epitomized by the film *Dances with Wolves* (1990). In this case, however, he claims that there is a striving for a 'new sincerity', which is almost an attempt to rediscover a lost generic purity. These films lack eclectic irony and take themselves very seriously. He cites both *Field of Dreams* (1989) and *Hook* (1991) as further examples of this trend.

Both of the tendencies identified by Collins within contemporary Hollywood film-making firmly acknowledge the intertextual knowledge of today's audiences. In the case of those that present an 'eclectic irony' there seems to be a need for audiences to share, at least some of, the intertextual knowledge referenced by the films in order to gain maximum pleasure from them. In those texts that display the 'new sincerity' Collins talks of, there is a sense that audiences share with the film-makers a desire to return to a purer version of genre. This must be dependent upon them sharing a knowledge of what cinema has gone before if they are to understand what makes a 'purer', more authentic genre film. So, whatever the tendency, there is a strong awareness that the contemporary consumer has a great deal of cinematic knowledge to bring to bear on their reading of new film texts. Much of this is due to the prevalence of new technologies which allow viewers to watch and re-watch older generic films at times of their choice. The reappearance of older generic films, many of which are now seen as classics, on TV, video and laser disc has meant that audiences have much more opportunity to view the history of cinema. This, in turn, allows them to view across genres at their leisure. It is therefore possible to argue that these contemporary genre films help to create a cinematic culture that is as introspective as the world of Italian television described by Eco as 'Neo-TV'.

Increasingly, it is the case that both film-makers and critics are interested in the reactivation of older styles and genres. This in turn contributes to the creation of a self-reflective tendency within contemporary Hollywood film-making. Examples of this are the renewed interest in film *noir* and so called 'neo-*noir*' shown by critics and film-makers in the late 1990s, and the acceptance of a new level of cultural capital for the western which is reflected by the Oscars awarded to *Dances with Wolves* (1990) and Clint Eastwood's genre-conscious *Unforgiven* (1992). However, in this intertextual media world it is fair to say that both film and television, as well as other media, cannot be media-specific with their inward-looking gaze; it is cast across different media, with films referencing television and television referencing film. But, as Eco argues, this creates an unbroken circle between the media and excludes the outside, 'real' world. Films such as *Street Fighter* (1994), *Super Mario Bros* (1993) and *Mortal Kombat* (1995) are examples of this multi-media intertextuality. They depend upon other media forms such as the computer game, the comic book and the animated cartoon for their source, and this informs the ways in which they are read by audiences. However, this manifestation of intertextuality can be examined and analysed outside the realm of the text, which is something that Eco does not do. The inward-looking reality of such intertextuality in fact lies in the economics of the contemporary media world. However 'unreal' this world may seem, it does exist within an economic reality based upon the profit motive of large media conglomerates. To understand fully media texts like *Street Fighter* (1994) we need to acknowledge the enormous influence of the industrial context of production upon them. Whilst critics may sneer at the perceived lack of originality in films which began as computer games, such as *Street Fighter* (1994) and *Mortal Kombat* (1995), their intertextuality in part depends upon the fact that profit can be made from the intertextual knowledge of the consumer. Whilst that knowledge is clearly present in the consumer marketplace, films will be made from sources such as computer games, comics will be developed that draw on films and television, and cartoons will be made from popular comic books.

L. Taylor and A. Willis, *Media Studies: Texts, Institutions and Audiences*, Blackwell, 1999, pp. 84–7

ACTIVITIES

➤ Some of the examples given in the above extract are a little out of date. Consider three current examples of intertextuality in advertising and explain how you think it works with audiences.

➤ Look at a recent example of a marketing campaign for the launch of a new media text. Make a list of the promotional techniques that have been used. Explain how each is used to relate to the text being promoted.

➤ Below is a copy of the *Sun* front page published in 2001. Study it carefully and then offer a detailed explanation of how the intertextual elements on it are likely to appeal to its readership.

THE Sun

Saturday, May 5, 2001   40p   www.thesun.co.uk

DANDO

Bizarre world of the 'killer who executed Jill on her doorstep'

SPECIAL TRIAL REPORT: PAGES 4,5,6 & 7

Sad . . . chat star Judy

Richard and Judy quit ITV

By DOMINIC MOHAN

TELLY stars Richard Madeley and Judy Finnigan are leaving ITV's This Morning in a £4million deal with Channel 4.

The husband-and-wife team – at This Morning for 13 years – will front a daily afternoon chat show from the autumn.

Judy, 52, said: "It's very sad, but we want to try something different."

Full story – Page Nine

FREE

star

MAG TODAY
VOUCHER PAGE 16

WORLD EXCLUSIVE

WE'RE RON OUR WAY

Go get him . . . Sun jet takes off yesterday to fetch Biggs (right)

Sun jets off to bring Biggs back to justice

From MIKE SULLIVAN on Sun jet

A PRIVATE Sun plane took off yesterday on a dramatic mission to bring Ronnie Biggs back to British justice.

Great Train Robbery gang leader Bruce Reynolds joined a Sun team on the jet as it headed to South America.

Fugitive Biggs, 71, will board the return flight. An emotional Reynolds, 69, said: "It's time for Ronnie to face the music."

Full story – Pages Two and Three

FURTHER READING

Casey, B., Casey, N., Calvert, B., French, L., and Lewis, J. (2002) *Television Studies: the Key Concepts*, Routledge.
Offers insight into the nature of intertexuality and explores the concept in relation to the *X-files*.

Rayner, P., Wall, P., and Kruger, S. (2001) *Media Studies: The Essential Introduction*, Routledge.
Contains a short section on media intertextuality.

Storey,J. (1993) *An Introductory Guide to Cultural Theory and Popular Culture*, Harvester Wheatsheaf.
Explores the nature of intertextuality in the chapter on postmodernism.

Strinati, D. (1995) *An Introduction to Theories of Popular Culture*, Routledge.
Provides some useful material.

▼ 8 IDEOLOGY AND ADVERTISING

Advertisements are signs, and through their systems of codes are a powerful carrier of ideology. Ideology is one of the key concepts of Media Studies, and advertisements are key texts in any analysis of the way in which ideology works. Roland Barthes labelled the ideological meaning of signs as the third level of interpretation after denotation and connotation (see p. 16). He described this third ideological level as 'mythic' – because at this level 'meaning' appears as natural or commonsense.

Because these ideological or mythic meanings can appear to be so natural, it is sometimes difficult to stand back and identify them. It is often easier to identify the ideology at work in particular advertisements if we look at examples from periods different to our own. For example, a series of adverts from the 1950s appear to present particular ideologies about male/female gender roles that we would probably want to challenge today. At the time they were published, however, these representations would have appeared to many people as 'natural' or commonsense.

IDEOLOGY

The term 'ideology', first used in France at the end of the eighteenth century, meant the 'study of ideas' but later developed to mean a 'belief system'. As the John Fiske extract highlights, much of the earliest and most influential work on ideology comes from Marx and Engels (see below). However, as Marx and Engels did not write specifically about the media, the concept of ideology as we understand it today has been developed by other theorists. The Fiske article considers two of the most influential modern writers on ideology, Antonio Gramsci and Louis Althusser.

He wears the
cleanest shirts in town

...his *"Missus"* swears by TIDE!

He wears the cleanest shirts in town!
There isn't any doubt
That all his shirts are washed with TIDE
'Cause when TIDE's in . . . dirt's out!

UNDERSTANDING IDEOLOGY

The theory of ideology as a practice was developed by Louis Althusser, a second-generation Marxist who had been influenced by the ideas of Saussure and Freud, and who thus brought theories of structure and of the unconscious to bear upon Marx's more economistic theories. For Marx, ideology was a relatively straightforward concept. It was the means by which the ideas of the ruling classes became accepted throughout society as natural and normal. All knowledge is class-based: it has scribed within it its class origins and it works to prefer the interests of that class. Marx understood that the members of the subordinate class, that is the working class, were led to understand their social experience, their social relationships, and therefore themselves by means of a set of ideas that were not *theirs*, that came from a class whose economic, and therefore political and social, interests not only differed from theirs but were actively opposed to them.

According to Marx the ideology of the bourgeoisie kept the workers, or proletariat, in a state of *false consciousness*. People's consciousness of who they are, of how they relate to the rest of society, and therefore of the sense they make of their social experience is produced by society, not by nature or biology. Our consciousness is determined by the society we have been born into, not by our nature or individual psychology. . . .

CONTINUED

Cooking's more fun in a gay kitchen

See how 'ALKATHENE' Houseware brightens things up!

BRIGHT COLOURS make a lot of difference to your home, to your mood, and to *you*! Gay, lovely kitchen things made from 'Alkathene' make cooking more attractive, less like hard work.

'Alkathene' is long-lasting, hygienic, virtually unbreakable. It will not chip, or dent or scratch. It can be washed clean in a jiffy with soap and water. It is as light as a feather.

'Alkathene' household goods come in a wide range of cheerful colours, made by many manufacturers. Whichever brand you choose, look for the label that says Made From 'Alkathene'.

It's light! It's bright!

IT'S MADE FROM

LOOK FOR THIS LABEL

MADE FROM
'ALKATHENE'
ICI POLYTHENE

Articles bearing this label are made from 'Alkathene', the sign of the highest quality.

❋ *'Alkathene' is the registered trade mark for the polythene made by I.C.I.*

IMPERIAL CHEMICAL INDUSTRIES LIMITED · LONDON · S.W.1

AH.8

The concept of ideology as false consciousness was so important in Marx's theory because it appeared to explain why it was that the majority in capitalist societies accepted a social system that disadvantaged them. Marx believed, however, that economic 'reality' was more influential, at least in the long run, than ideology, and that inevitably the workers would overthrow the bourgeoisie and produce a society where one class did not dominate and exploit the majority and so would not need to keep them in a state of false consciousness. In a fair and equal society there is no need for ideology because everyone will have a 'true' consciousness of themselves and their social relations. The bitterness of the black youths would be seen in this theory as a sign that their socio-economic 'reality' was stronger than the attempt of the dominant ideology to make them accept it.

As the twentieth century progressed, however, it became more and more clear that capitalism was not going to be overthrown by internal revolution, and that the socialist revolution in Russia was not going to spread to the rest of Europe and the western world. Yet capitalism still disadvantaged the majority of its members and exploited them for the benefit of a minority. To help account for this, Marxist thinkers such as Althusser developed a more sophisticated theory of ideology that freed it from such a close cause-and-effect relationship with the economic base of society, and redefined it as an ongoing and all-pervasive set of practices in which all classes participate, rather than a set of ideas imposed by one class upon the other. The fact that all classes participate in these practices does not mean that the practices themselves no longer serve the interests of the dominant, for they most certainly do: what it means is that ideology is much more effective than Marx gave it credit for because it works from within rather than without – it is deeply inscribed in the ways of thinking and ways of living of all classes.

A pair of high-heel shoes, to take an example, does not impose upon women from outside the ideas of the ruling gender (men); but wearing them is an ideological practice of patriarchy in which women participate, possibly even more than the ideology would require. Wearing them accentuates the parts of the female body that patriarchy has trained us into thinking of as attractive to men – the buttocks, thighs, and breasts. The woman thus participates in constructing herself as an attractive object for the male look, and therefore puts herself under the male power (of granting or withholding approval). Wearing them also limits her physical activity and strength – they hobble her and make her move precariously; so wearing them is practising the subordination of women in patriarchy. A woman in high heels is active in reproducing and recirculating the patriarchal meanings of gender that propose masculinity as stronger and more active, and femininity as weaker and more passive.

One of the most ubiquitous and insidious ideological practices is what Althusser calls 'interpellation' or 'hailing'. It is particularly relevant to this book because it is practised in every act of communication. All communication addresses someone, and in addressing them it places them in a social relationship. In recognizing ourself as the addressee and in responding to the communication, we participate in our own social, and therefore ideological, construction. If you hear in the street a shout 'Hey you!', you can either turn in the belief that you are being addressed or you can ignore it because you know that 'nobody, but nobody' speaks to you like that: you thus reject the relationship implicit in the call. All communication inrrepellates or hails us in some way: a pair of high-heel shoes, for example, hails the woman (or man) who answers them by liking or wearing them as a patriarchal subject. The woman who recognizes 'herself' as their addressee by wearing them positions herself submissively within gender relations; the man who likes to see her wearing them is equally but differently positioned – he is hailed as one with power . . .

Althusser's theory of ideology as practice is a development of Marx's theory of it as false consciousness, but still emphasizes its role of maintaining the power of the minority over the majority by non-coercive means. Another European second-generation Marxist, Antonio Gramsci, introduced into this area another term – *hegemony*, which we might like to think of as ideology as struggle. Briefly, hegemony involves the constant winning and rewinning of the consent of the majority to the system that subordinates them. The two elements that Gramsci emphasizes more than Marx or Althusser are resistance and instability.

Hegemony is necessary, and has to work so hard, because the social experience of subordinated groups (whether by class, gender, race, age, or any other factor) constantly contradicts the picture that the dominant ideology paints for them of themselves and their social relations. In other words, the dominant ideology constantly meets resistances that it has to overcome in order to win people's consent to the social order that it is promoting. These resistances may be overcome, but they are never eliminated. So any hegemonic victory, any consent that it wins, is necessarily unstable; it can never be taken for granted, so it has to be constantly rewon and struggled over.

One of the key hegemonic strategies is the construction of 'common sense'. If the ideas of the ruling class can be accepted as *common* (i.e. not class-based) sense, then their ideological object is achieved and their ideological work is disguised. It is, for example, 'common sense' in our society that criminals are wicked or deficient individuals who need punishment or correction. Such common sense disguises the fact that lawbreakers are disproportionately men from disadvantaged or disempowered social groups – they are of the 'wrong' race, class, or age. Common sense thus rules out the possible sense that the causes of criminality are social rather than individual, that our society teaches men that their masculinity depends upon successful performance (which is typically measured by material rewards and social esteem), and then denies many of them the means of achieving this success. The 'law-abiding citizens', who 'happen', generally, to belong to those classes which have many avenues to socially successful performance, are thus relieved of the responsibility of thinking that criminality may be the product of the system that provides them with so many advantages, and that the solution to the problem may involve them in forgoing some of their privileges. The common sense that criminality is a function of the wicked individual rather than the unfair society is thus part of bourgeois ideology, and, in so far as it is accepted by the subordinate (and even by the criminals themselves, who may well believe that they deserve their punishment and that the criminal justice system is therefore fair to all), it is hegemony at work. Their consent to the common wisdom is a hegemonic victory, if only a momentary one.

Ideological theories stress that all communication and all meanings have a socio-political dimension, and that they cannot be understood outside their social context. This ideological work always favours the status quo, for the classes with power dominate the production and distribution not only of goods but also of ideas and meanings. The economic system is organized in their interest, and the ideological system derives from it and works to promote, naturalize, and disguise it. Whatever their differences, all ideological theories agree that ideology works to maintain class domination; their differences lie in the ways in which this domination is exercised, the degree of its effectiveness, and the extent of the resistances it meets.

To summarize it briefly, we may say that Marx's theory of ideology as false consciousness tied it closely to the economic base of society and posited that its falseness to the material conditions of the working class would inevitably result in the overthrow of the economic order that produced it. He saw it as the imposition of the ideas of the dominant minority upon the subordinate majority. This majority must eventually see through this false consciousness and change the social order that imposes it upon them.

Althusser's theory of ideology as practice, however, appeared to see no limits to ideology, neither in its reach into every aspect of our lives, nor historically. Its power lay in its ability to engage the subordinate in its practices and thus to lead them to construct social identities or subjectivities for themselves that were complicit with it, and against their own socio-political interests. The logical conclusion of his theory is that there is no way of escaping ideology, for although our material social experience may contradict it, the only means we have of making sense of that experience are always ideologically loaded, so the only sense we can make of our selves, our social relations, and our social experience is one that is a practice of the dominant ideology.

Gramsci's theory of hegemony, or ideology as struggle, however, lays far greater emphasis on resistance. While in broad agreement with Althusser that the subordinate may consent to the dominant ideology and thus participate in its propagation, his theory also insists that their material social conditions

contradict that dominant sense, and thus produce resistances to it. His account of the structures of domination is as subtle and convincing as Althusser's; but because he lays greater stress on the resistances that ideology has to overcome, but can never eliminate, his theory is finally the more satisfying, for it takes into account more of the contradictions that go to make up our social experience. Gramsci's theory makes social change appear possible, Marx's makes it inevitable, and Althusser's improbable.

J. Fiske, 'Ideology and Meaning', *Introduction to Communication Studies*, Routledge, 1990, pp. 172–8

Karl Marx and Engels' explanation of ideology is based on the idea that the ruling classes (i.e. the aristocracy, the bourgeoisie and the government) not only controlled economic wealth but also controlled the production and distribution of ideas. According to Marx and Engels (1970), the ruling class was able to rule not by force but through ideas.

The ideas of the ruling class are in every epoch the ruling ideas, i.e. the class that is the ruling material force of society is at the same time its ruling intellectual force. The class that has the means of material production at its disposal has control at the same time over the means of mental production.

Fiske explains Marx and Engels' notion of false consciousness, which occurs when the ruling ideas protect ruling-class interests by making sure the working classes see the economic relations of production as natural and ideologically neutral.

Althusser saw ideology not as something imposed on the majority from outside, from the ruling classes, but rather as practice, as something that works within and is part of our daily lives. Althusser used the term 'ideological state apparatus' to refer to the social institutions, including the media, that reproduce ideology to represent a particular social and economic order as natural and inevitable. We've seen an example of this earlier, in the way television news is taken as objective, authoritative and somehow speaking for us.

Fiske explains Althusser's concept of interpellation, or 'hailing', to describe the way in which the media construct our consent and address us in a complicitous way. If we accept the way in which we are hailed, according to Fiske, we are drawn into a form of compliance or agreement with whoever is hailing us, and with their ideological construction of us.

For instance, many advertisements for products aimed at women consumers interpellate women as wanting to look attractive. If women accept this interpellation, they are participating in an ideology that says women must construct themselves as attractive objects for the male gaze, and therefore acquiesce in the notion of a male power that can grant or withhold approval. The male is also acquiescing in this power relationship by his acceptance of media-promoted notions of what defines female beauty.

MEDIA STUDIES: THE ESSENTIAL RESOURCE

Hegemony is the process by which a dominant class or group maintains power by making everyone accept their ideology as normal or neutral, through cultural influence rather than force.

Antonio Gramsci used the idea of hegemony to describe how people are persuaded to accept the domination of a power elite who impose their will and world view. Hegemony is a way of seeing ideology as a struggle. Gramsci challenges the idea that ideology is uncritically accepted by subordinated groups. According to Gramsci, there is a constant state of struggle where dominant ideology is involved in a continual winning and rewinning of the consent of the majority. If a dominant ideology is challenged, it incorporates the challenging ideas, thus neutralising those that threaten its supremacy. This means that a particular dominant ideology can change and evolve as it accepts or rejects new elements.

If we look at many of today's advertisements aimed at women, we can see that they often show women as positive, active and independent; this suggests that some elements of feminist and post-feminist thought have been taken on board by advertisers. Yet often when we look more closely at the adverts, they are still selling the same ideas that women are to be judged by their appearance and that they must look 'good' in particular ways. This could be seen as an example of hegemony, where a dominant patriarchal ideology has managed to absorb some of the ideas of feminism and incorporate these in a new form of ideology that looks different but is fundamentally the same.

Fiske adds that one of the key strategies of hegemony is the construction of 'common sense', where a particular set of ideas that make up the dominant ideology are seen as natural and common sense. Fiske uses the example of law and order where it is 'common sense' that criminals should be punished for committing crimes; yet we do not consider the reasons why so many criminals come from disenfranchised or disempowered groups.

Levi's Jeans as Signs

In 'The Jeaning of America' from *Understanding Popular Culture*, Fiske considers the ideological underpinning of jeans. He asked his students what jeans meant to them and why they wore them. According to the students, jeans were seen to be among other things:

- Informal
- Classless
- Sexless
- Fashionable
- Ordinary
- Functional
- Rugged

Fiske then goes on to suggest that when we buy particular brands or styles of jeans we are not just buying jeans but products that, to some degree, reflect our own sets of ideas and values. The jeans we buy have become in some way a sign signifying how we see ourselves.

Jeans are no longer, if they ever were, a generic denim garment. Like all commodities, they are given brand names to compete among themselves for specific segments of the

market. Manufacturers try to identify social differences and then to construct equivalent differences in the product so that social differentiation and product differentiation become mapped on to each other.

Advertising is used in an attempt to give meanings to these product differences that will enable people in the targeted social formation to recognise that they are being spoken to, or even to recognise their own social identity and values in the product. The different meanings (and therefore market segments) of 501s and 505s are created at least as much by the advertising as by any differences in the jeans themselves.

ACTIVITY

➤ Think about yourself and your fellow students. How many of you regularly wear jeans? Why? Do you all wear the same brand of jeans? Does it matter which brand you wear? If so, why? Do different brands have different connotations? If so how are these identified? Do different groups of students wear different types of clothes?

➤ Often students will cite fashionableness as a reason for wearing particular clothes and particular brands; think about where these ideas of what is (or is not) fashionable come from. How do we know what is and what is not fashionable?

Levi's jeans are famous for their advertisements, from Nick Kamen in his boxer shorts in 1985 to the use of computer-generated images for the Twisted and Bold New Breed ranges of jeans today. If we think about the advertisements for Levi's jeans over the years we can identify a series of principles that can be seen to be prominent. These might include:

■ Ruggedness
■ Personal freedom
■ Sexual success
■ Independence
■ Acting against the norm/majority
■ Looking good

If you go to the Levi's website www.levistrauss.com/about/vision, you will see that Levi's themselves identify a set of four common values for their company and its products. These are:

■ Empathy – Walking in other people's shoes
■ Originality – Being authentic and innovative
■ Integrity – Doing the right thing
■ Courage – Standing up for what we believe

> ➤ Think about these two lists. Can you identify any other values that the Levi's advertisements promote? To what extent do you think the two lists are compatible? Why do you think Levi's as a company would want to promote a set of values? How do these reflect on their products? Think about the extent to which the people who purchase Levi's products are aware of the Levi's values and the extent to which people who purchase Levi's products are buying a set of principles or values that they associate with the products. Do you think that this is a successful advertising strategy?
> ➤ Consider other brands and products to try and identify similar ways of 'mapping together' social identity and consumer products.

According to Judith Williamson (1978), 'Advertisements are selling us something more than consumer goods. In providing us with a structure in which we and those goods are interchangeable, they are selling us ourselves.'

The final article by Gillian Dyer takes these ideas further. In talking about the purpose and effects of advertising Dyer suggests that increasingly who we are is being determined by what we purchase, and that advertising supports a consumerist ideology.

Advertisers play a major part in shaping society's values, habits and direction. They are also partly responsible for influencing the character and development of the media system. The traditional media are in decline as a result of advertising allocation, and advertising has encouraged the conservative domination of the press, orienting it more and more towards the young middle class and in the process depriving a substantial section of the population of a serious newspaper. Advertising threatens the UK public-service broadcasting institution and has caused both kinds of television service to limit their programming, 'play safe' and go for large, predictable audiences. Newspapers and magazines are increasingly forced into creating the right 'editorial environment' for advertisers, and in addition we can see a growing polarization between popular and quality newspapers.

The future of the media as organs of public communication looks extremely gloomy because of the narrow and competitive needs of large corporations. We might applaud the aesthetic and technical standards of many of the ads themselves or at worst regard them as superficial, unreliable and intrusive, but it is hard to get away from them and to resist the general temptations and advantages of the consumer society. It is often hard to pin down what is actually objectionable about ads. Who seriously believes, for instance, that 'Heineken reaches the parts that other beers can't reach' or that 'Four out of five people

CONTINUED

can't tell Stork from butter' or does 'The Daz blue whitener window test' with their washing?

To be fair, advertisements rarely perpetrate downright lies. The ads in magazines and newspapers, on posters and at the cinema are bound by a code of practice administered by the Advertising Standards Authority. The IBA is responsible for television commercials and makes sure that they are not misleading or offensive and that they are confined to 'natural breaks'. The ASA judges the validity of complaints that come from the general public and publishes its verdicts in its own literature and in the press. (It also advertises itself in the press.) If a complaint is upheld the ASA can tell the advertiser to amend or remove offending material. It is particularly keen to uphold standards in sensitive areas such as those for slimming products, alcohol, tobacco and ads aimed at children. Ads for these products come in for special scrutiny, but as this book has argued, it is often not the overt message of an ad that is misleading or dangerous but its subtle, hidden message, which presumably the ASA is unable or unwilling to do much about.

As you might imagine, a lot of advertisements fall through the ASA's net. Many ads that might be seen as an attack on or demeaning to women are not considered so by the ASA. For instance, while many ads that appear in magazines, on posters and on television might not be too objectionable as far as women's roles in society are concerned, some ads that appear in trade or industrial journals, car, motorbike or girlie magazines often feature pictures of scantily-dressed or naked women, and captions such as 'Like a bit of spare' (from an ad for motorbike accessories), 'We'll never let you down' (an ad in a car magazine accompanying a picture of a woman with her knickers down) and 'Abbey carpets lay best' (alongside a woman lying down with few clothes on). Frequently the ASA dismisses complaints about these sorts of ads because 'they do not cause grave or widespread offence'; they have been known to dismiss complaints about the sexist portrayal of women in ads because they argue that the woman is there as decoration and is irrelevent to the product (and therefore presumably without significance), or because the ad is not addressed to women but to motorcycle enthusiasts, or long-distance lorry-drivers.

In general, the success of advertising depends not on its logical propositions but on the kinds of fantasies it offers. The world of ads is a dream world where people and objects are taken out of their material context and given new, symbolic meanings, placed on hoardings or on the screen where they become signs. Advertising appropriates things from the real world, from society and history and sets them to its own work. In doing so it mystifies the real world and deprives us of any understanding of it. We are invited to live an unreal life through the ads. The more we are isolated from the real world by the media, the more we seek images from them to give us a sense of social reality. Advertising helps us to make sense of things. It validates consumer commodities and a consumer life-style by associating goods with personal and social meanings and those aspirations and needs which are not fulfilled in real life. We come to think that consuming commodities will give us our identities. In this sense advertising is capable of some success. People may admire us if we have made the right purchases within a system to which we are trained to respond. Ads may provide a magic which displaces our feelings and resolves our dilemmas but only at a personal and social cost. We become part of the symbolism of the ad world; not real people but identified in terms of what we consume: Raymond Williams sums this up when he says:

> Fantasy seems to be validated at a personal level but only at the cost of preserving the general unreality which it obscures: the real failures of society . . . if the meanings and values generally operative in society give no answers to, no means of negotiating, problems of death, loneliness, frustration, the need for identity and respect, then the magic system must come and mixing its charms and expedients with reality in easily available forms and binding the weakness to the condition which has created it. (1980: 191)

The condition which has need of this fantasy is one which isolates us, the consumers, from real information and decision-making about the production and distribution of goods. Advertising, according to Williams, has become 'a mimed celebration of other people's decisions', not the consumers.

One of the ways in which advertising rebuffs criticism and validates its own existence is by appropriating hostile criticism and counter-ideologies, Some advertisers, aware of the objections of the feminist movement to traditional images of women in ads, have incorporated the criticism into their ads, many of which now present an alternative stereotype of the cool, professional, liberated woman. On the whole, however, advertising hasn't been able to keep pace with women's changing roles and aspirations and, unsure about what to do about criticism, has fallen back on tried and tested clichés. Some agencies, trying to accommodate new attitudes in their campaigns, often miss the point and equate 'liberation' with a type of aggressive sexuality and very unliberated coy sexiness. So we have seen in the past few years campaigns like 'Underneath they're all Lovable' (for frilly underwear), or ads showing cool, professional women who really have weak spots, be they for a man's aftershave lotion, a gift of chocolates or 'sexy' underwear.

Another example of the way that ads escape real criticism is by self-reference; that is, by incorporating criticism or by showing up the ad system as rather dishonest and silly. The actor John Cleese's presentation of Sony products incorporates a kind of cynicism about the process of celebrities endorsing products – no doubt with great commercial success, since his image on his comedy programmes is that of a cynic. A shampoo commercial on TV shows a young couple running towards each other on a deserted beach in slow motion

to the sound of an orchestra in full romantic flood; but instead of falling into each other's arms as we might have expected from watching countless similar ads and romantic films, they run past each other. The voice-over remarks that this shampoo will not get you a lover (as we have been led to believe from other shampoo ads) but will make your hair clean and beautiful. This is a parody of other, much criticized ads for beauty products. It is self-validating because we are disarmed by its honesty and its apparent self-criticism. Another example of an ad which refers to the genre of ads is a poster for sausages which says: 'I'm meaty. Fry me', a take-off of the offensive series of airline ads which said 'I'm Suzie/Cheryl/Lorraine. Fly me'. These kinds of ad often set themselves up as more aware, down-to-earth, honest and credible.

This leads us to a further point about advertising's resistance to criticism. The reason why ads are rarely dishonest in any 'legal' sense is that they don't function at the manifest level but at the level of the signifier. Few people believe or take seriously the (dishonest) slogans of ads: 'I was Mr Holmes of Household Linens until I discovered Smirnoff', 'Fairy tales come true' (Martini), 'Daz with the blue whitener washes cleanest'. But the *signifiers* of the image of these ads are usually the kind of people who are seen using the product – smart, young people, caring mothers or happy families. And it is at this level that ads are hard to resist because they offer the chance to obtain perfect relationships, handsome lovers, luxurious surroundings, appreciative husbands and happy children. We remember these images rather than the claims made on behalf of the product. We don't use a product for what it is; we identify with the result. The product can make us like the signifier in the ads.

It is possible to attempt to ban deceitful, sexist or racist slogans from ads. For instance, the ASA made the original 'I was only until I discovered . . .' Smirnoff ads unlawful, because of the overt implication that drinking Smirnoff would bring sexual and material success. Some Smirnoff ads now show the successfully transformed Smirnoff person saying 'They say Smirnoff won't . . . I'll drink to that', referring to the old series of ads and to the restriction imposed on them. This again shows how 'daring' ads are and how they can rebut criticism by criticising themselves. It is impossible to ban the use of images and symbols in ads and the interconnections they make between things of value. It is ultimately the images that ads leave us with, and the images of the slogans, not the slogans themselves, that make ads so successful.

This is why it is important to be aware not just of the content, but also of the structure of signs in ads, the way meanings are exchanged, the way signifier and signified work, the way ads incorporate other referent systems and ideologies (even advertising itself), and the way they structure us into the ad and call upon us to create meaning. Only in this way can we understand the way ideology works and ties advertising to the existing conditions of society.

G. Dyer, 'Conclusion', *Advertising as Communication*, Routledge, 1982, pp. 183–7

MEDIA STUDIES: THE ESSENTIAL RESOURCE

In the final paragraph of her book, Dyer claims that it is important to be aware of the way in which advertisements work, not just their content but the way in which meanings are exchanged and the way in which adverts incorporate other referent systems and ideologies.

Dyer explains that 'Advertisers play a major part in shaping society's values, habits and direction'. She goes on to say that the success of advertising depends not on its logical propositions (we do not really believe that Heineken beer can reach the parts other beers cannot) but rather on the kind of fantasies that adverts offer.

> It [advertising] validates consumer commodities and a consumer lifestyle by associating goods with personal and social meanings and those aspirations and needs which are not fulfilled in real life. We come to think that consuming commodities will give us our identities. . . . Ads may provide a magic which displaces our feelings and resolves our dilemmas but only at a personal and social cost. We become part of the symbolism of the ad world; not real people but identified in terms of what we consume . . . (Dyer 1982: 185).

And then there were the companies that had always understood that they were selling brands before product. Coke, Pepsi, McDonald's, Burger King and Disney weren't fazed by the brand crisis, opting instead to escalate the brand war, especially since they had their eyes firmly fixed on global expansion. They were joined in this project by a wave of sophisticated producer/retailers who hit full stride in the late eighties and early nineties. The Gap, Ikea and the Body Shop were spreading like wildfire during this period, masterfully transforming the generic into the brand-specific, largely through bold, carefully branded packaging and the promotion of an 'experiential' shopping environment. The Body Shop had been a presence in Britain since the seventies, but it wasn't until 1988 that it began sprouting like a green weed on every street corner in the US. Even during the darkest years of the recession, the company opened between forty and fifty American stores a year. Most baffling of all to Wall Street, it pulled off the expansion without spending a dime on advertising. Who needed billboards and magazine ads when retail outlets were three-dimensional advertisements for an ethical and ecological approach to cosmetics? The Body Shop was all brand.

The Starbucks coffee chain, meanwhile, was also expanding during this period without laying out much in advertising; instead, it was spinning off its name into a wide range of branded projects: Starbucks airline coffee, office coffee, coffee ice cream, coffee beer. Starbucks seemed to understand brand names at a level even deeper than Madison Avenue, incorporating marketing into every fiber of its corporate concept – from the chain's strategic association with books, blues and jazz to its Euro-latte lingo. What the success of both the Body Shop and Starbucks showed was how far the branding project had come in moving beyond splashing one's logo on a billboard. Here were two companies that had fostered

CONTINUED

powerful identities by making their brand concept into a virus and sending it out into the culture via a variety of channels: cultural sponsorship, political controversy, the consumer experience and brand extensions. Direct advertising, in this context, was viewed as a rather clumsy intrusion into a much more organic approach to image building.

Scott Bedbury, Starbucks' vice president of marketing, openly recognized that 'consumers don't truly believe there's a huge difference between products,' which is why brands must 'establish emotional ties' with their customers through 'the Starbucks Experience.' The people who line up for Starbucks, writes CEO Howard Shultz, aren't just there for the coffee. 'It's the romance of the coffee experience, the feeling of warmth and community people get in Starbucks stores'.

Interestingly, before moving to Starbucks, Bedbury was head of marketing at Nike, where he oversaw the launch of the 'Just Do It!' slogan, among other watershed branding moments. in the following passage, he explains the common techniques used to infuse the two very different brands with meaning:

> Nike, for example, is leveraging the deep emotional connection that people have with sports and fitness. With Starbucks, we see how coffee has woven itself into the fabric of people's lives, and that's our opportunity for emotional leverage . . . A great brand raises the bar – it adds a greater sense of purpose to the experience, whether it's the challenge to do your best in sports and fitness or the affirmation that the cup of coffee you're drinking really matters.

> N. Klein, *No Logo*, Flamingo, 2001, pp. 20–1

ACTIVITIES

➤ The extract by Naomi Klein considers the way in which shops like the Body Shop, Gap, Disney and Starbucks promote themselves as 'brands'. If you can visit one of these stores consider the ways in which they promote themselves, for example through the use of particular types of shopping 'environments', the way in which they display their goods, 'address' customers and package their products

➤ 'All media products are, in fact, promoting something or someone'. Do you agree? Give detailed examples to support your views (AQA Unit 2, May 2002).

FURTHER READING

Dyer, G. (1989) *Advertising as Communication*, Routledge.
A good and accessible introduction to the analysis of advertisements as signs and the ways in which advertisements construct both meanings and particular responses from audiences. The book also contains some details on the regulation and economic impact of advertising.

Fiske, J. (1990). *Introduction to Communication Studies*, 2nd edn, Routledge.
Primarily a text aimed at providing a basic introduction to various communications theories. Has some good sections on uses and gratifications etc. but perhaps not the best way in.

Fiske, J. (1991) *Understanding Popular Culture*, Routledge.
Although the examples are a little dated, this is an interesting and persuasively political book that argues a case for popular culture.

Geraghty, C. (2000) *British Cinema in the Fifties: Gender, Genre and the 'New Look'*, Routledge.
Although dealing with other issues, this is an interesting and informative text on the ideology of the housewife in the 1950s.

Klein, N. (2000) *No Logo*, Flamingo.
A very accessible and detailed examination of the way in which large multinational corporations like Nike or Gap market their goods as 'lifestyle' brands.

Marx, K. and Engels, F. (1970) *The German Ideology*, Lawrence & Wishart.
It is probably wise not to try and read the original works by Marx and Engels but instead to read modern explanations of their work such as Chapter 5 'Marxism' in J. Storey (1993) *An Introductory Guide to Cultural Theory and Popular Culture*, Harvester Wheatsheaf.

▼   **1 INTRODUCTION**

An extensive amount of audience research is carried out by the media industries themselves in order to quantify and profile consumers of media products. Typically, the findings of such research might take the form of viewing figures for prime-time television or the circulation figures of newspapers and magazines. Such statistics, usually complied by independent industry-funded bodies, are an important barometer of the success of specific media products. They can fuel and monitor market competition, as evidenced in the 'ratings wars' between soap operas, the circulation battle between tabloid newspapers, or record labels and producers fighting to produce the Number 1 single in the Christmas charts.

In addition to measuring audiences quantitatively, that is, in terms of their numbers, media producers also collect qualitative data, taking into account characteristics of their audience such as social class, gender, life-stage and disposable income. Such information is aimed primarily at convincing would-be advertisers that the audience they wish to reach is being delivered through a specific media product.

A third type of media research is conducted by media academics. This type of research is less concerned with the volume and nature of audiences, focusing instead on the relationship between media products and the audiences that consume them. A particularly popular area of research concerns the effects that media products allegedly have on their audience. For example, studies at Middlesex University recently claimed that children become more aggressive the more they play video games; in 2002, this study indirectly led to the adoption of a regulation system where games are classified in terms of content, in much the same way as films are. As well as looking at the potentially negative effects of media products, academic research into audiences also examines the ways in which people consume the media, and their likes and dislikes.

Interest from both industrial and academic sources has led to the development and application of a range of methodologies in media research. It is important that a media researcher is clear about the precise methodology that he or she is using in audience research. The main reason for this is to allow other commentators to assess the validity of their findings and, where necessary, to replicate the research to test it further.

Methodologies can be divided into two broad categories:

- **Quantitative research** relies on the processing of large amounts of data. Content analysis is an example of this type of research, whereby large amounts of media output, such as television advertisements, are examined to identify recurring features. This methodology might be used to explore gender roles in contemporary television advertising by looking at a large number of advertisements from the perspective of how men and women are represented.
- **Qualitative research** usually requires a more in-depth engagement with the audience itself. This might include such techniques as interview or observation in order to arrive at conclusions about audience behaviour in relation to media consumption.

In the following section we explore some of the approaches to audience study which have been adopted both by academic researchers and by the industry itself.

▼ 2 ENCODING AND DECODING

One of the key issues in audience studies concerns the relationship between producer, text and audience. In many ways this equation is about a balance of power: assessing the extent to which audiences are influenced and swayed by media texts, and to what extent they appropriate them in ways quite different to the producers' intentions.

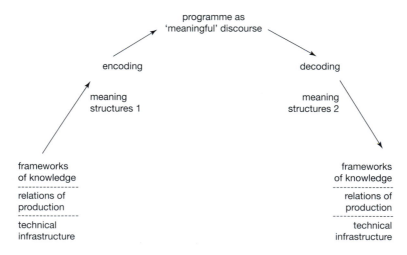

Extract 29

Source: S. Hall, 'Encoding/Decoding', in S. Hall *et al.* (eds), *Culture, Media, Language*, Hutchinson, 1980, p. 130

One of the earliest explorations of this relationship comes in Stuart Hall's Encoding/ Decoding model. In the diagram reproduced above, he represents the two sides: encoding, which is the domain of the producer, and decoding, the domain of the audience. The process of communicating a message requires that it be encoded in such a way that the receiver of the message is able to decode it. For example, a televisual message is encoded through the use of camera technology, transmitted as a signal and then decoded using a television set. If you do not have a television set, then you don't have the means to understand or decode the televisual message.

Examine the symmetry between the two sides in the diagram above. Both encoding and decoding take place within the similar contexts, which ultimately provide the means by which the message can be transmitted and received. One reason that the encoded and decoded messages may not be the same is the capacity of the audience to vary its response to media messages. Hall identified three possible types of response that an audience might make to a media message, as Bell, Joyce and Rivers also point out in the extract below.

The **encoding/decoding** model put forward by Stuart Hall and David Morley centred on the idea that audiences vary in their response to media messages. This is because they are influenced by their social position, gender, age, ethnicity, occupation, experience and beliefs as well as where they are and what they are doing when they receive a message. In this model, media texts are seen to be encoded in such a way as to present a **preferred reading** to the audience but the audience does not necessarily accept that preferred reading. Hall categorised three kinds of audience response.

- Dominant – the audience agree with the dominant values expressed within the preferred reading of the text
- Negotiated – the audience generally agree with the dominant values expressed within the preferred reading but they may disagree with certain aspects according to their social background
- Oppositional – the audience disagree with dominant values expressed within the preferred reading of the text

A. Bell, M. Joyce and D. Rivers, *Advanced Media Studies*, Hodder & Stoughton, 1999, p. 21

One concept that has been challenged subsequently by theorists is the notion of Hall's 'preferred reading'. This refers to the way the encoder would prefer the audience to interpret a media message, above all other possible readings. However, it could be argued that some texts are deliberately created to remain open to interpretation. The films of David Lynch, such as *Lost Highway* or *Mulholland Drive*, are examples of texts that deliberately leave it up to the audience to make their own individual readings.

A theorist who developed the ideas behind Hall's Encoding and Decoding model was John Fiske. He explained the distinction between the two sides of the model as an opposition

between the 'power bloc' of a dominant cultural, political and social order and 'the people'. The power bloc produces mass products that the people change by their resistance to them. As Nick Stevenson explains in his essay, 'Critical Perspectives with Audience Research': 'popular culture is made by the people, not produced by the cultural industry'.

From this perspective, the audience is empowered in a way that might not be readily observed. Stevenson goes on to cite Fiske's use of Madonna's music to exemplify the way in which 'the act of consumption always entails the production of meaning'.

The circulation of meaning requires us to study three levels of textuality while teasing out the specific relations between them. First there are the cultural forms that are produced along with the new Madonna album to create the idea of a media event. These can include concerts, books, posters and videos. At the next level, there is a variety of media talk in popular magazines and newspapers, television pop programmes and radio shows all offering a variety of critical commentary upon Madonna. The final level of textuality, the one that Fiske claims to be most attentive to, involves the ways in which Madonna becomes part of our everyday life. According to Fiske, Madonna's career was launched by a rock video of an early song 'Lucky Star'. She became established in 1985 as a cultural icon through a series of successful LPs and singles, the film *Desperately Seeking Susan*, nude shots that appeared in *Penthouse* and *Playboy*, as well as the successful marketing of a certain 'look'. Fiske argues that Madonna symbolically plays with traditional male-dominated stereotypes of the virgin and the whore in order to subtly subvert patriarchal meanings. That is, the textuality of Madonna ideologically destabilises traditional representations of women. Fiske accounts for Madonna's success by arguing that she is an open or writerly text rather than a closed readerly one. In this way, Madonna is able to challenge her fans to reinvent their own sexual identities out of the cultural resources that she and patriarchal capitalism provides. Hence Madonna as a text is polysemic, patriarchal and sceptical. In the final analysis, Madonna is not popular because she is promoted by the culture industry, but because her attempts to forge her own identity within a male-defined culture have a certain relevance for her fans.

N. Stevenson, 'Critical Perspectives within Audience Research' in T. O'Sullivan and Y. Jewkes (eds), *The Media Studies Reader*, Arnold, 1997, p. 235

ACTIVITY

Choose a more up-to-date example of a product of mass culture that you think has been appropriated by people as 'a cultural resource'. Explain how you think that audiences may have used it differently from the way the producers intended.

▼ 3 RESEARCHING AUDIENCES

Commercially motivated market research makes up a large part of studies into media audiences. This type of research is primarily concerned with measuring the number of people who consume specific media products. As mentioned earlier when we defined quantitative research, this is useful in determining which programmes and other media products are successful. A prime-time television programme that attracts an audience of 15 million viewers will be considered more successful than one that attracts only 12 million, despite what critics and reviewers have to say about its quality. Having precise information about the size of audiences for individual programmes is an important weapon in the 'ratings war' where television channels compete with one another for audience ratings, especially during the early evening prime-time slots.

A measure of the size of an audience may not provide sufficient information for another interested group, however – the advertisers. Commercial television channels are funded mostly through the sale of advertising time during commercial breaks in their programmes. Clearly, the more successful a show becomes at pulling in an audience, the more money a station can charge in advertising fees. However, the sheer size of the audience may be less important than the people who constitute it, as we shall see when we look at audience segmentation (p. 104). It is in advertisers' interest to aim their advertising at the specific groups who are most likely to buy their products. For example, advertisements for insurance companies and banks are more likely to reach their target market during the ad breaks of television programmes whose viewers are largely working adults. Similarly, Saturday morning kids' TV shows are more likely to have adverts for toys, compilation CDs, and nappies, in order to capture their target market of young children and their parents, who will be spending money on these products. Finding out the lifestyles, preferences, ages and values of a certain segment of the audience is called profiling.

Most audience research is carried out by market research companies, and the information can be used to persuade advertisers to use advertising space in order to reach an audience whose profile suggests that they would find the advertiser's product appealing.

The extracts below offer some insight into this process of collecting and presenting information about audiences. The first is taken from the Broadcaster Audience Research Board (BARB) website. It shows us how information about the size and nature of audiences is gathered. The measurement is on a sampling basis, with the households carefully chosen to represent the viewing public as a whole. Information about viewing figures is available on the BARB website and in such publications as the *Radio Times* and *Heat* magazine. More detailed information, as set out below, is provided by BARB for organisations which subscribe to its service.

The measurement service provides television audience data on a minute-by-minute basis for channels received within the UK. These data are available for reporting nationally as well as at the ITV and BBC regional level.

Viewing estimates are obtained from panels of television owning households representing the viewing behaviour of the 24+ million households within the UK. The panels are selected to be representative of each ITV and BBC region.

Panel homes are selected via a multi-stage stratified and unclustered sample design. This ensures that the panel is fully representative of households across the whole of the UK. Each panel is maintained against a range of individual and household characteristics (panel controls). As the estimates for the large majority of the panel controls are not available from census data, it is necessary to conduct surveys (the Establishment Survey) to obtain this information.

The Establishment Survey is a random probability survey carried out on a continuous basis and involving some 50,000 interviews per year. The nature of this survey ensures that any changes within the characteristics of the population can be identified. Panel controls can therefore be updated and panel household representation adjusted to ensure representativeness is maintained. In addition to being the prime source of television population information, the Establishment Survey also generates a pool of potential recruits from which panel member homes are recruited. Each of the panel member households have all their television receiving equipment (sets, video cassette recorders, set-top box decoders etc.) electronically monitored by a 'peoplemeter' monitoring system. This system automatically identifies and records the channel to which each television set is tuned when switched on and all viewing involving a VCR (recording, playback, viewing through the VCR etc.). In addition the metering system incorporates the capability to 'fingerprint' videotapes during recording sessions and to subsequently identify such recorded material when played back (time-shifted viewing).

All permanent household residents and guests declare their presence in a room whilst a television set is on by pressing an allocated button on a handset. The metering system monitors all registrations made by each individual.

Throughout each day the meter system stores all the viewing undertaken by the entire household. Each night the panel household is contacted by the processing centre by telephone to collect the stored data. This procedure is carried out on every home each day to produce 'overnight' television viewing data.

Extract from BARB website – www.barb.co.uk

➤ Imagine that your household has been selected for measuring by BARB. What sort of results do you think it would have produced over the last week? Do you think you are typical of other viewers in your pattern of using television?

➤ How accurate a picture of television consumption do you thinkthe BARB system of measuring audiences provides?

Another organisation that collects and publishes data is JICREG, the Joint Industry Committee for Regional Press Research. This organisation is concerned with researching audience information about the regional press. Like BARB, it offers a limited amount of information free on its website, but operates a subscription service for the media industries if they require more information.

Below is an example of a JICREG report on a regional newspaper, in this case the *Wakefield Express*.

JICREG NEWSPAPER READERSHIP REPORT FOR THE WAKEFIELD EXPRESS

Total readerships by demographic group:

Adults	Men	Women	FMS	Age 15-24	Age 25-34	Age 35-44	Age 45-54	Age 55-64	Age 65 plus	ABC1	C2DE	AB	C1	C2	DE
104450	49532	54918	36172	14566	20727	19983	15948	13629	19597	51065	55319	17196	31133	25707	30414

Demographic profile of the area:

Total aged 15+: 148581 | Total households: 76888

Total men	Total women	Total female main shoppers	Total aged between 15 and 24	Total aged between 25 and 34	Total aged between 35 and 44	Total aged between 45 and 54	Total aged between 55 and 64	Total aged 65 or more	Total ABC1	Total C2DE	Total AB	Total C1	Total C2	Total DE
73448	75133	65518	20523	26553	29642	24631	20312	26920	65903	82678	25981	39922	34270	48408

Readerships by location:

Location	Pop	HH	Adult AIR	AIR %	RPC	Men	Women	FMS	Age 15-24	Age 25-34	Age 35-44	Age 45-54	Age 55-64	Age 65 plus	ABC1	C2DE	AB	C1	C2	DE	Circ
NORMANTON	16235	8650	8380	51.62	3.1	3950	4431	2843	1156	1872	1540	1134	1052	1627	3457	4923	973	2484	2274	2649	2687
OSSETT	17389	8889	7063	40.61	3.2	3279	3784	2427	962	1486	1397	1137	874	1207	3647	3415	1179	2468	1824	1591	2216
SOUTH WAKEFIELD RURAL	48530	24587	29170	60.11	3.1	13619	15551	10353	3990	5400	5603	4818	4003	5356	16160	13873	6216	9228	6571	7155	9530
WAKEFIELD	66427	34762	59837	90.08	3.1	28684	31153	20549	8459	11969	11442	8860	7701	11407	27800	33108	8828	16953	15037	19019	19453

JICREG data as at 28/01/2003

➤ Study the information carefully. Does it help you form a picture of a typical *Wakefield Express* reader? Why do you think the column headed 'total female main shoppers' might be important to advertisers considering taking space in the newspaper?

▼ 4 ETHNOGRAPHIC RESEARCH

Ethnographic research is an approach to audience studies that relies heavily on qualitative methodologies. Popular in the 1980s, the ethnographic approach placed a great deal of emphasis on the conditions under which audiences consumed media products. Television viewing by such groups as families became a particular target for ethnographic researchers. David Morley carried out a major ethnographic survey in 1978, in which he explored audience readings of the popular current affairs programme *Nationwide*. His research findings did not wholly fit with Hall's categories in the Encoding/Decoding model, not least because many in the sample thought the programme irrelevant or that it made little sense to them.

The following extract from James Lull's essay 'How Families Select Programs', offers an example of a mass observational study. In the extract, Lull explains the method used to set up the study.

METHOD

The present research was designed systematically to focus the attention of nearly 100 observers on how families turn on, change channels and turn off the main television set in their homes. Undergraduate students from an upper division theoretical course in mass communication at a West Coast University were trained to observe the families who served as subjects for the study. Training of student observers involved participation in family simulation exercises as well as the observing and reporting of family communicative behavior which was viewed by the group on film. Personal contact was made with the families in the sample by the researchers prior to the observational period.

Observers spent most of two days with the families which were randomly assigned to them and returned a third day to conduct interviews with each family member. Families that took part in the study were members of the Goleta Valley Boys Club, a large, heterogeneous organization that exists in the vicinity of the University of California, Santa Barbara. In order to achieve the desired sample size, more than 500 families were contacted by telephone. Random procedures were used to develop the phone list and a high rate of rejection took place as it always does when this type of research is conducted.

Observers spent two consecutive late afternoons and evenings with the families to which they were assigned. They ate dinner with the families and generally took part in all their activities. To the degree it was possible, families were asked to ignore the presence of the observer and carry out their routines in normal fashion. Previous data indicate that families' basic activities, including their television viewing, are not greatly disrupted by the presence of a trained observer. The observers took written notes in order to document as accurately as possible the activities that occurred. Since this study focused on the specific actions that surround the operation of the main television set, the observers were able to limit their observations and documentations to particular instances of interaction.

Families were not informed in advance that the intent of the observer was to examine television-related behavior. They were told that the observer was interested in studying 'family life' for a college class. Families watched television in great abundance during the observational sessions. Of the families that had a television set (all but two in the eventual sample), only one family failed to turn the set on at least once during the observational period.

Some 93 families were observed during the same week during late Autumn 1980. Of these groups, 74 were two-parent families. The one-parent families have been removed from the sample for this analysis. Most one-parent families had a woman as head of the household, and this condition could have systematically distorted an understanding of the role of fathers and mothers in the normative two-parent groups. This analysis then, considers 74 families comprised of 286 members. In total 74 fathers and 73 mothers were analyzed, the small discrepancy due to the failure of one of the mothers to complete a postobservational questionnaire. Child subjects numbered 139, comprising 48 percent of the sample.

Observers returned to the homes of the families with whom they stayed on a third day in order to interview each person. Family members were asked to report their perceptions of family position and communication patterns in their homes, to describe and evaluate the program selection processes in which they participate, to indicate the degree of selectivity employed in personal viewing, and to provide fundamental demographic information.

J. Lull, 'How Families Select Programs', *Inside Television*, Routledge, 1990, pp. 88–9

ACTIVITY

➤ Devise a small ethnographic study of a social group to which you are affiliated, e.g. your family or your classmates. Base your study on their responses to one television programme or other media text. Through questioning or observation, try to establish some of the differences in the readings of texts that are apparent. How do you explain these?

FURTHER READING

Geraghty, C. (1998) 'Audiences and Ethnography: Questions of Practice', in C. Geraghty and
D. Lusted (eds), *The Television Studies Book*, Arnold.
A particularly useful survey of key research.

Gray, A. (1991) *Video Playtime*, Routledge.
Explores gendered attitudes to video technology.

Moores, S. (1993) *Interpreting Audiences*, Sage.
A succinct book that provides a good overview of reception theory, in particular the way in which
media theorists and researchers have focused on how audiences consume and interpret media texts.

Morley, D. (1992) *Television Audiences and Cultural Studies*, Routledge.
Offers a useful overview.

▼ 5 AUDIENCE SEGMENTATION

Traditionally on television there have been a number of highly popular programmes that could be guaranteed to attract huge audiences. These included soap operas such as *Coronation Street* and *EastEnders*, which played a key role in the scheduling of peak-time early evening programmes. However, an increasing number of viewing options available through digital and satellite channels have begun to chip away at the mass audience in recent years. On commercial channels this has been accompanied by a reduction in the rates that can be charged for advertising slots during these programmes, meaning that the stations no longer make as much money from them. The decision by Channel 4 to scrap the popular soap *Brookside* is symptomatic of this decline.

In a similar way, the circulation of popular tabloid titles such as the *Sun* and the *Mirror* has also steadily declined. One of the reasons for the reduction in the size of the mass audience is competition from other sources of information and entertainment. The Internet, for example, has become for many people an alternative source of information and entertainment, presumably at the expense of more established media forms such as television and print.

Another reason given for the decline of mass audiences is the increasing degree of choice now available to media consumers. This has come about largely because of technological innovation in the production and delivery of media texts. Changes in print technology and industrial working practices now make it possible to produce much shorter print runs without incurring the heavy initial costs, as was previously the case. For example, small circulation specialist interest magazines aimed at niche markets have cropped up all over, often at the expense of mass circulation titles.

The advent of satellite, cable and digital technology as methods of delivering television channels into our homes has resulted in a plethora of channels mostly produced on minimal budgets and aimed at niche markets. Similarly, radio broadcasting has seen increasing numbers of specialist interest channels broadcast nationally, using digital technology as well as small community-based stations aimed at compact geographical areas. This again has resulted in a decline in audiences for the larger, nationally broadcast channels such as Radio 1.

Of course, such developments have implications for the advertising industry. The breaking down of mass audiences into specific niches, whether geographically or by means of lifestyle and interest, presents an ideal opportunity for the advertiser to target particular segments of the market. The process of breaking audiences down in this way is known as segmentation. The more information advertisers have about the nature and composition of an audience, the more effectively can they target that audience with products that they are likely to buy.

In the extract that follows, Shaun Moores explains some of the ways in which audiences can be segmented into different groups. The work is based on methods used by market researchers.

MARKET SEGMENTATION IN THE COMMERCIAL SPHERE

Outside of sociology and cultural studies, of course, there lies a whole field of commercial research which is concerned with issues of taste and consumption that are similar to those raised in Bourdieu's *Distinction*. Even though market researchers are motivated by a desire to identify potential purchasers for commodities and business services – rather than by an academic or political interest in providing accounts of cultural power and social reproduction – I want to propose that the work they do may still be of relevance to academics engaged in the analysis of consumer practices. In fact, marketing discourses can be read as signs of quite fundamental shifts in capitalist modes of production and consumption during the twentieth century. The growth of marketing as a profession parallels the movement from an era of so-called 'mass consumption' to newer, flexible and specialized, forms of production – with correspondingly more diverse and fragmented consumer subgroups. It is highly appropriate that in the jargon of recent debates on the Left of British politics, this has come to be known as a transformation from 'Fordism' to 'Post-Fordism', because the car industry shows clear evidence of the changes taking place. When the Ford Motor Company once said of its famous 'Model T' that buyers could have any colour they wanted so long as it was black, few foresaw the day when, counting all the multiple combinations of engine and optional accessories, one type of car would be available in over 69,000 varieties. Car advertising campaigns are increasingly targeted at specific audiences – promoting the spacious saloon for family use,

CONTINUED

sports performance for the young executive or a stylish hatchback for the independent woman about town.

Whilst they share no common consensus on exactly how to conceptualize consumer divisions, all commercial market researchers are involved in a process known as 'segmentation'. It entails an 'overt recognition that consumers are not homogeneous'. Peter Chisnall, in his text written for business students, explains that strategies of this sort are 'a deliberate policy of maximising market demand by directing marketing efforts at significant subgroups of customers' – and in the following notes, I consider various models of market segmentation which have proved influential in the commercial sector over the last twenty years or so. I begin with those that divide consumers by socioeconomic status or geographical location, before going on to assess recent approaches which disaggregate markets into lifestyle categories with particular 'psychographic' profiles. Work on family purchasing decisions is also considered for its pertinence to the critical study of domestic cultures.

Amongst market researchers in Britain, the most widely employed classification of socioeconomic groupings is still the six category JICNARS scale. This was originally used for an investigation into the distribution of newspaper and magazine sales – now administered by the Joint Industry Committee for National Readership Surveys, which represents a range of publishing and advertising organizations. The model is basically a segmentation of the population by occupation. Group 'A' are described in the JICNARS scale as upper middle class: 'the head of the household is a successful business or professional man . . . or has considerable private means'. 'Bs' – middle class – are also 'senior people but not at the very top of their profession or business . . . quite well off, but their style of life is generally respectable rather than rich or luxurious'. The 'C1' category denotes 'white collar', lower middle-class consumers who are 'in general . . . the families of small tradespeople and non-manual workers who carry out less important administrative, supervisory or clerical jobs'. 'C2s', meanwhile, are the skilled working class in 'blue collar' jobs ('serving of an apprenticeship may be a guide to membership of this class') – and category 'D' consists of semi- or unskilled manual workers. Lastly, 'Es' are those at the lowest levels of subsistence, 'casual workers or those who, through sickness or unemployment, are dependent on social security schemes'.

Although the JICNARS divisions remain an important element of marketing discourse, a series of objections have now been made to the use of this classi-fication system – reflecting doubts in the industry about whether occupational differences alone can enable an accurate 'carving up' of contemporary consumer markets. An evident shortcoming of the model is its sole reliance on the job done by 'heads of household' – assumed to be male – as an indicator of family consumption habits. It takes no account either of women's paid work or of households without a male breadwinner (in addition, it mistakenly sees 'the family' as a single, uncontradictory consuming unit). Another crucial problem is the failure fully to recognize generational, or life-stage, distinctions. For that particular reason, in the early 1980s, a company named Research Services developed the 'Sagacity' segmentation. Rather than relying just on occupation, the consumer categories they introduced treated demographics 'multi-variately' – producing a twelve-scale framework which sought to combine data on positions within the life-cycle, along with income (allowing for the working status of spouses and levels of disposable income), and occupation too. So, for instance, the Sagacity categories incorporate stages such as 'Dependent', 'Pre-family', 'Family' or 'Late'. They indicate whether households are 'Better off' or 'Worse off', and they distinguish 'White' from 'Blue' collar.

The last decade has also witnessed the arrival of market segmentation models which differentiate between areas of housing, or else between broader geographical spaces and communities. ACORN (A Classification of Residential Neighbourhoods) is a British system that seeks to map geographically the concentrated clustering of certain types of consumers in certain residential districts. Gordon Oliver explains how 'advocates for this segment base would argue that where we live is intimately connected with how we live, and how we live subsumes what we consume'. The neighbourhood context might also tell us something about how a cultural object gets utilized and made sense of – hence my own interest in geographical segmentations as a starting point for ethnographic research on the household consumption of satellite TV. In promotional material for their ACORN model, CACI Market Analysis (1985) describe the way in which it applies published census statistics and classifies small enumeration districts of around 150 homes into one of eleven neigh-bourhood groupings. For each of these alphabetically ordered segments, specific kinds of lifestyles and cultural practices are identified. So in group 'B' here – 'modern family housing, higher incomes' – there are 'relatively weak community networks and a fairly high expenditure on consumer goods and family leisure'. For the 'better off council estates' that form group 'E', 'movement away from relatives and the close community networks of the inner city often results in a weakening of traditional social attitudes, leisure patterns and consumer preferences . . . households become more confident in their ability to use credit'. And in the 'high status non-family areas' of group 'I', residents 'tend to be frequent readers of books and journals, receptive to new ideas and products and, especially if they are single, likely to spend much of their leisure time and money on outside entertainment and on eating out'. A potential difficulty for this sort of analysis is in dealing with divided and contested areas . . . Nevertheless, in the business world, many companies have drawn on ACORN data in deciding where to locate a new store or how to focus the distribution of mailshot advertising.

PRIZM (Potential Rating Index by Zip Market) is a close relative of ACORN's on the other side of the Atlantic. A 'zip' number is the five-digit American postal

code, and PRIZM divides a total of over 35,000 neighbourhood codes into forty 'zip market clusters' – with titles ranging from 'Pools and Patios' to 'Bohemian Mix' to 'Norma Rae-Ville'. These clusters are constituted with reference to a combination of demographic and social variables – such as housing stock, education, ethnicity and urban/rural divisions. A rather different form of geographical segmentation in operation there is Joel Garreau's 'Nine Nations of North America' chart. He encourages marketers to forget about formal political boundaries between countries and states, and in their place he constructs nine regional categories called 'The Foundry', 'Dixie', 'Breadbasket', 'Ecotopia', and so on. Each is seen to have a capital city and its own distinctive way of life. . . . This is certainly an ambitious effort to map out imagined communities, although there has been a good deal of debate amongst American market researchers concerning its practical application to consumer targeting.

At this juncture, before moving on to consider the emergence of a currently fashionable method of segmentation known as psychographics, it may be appropriate to discuss just briefly a general problem with models like JICNARS, Sagacity, ACORN and PRIZM – which is the tendency they have to view the household as a taken-for-granted unit of consumption. I am not disputing the fact that the private sphere of family life is indeed a major domain in which commodities are consumed . . . [but] households are best understood as places where there are key differences in taste and consumer activity. Some market researchers have, it is true to say, done interesting work on the question of domestic dynamics by investigating processes of decision-making in families. For example, James Engel and Roger Blackwell (1982) comment on research carried out in Belgium during the 1970s on the relative influence of husbands and wives in purchasing decisions for twenty-five specified product-types (including food, furniture, clothing, car, etc.). Four sorts of decision were identified – 'husband dominant', 'wife dominant', 'syncratic' and 'autonomic'. The first two of these are fairly self-explanatory, whilst a 'syncratic' decision is one which over half of the survey respondents said they took jointly, and 'autonomic' refers to instances where less than half decided together. In principle, that survey approach seems to be quite promising. However, in practice, it is both conceptually and politically dubious. It needs to go further by asking more directly about power relations between men and women in domestic life. So who is controlling the large items of household expenditure and who looks after, say, the day-to-day shopping for foodstuffs? Even there, might the person buying and preparing the food for meals make choices on the basis of satisfying others' preferences?

Psychographics – the latest trend in market segmentation to be imported from the USA – makes a fundamental break with the socioeconomic and demographic models I have been describing up to now. It distinguishes consumers according to 'cognitive styles' rather than by the jobs they do or the places where they live, and it involves researching into their activities, interests and opinions (AIOs).

At root this is a psychological approach to cultural consumption – one that posits the determining influence of particular personality traits or 'consumer profiles'. Typically, such research is done by mailing questionnaires to members of a panel who are invited to respond positively or negatively to a large number of AIO statements like, for instance, 'a woman's place is in the home', 'premarital sex is immoral', 'the use of marijuana should be made legal' or 'I buy many things with a credit card'. Working with the responses given, psychographic segmentations proceed to put consumers into a variety of lifestyle categories. Although these classificatory schemes display a profoundly dangerous tendency towards psychological reductionism, their popularity within the marketing community is growing – and while my argument will be that the overall approach is seriously flawed, I nevertheless believe that psychographics may deliver a few productive insights into cultures of consumption.

'Needham Harper Worldwide' is the title of a US classification which separates out over 3,000 survey respondents into ten lifestyle groups, each given a different name to denote a certain sort of personality. Half are male – Herman the retiring homebody, Dale the devoted family man, and so forth. The other half are female, with examples here being Mildred the militant mother, or Eleanor the elegant socialite. Indexes of predicted product consumption are then linked up to the ten profiles. VALS (Values and Lifestyles) is another well known American system, employing a form of 'attitudinal cluster analysis' and thereby constructing a typology which comprises four main market components – need driven, outer directed, inner directed and integrated individuals. This ordering is derived from the notion that there exists a universal 'hierarchy of needs' in human societies. So need-driven individuals are concerned with satisfying the basic physiological requirements for nutrition and shelter. Outer-directed personalities invest most value in the possession of material goods, and inner-directed individuals are thought to have a more 'spiritual' set of concerns with self-realization. Meanwhile, those credited with an integrated personality manage to combine both material values and spiritual or social awareness. Within the four main categories is a series of subdivisions – for instance, the outer-directed segment is made up of 'Belongers', 'Emulators' and 'Achievers'. It is worth mentioning, incidentally, that public arts organizations outside the business sector have also begun to use the VALS research in an attempt to define their existing and target audiences.

On British shores, the 'Monitor' social value group model – devised by the Taylor Nelson agency – provides something of a parallel to VALS. Based on an annual survey of attitudes, Monitor is a 'seven cluster solution' to the problem of charting values and beliefs. Once again, each cluster has a label (e.g. 'self-explorers', 'conspicuous consumers', 'survivors'). In addition, each name is accompanied by a key phrase which is supposed to typify the outlook of a specified consumer grouping – 'I'll try it', 'Look at me' and 'My family comes first' are three of the seven. Actually this style of drawing on brief, indicative phrases

is not dissimilar to Bourdieu's writing strategy in parts of *Distinction*. . . . He was interested in precisely what market researchers call 'attitudinal clusters' – choosing instead to use terms like disposition or habitus – but the telling difference with Bourdieu's work is his insistence on always seeking to relate cultural values and perceptions back to the socioeconomic level. If, as I suggested earlier, he has been open to accusations of sociological essentialism, that is still far preferable in my view to the kind of reductionist psychology we find in much psychographic market research. The question is surely how the VALS and Monitor classifications connect with older occupational segmentations – or with the geographical divisions of ACORN and PRIZM. What should concern us in studying patterns of cultural consumption is exactly how social demography and social psychology intersect.

S. Moores, 'On Cultural Consumption', *Interpreting Audiences*, Sage, 1993, pp. 124–9

A glance at the range of publications available in any large newsagents or the listings for a local multiplex cinema testify to the range of media products available. However, there are commentators who question whether segmentation of markets and audiences has provided choice and variety in the media, or simply more of the same in different packaging.

Television magazines and guides now tend to list channels according to genre, providing shortcuts for the segmented audience to find the sort of programming they may like. In addition to programmes for the major terrestrial channels, listings are also given for satellite and cable under the following headings:

Entertainment
Gold
Lifestyle
Music
Factual
Kids
Movie Channels
Pay per view movies
Sport

ACTIVITY

➤ Look at the page reproduced below from the entertainment section of *TV and Satellite Week*. Choose three or four of the channels and try to draw up a profile of the audience you think most likely to tune in. What sort of advertising do you think the channel would seek to attract? Do you think the type of advertising might vary at different times of day?

MEDIA STUDIES: THE ESSENTIAL RESOURCE

10 DECEMBER TUESDAY

ENTERTAINMENT

PARAMOUNT
Cab DigCab SkyDig 127

9.00am Moonlighting 10.00 Ellen 10.30 Moesha 11.00 The Cosby Show 11.30 A Different World

12.00noon Clueless 72314132 **12.30pm Happy Days** 98723045 **1.00 What About Joan** 39027749 **1.30 Married... With Children** 98722316 **2.00 M*A*S*H** 23922671 **2.30 Ellen** 58534855 **3.00 Mad About You** 23918478 **3.30 Spin City** 58539300 **4.00 3rd Rock from the Sun** US sci-fi sitcom. 58525107 **4.30 Cheers** 58627519 **5.00 Frasier** 23913923 **5.30 Becker** 58538671

6.00 Happy Days
In order to join the college fraternity house, Richie must dump his blackballed pals. 58535584

6.30 Roseanne
Roseanne cajoles Dan into joining her in a weight-loss campaign involving much exercise. 58526836

7.00 M*A*S*H
Hawkeye dictates a letter to the president asking him who is responsible for the Korean War. 23006687

7.30 M*A*S*H
A South Korean boy is brought into the hospital to have shrapnel removed from his leg. 58515720

8.00 Seinfeld
The Dog: When Jerry looks after a boisterous dog, Elaine and George discover just how dependent their relationship is on him. 23919107

8.30 Mad About You
Paul and Jamie cannot decide on a name for their daughter. 23921942

9.00 Becker
Becker becomes aware that his sex life is non-existent. 59791519

9.30 Frasier
Frasier jumps to the wrong conclusion and tells Niles that Maris is having an affair. 98630381

10.00 Frasier
Frasier's agent attempts to negotiate a new contract for him. 72315861

10.30 Harry Enfield's Brand Spanking New Show
Comedy sketches. 72228381

11.00 The New Statesman
Alan's position as the most right-wing MP is threatened. 59690836

11.30 Drop the Dead Donkey
Some hen and stag nights need careful planning. 14678584

12.00m't Spin City 12.30am Married... With Children 1.00 Moesha 1.30 Cheers 2.00 Roseanne 2.30 3rd Rock from the Sun 3.00 Clueless 3.30–4.00am What About Joan

EXTREME
DigCab SkyDig 422

6.00am World of Wakeboarding 6.30 Waveriderz 7.00 Board Wild 7.30 20 Inch 8.00 MXVM 8.30 High Octane 9.00 The Chilli Factor 9.30 Sportsworx 10.00 World of Wakeboarding 10.30 Sportsmax 11.30 Waveriderz

12.00noon Core Culture USA 1.00pm 20 Inch 1.30 Sportsworx 2.00 Chilli Factor 2.30 High Octane 3.00 Wakeboarding 3.30 FORE & Friends 4.30 Board Wild 5.00 FORE & Friends 5.30 High Octane

6.00pm Sick Air 6.30 The Chilli Factor 7.00 Third Down 7.30 Logic 10 8.00 Core Culture USA 9.00 16mm 9.30 Board Wild 10.00 Time Machine 10.30 High Octane 11.00 Snowbombing 12.00m't Third Down 12.30am Logic 10 1.00 Core Culture USA 2.00 16mm 2.30 Sportsworx 3.00 Waveriderz 3.30 World of Wakeboarding 4.00 Sportsmax 5.00 Board Wild 5.30–6.00am 16mm

LIVING
Cab DigCab SkyDig 112

6.00am Home Shopping 7.00 Billy 7.10 Tiny and Crew 7.30 Oswald 7.45 Busy Buses 7.55 Barney and Friends 8.25 Hi-5 9.00 Maury Povich 9.50 Maury Povich 10.40 Ricki Lake 11.30 The Golden Girls

12.00noon Hollywood Star Treatment 4180652 **12.30pm Sixth Sense with Colin Fry** 9511132 **1.00 Crossing Over with John Edward** 6516687 **2.00 The Golden Girls** 7671774 **2.30 The Cosby Show** 5394045 **3.00 Maury Povich** 1875584 **4.00 Maury Povich** 3364590 **4.50 Ricki Lake** 1777010 **5.40 The Jerry Springer Show** 5139720

6.30 Sixth Sense with Colin Fry
Series in which the psychic attempts to reunited members of a studio audience with the spirits of departed loved ones. 5213126

7.00 Crossing Over with John Edward 6195687

8.00 Charmed
A vampire queen attempts to oust Cole as ruler of the underworld. Stars Julian McMahon. 7555836

9.00 The Three Mediums
Special with the three tenors of the spirit world: Colin Fry, Tony Stockwell and Derek Acorah. 6011671

10.00 CSI: Crime Scene Investigation
The team attempts to piece together clues from the scene of a brutal carjacking, but are hampered by a storm that threatens to wash away the evidence. 6194958

11.00 Bedtime Stories
Adult entertainment. 5901316

11.30 Sex Goddesses of the World 4846478

12.00m't Unsolved Mysteries 12.30am Family Law 1.30 The Geena Davis Show 2.00 The Fifth Wheel 2.30 The Bold and the Beautiful 3.00 Strong Medicine 4.00 Judge Judy 4.30 Birth Day Girls 5.00 The Geena Davis Show 5.30–6.00am Home Shopping

CHALLENGE
Cab DigCab SkyDig 121

6.00am Teleshopping 7.00 Treasure Hunt 8.00 Under Offer 8.30 Boot Sale Challenge 9.00 Soft Sell 9.30 HouseBusters 10.00 What's My Line? 10.30 It's Anybody's Guess 11.00 Stars in Their Eyes 11.45 Comedy of Errors

12.00noon Family Fortunes 12.30pm 100% 1.00 Wheel of Fortune 1.30 Beadle's About 2.00 Under Offer 2.30 Boot Sale Challenge 3.00 Soft Sell 3.30 HouseBusters 4.00 The Crystal Maze 5.00 Game Central 5.05 Bruce Forsyth's Play Your Cards Right 5.35 Game Central 5.40 Bruce's Price Is Right

6.10pm Game Central 6.15 Wheel of Fortune 6.45 Game Central 6.50 Fort Boyard Melinda Messenger presents the adventure game show set in a fortress. **7.50 Game Central** Interactive series. **7.55 The Crystal Maze** Game show set in a fantasy world. **8.55 Game Central 9.00 100%** Quick-fire quiz. **9.30 Family Fortunes 10.00 Bruce Forsyth's Play Your Cards Right 10.30 Bruce's Price is Right** Show in which contestants must guess the correct prices of consumer goods. **11.00 Game Central 11.05 Fort Boyard**

12.05am Game Central 12.10 Stars in Their Eyes 12.55 Who Dares Wins 1.25 Comedy of Errors 1.40 Treasure Hunt 2.40 What's My Line? 3.10 Family Fortunes 3.40 The Best of Beadle's About 3.50 It's Anybody's Guess 4.20 Comedy of Errors 4.30 Beadle's About 5.00 Sport Addicts Play Along 5.30–6.00am Wheel of Fortune

The magic number: Colin Fry is one of **The Three Mediums** in tonight's psychic special on Living at 9.00pm

TROUBLE
Cab DigCab SkyDig 607

6.00am Heartbreak High 6.55 Celebrity Extra 7.00 Saved by the Bell: The New Class 7.25 Hang Time 7.50 Malibu CA 8.20 City Guys 8.45 Baywatch 9.40 Home and Away 10.05 Saved by the Bell: The New Class 10.35 Malcolm and Eddie 11.00 City Guys 11.25 Sex Bomb 11.55 Fresh Prince of Bel Air

12.25pm Date My Sister 12.55 The Parkers 1.25 Steve Harvey Show 1.50 Malcolm and Eddie 2.20 Hang Time 2.50 Just Deal 3.15 Celebrity Extra 3.30 In the House 4.00 Fresh Prince of Bel Air 4.30 Two Guys, a Girl and a Pizza Place 5.00 Date My Sister 5.30 My Wife and Kids

6.00pm The Steve Harvey Show Comedy series about an inner-city music teacher. **6.30 Malibu CA** Teen drama series about two brothers who move to Malibu to start a new life with their father. **6.55 Saved by the Bell: The New Class** US comedy set in a high school. **7.20 Home and Away** Australian soap. **7.50 Celebrity Extra** Showbiz gossip with Tania Bryer. **8.00 Baywatch** Beach drama series starring David Hasselhoff. **8.55 The Parkers** US comedy series about a mother who goes back to high school and ends up at the same college as her daughter. **9.25 In the House 9.55 Date My Sister** Dating series. **10.25 My Wife and Kids 10.55 Sex Bomb 11.25 Two Guys, a Girl and a Pizza Place 11.55pm–12.00m't Celebrity Extra**

BBC FOUR
DigTerr DigCab SkyDig 161

7.00pm Business Confessions 7.10 America Documentary series. **8.00 News; Weather 8.30 Broadband Revolution?** An investigation into the possible benefits of broadband internet access, which allows for the fast transfer of data. **9.00 Storyville** This edition unravels the character and ambitions of Slobodan Milosevic, the former president of Yugoslavia who orchestrated one of Europe's most ruthless dictatorships since World War Two. **10.20 A Shadow Over Europe** Examining the consequences of the Benes Decree of 1945, whereby two and a half million ethnic Germans were driven from their homes in Czechoslovakia in a mass expulsion sanctioned by the wartime allies. **11.00 The Voynich Manuscript** Documentary telling the strange tale of the Voynich manuscript, a mysterious illustrated text that Polish book dealer Wilfried Voynich placed on the antiquarian book market in the 1920s. His claims that it was medieval, possibly by Roger Bacon, were dismissed by others as a hoax, and the manuscript remained unsold. But over the years a Voynich circle of scientists and scholars has attempted to crack the manuscript's code – but all disagree on what it means. **12.00m't Broadband** As 8.30pm. **12.30am Storyville** As shown above at 9.00pm. **1.50–2.50am A Shadow Over Europe** As shown above at 10.20pm.

HALLMARK
DigCab SkyDig 190

6.00am FILM: A Child's Cry for Help See below, 3.00pm. **8.00 Any Day Now 9.00 Judging Amy 10.00 Dr Quinn, Medicine Woman 11.00 Hamish Macbeth**

12.00noon Diagnosis Murder 43975590 **1.00pm FILM: Dalva** Drama. A woman with Sioux Indian ancestry looks for the child that she gave up 20 years earlier. *Stars Farrah Fawcett.* (1996, 15, 120min) ★★ 22338590 **3.00 FILM: A Child's Cry for Help** Medical drama. A doctor suspects that a woman is deliberately harming her child. *Stars Veronica Hamel, Pam Dawber.* (1994, PG, 120min) ★★ 73747359 **5.00 Dr Quinn, Medicine Woman** 60840836

6.00 Diagnosis Murder
Mark suspects sabotage when a motorcross rider has a fatal accident at a local track. 43971774

7.00 Judging Amy
Amy's college nemesis offers her a chance for an appellate court appointment if she agrees to compromise her principles. 26115519

8.00 Hamish Macbeth
Hamish is publicly denounced as the devil incarnate by the leader of a local church group. 26028039

9.00 Once and Again
Rick is forced to spend the weekend with Karen at Eli's basketball tournament. 26104403

10.00 Homicide: Life on the Street
Pressure mounts as a third near-naked murder victim is discovered. Stars Isabella Hoffman. 26107590

11.00 Are You Lonesome Tonight?
Thriller starring Jane Seymour. A lonely woman's husband disappears shortly after she learns he is obsessed with a girl who works on a phone-sex line. *With Parker Stevenson, Beth Broderick.* (1991, 15, 120min) ★★ 23646300

1.00am Once and Again 2.00 Lonesome Dove 4.00–6.00am FILM: Dalva See above, 1.00pm.

ARTSWORLD
SkyDig 199

2.00pm Outsider Art Looking at art made by people with no training. **3.00 Ariodante** See 8.00pm. **6.05 Erik Bruhn** Profile of the dancer and choreographer. **6.50 Tantalus**

7.00pm The Nude Series examining the nude in the visual arts. **7.30 Belcanto: The Singing Robot** The introduction of the gramophone record. **8.00 Ariodante** David Alden's critically-acclaimed English National Opera production of Handel's opera. Starring Ann Murray, Christopher Robso, Joan Rodgers and Lesley Garrett. **9.25 Passengers** Modern dance series. **9.55pm–12.00m't FILM: The Beekeeper** Greek drama. A retired teacher decides to follow in the footsteps of his father and grandfather by becoming a beekeeper. Subtitled. (1986, 18, 125min) ★★★

PERFORMANCE
Cab DigCab

7.00pm Abbado: Beethoven Symphony No 3 Claudio Abbado conducts the Berlin Philharmonic Orchestra. **8.00 The Monkees** Tracing the formation and success of the American pop group. **9.00 Neil Sedaka – Live** The American singer-songwriter at Birmingham's Symphony Hall. **10.00 The Pretenders Live from the Isle of View** The rock band performing in London, with a guest appearance by Blur's Damon Albarn. **11.00 Art Blakey** The jazz drummer at Ronnie Scott's nightclub in Soho, London. **12.00m't Chuck Mangioni and Koinonia 12.30–1.00am Teleshopping**

DISNEY
Cab DigCab SkyDig 613

6.00am The Little Mermaid 6.25 Goof Troop 6.50 Aladdin 7.15 Hercules 7.40 Tarzan 8.30 House of Mouse 9.00 Book of Pooh 9.20 Rolie Polie Olie 9.35 Bear in the Big Blue House 10.05 Stanley 10.25 Bite Size 10.35 Classic Toons 10.50 64 Zoo Lane 11.05 The Adventures of Spot 11.15 Sing Me a Story with Belle 11.45 Book of Pooh

12.00noon Rolie Polie Olie 9398958 **12.15pm Bear in the Big Blue House** 9204565 **12.35 Art Play** 15514132 **12.45 Stanley** 44965300 **12.55 Bite Size** 7032403 **1.15 Classic Toons** 37706687 **1.25 64 Zoo Lane** 37613923 **1.40 Adventures of Spot** 59132410 **1.50 Sing Me a Story with Belle** 73849300 **2.15 The Little Mermaid** 71590403 **2.40 Goof Troop** 2846213 **3.00 Buzz Lightyear of Star Command** 2037039 **3.25 Art Attack** 1691749 **3.45 Teamo Supremo** 3082749 **4.00 Recess** 3584 **4.30 Kim Possible** 9768 **5.00 That's So Raven** 6565 **5.30 Lizzie McGuire** 3720 **6.00 Smart Guy** 6861 **6.30 Boy Meets World** 4213

7.00 White Fang
Adventure based on a novel by Jack London set in the Alaskan gold rush. A young prospector teams up with a tough Klondike guide and tames a vicious wolf-dog called White Fang. *Starring Klaus Maria Brandauer, Ethan Hawke.* (1990, PG, 105min) ★★ 99577403

8.45 House of Mouse
Animated series. 445478

9.00 Honey, I Shrunk the Kids – The TV Show
When Amy develops a crush on her history teacher, she decides her only hope is to travel back in time and rewrite his history. 532720

9.50 Untalkative Bunny
Animated adventures. 737861

10.00 Home Improvement
Tim must convince Jill that, even though she does not measure up to his idea of an ideal woman, he loves her exactly as she is. 70355

10.30 Home Improvement
Tim faces stiff competition when he goes head-to-head in a quiz with the female foreman of a large construction company. 85403

11.00 Sweet Valley High
Jessica needs a good grade in her chemistry test or she risks losing her star place on the cheerleading squad. Starring Cynthia Daniel and Brittany Daniel. 27316

11.30pm–12.00m't Caitlin's Way
Caitlin's decision to look for her real father upsets her new family. Starring Lindsay Felton. 53923

ZEETV
Cab DigCab SkyDig 808

6.00am Jagraan 6.30 Ramadhan Reflections 7.00 Gujarati News 7.30 Daily News 8.00 Love Marriage 8.30 Gharana 9.00 Yoga For Life 9.30 Aa Gale Lag Ja 10.00 Colony 52 11.00 Saath Saath 11.30 Kittie Party 12.00noon FILM: Kaash 3.00pm Aati Rahengi Baharein 3.30 Kammal 4.00 Archana Aa Haa 5.00 Dream Destinations 5.30 Kohi Apna Sa

6.00pm Chandan Ka Paina Resham Ki Dori 7.00 Gharana 7.30 Love Marriage 8.00 News 8.30 Aati Rahengi Baharein 9.00 Kohi Apni Sa 9.30 Kammal 10.00 Kittie Party 10.30 Simply Shekhar 11.00 Lipstick 11.30 Nostalgia 12.00m't News 12.30am FILM: Mera Farz 3.30 Yehi To Pyar Hai 4.00 Aangan 4.30 Chingari 5.00 Lakeerein 5.30–6.00am Kasak

58 TV & SATELLITE WEEK

FILM RATINGS ★★★★ Excellent ★★★ Good ★★ Fair ★ Poor

▼ 6 QUESTIONING 'EFFECTS'

In addition to commercial market research, another kind of research into media audiences is that carried out by academic researchers. As mentioned in the introduction to this part of the book, an important aspect of this research is determining the effects that media texts have upon their audiences. The controversy about the extent to which the media can be held responsible for societal problems is referred to as the 'effects debate', and has implications beyond the confines of academic Media Studies. Thinking about media effects has moved from early models, which claimed that the media had a very direct impact on its audience, through to more contemporary thinking which focuses more on how audiences use the media.

As both Martin Barker and David Gauntlett point out, much of this 'effects' research is carried out by people who already have a particular opinion or axe to grind regarding the effects and influence of the media and who wish to use their research to confirm a particular, often political, position.

In the following extracts, both Barker and Gauntlett are sceptical about the current state of effects research. In the first extract, 'Ten Things Wrong with the Effects Model', Gauntlett argues that this research is often ideologically flawed. Barker's criticisms in his article 'Critique: Audiences 'Я' Us', are focused on the gap that he perceives between the ways in which the research is conducted and the ways in which we consume and interact with media texts.

TEN THINGS WRONG WITH THE 'EFFECTS MODEL'

It has become something of a cliché to observe that despite many decades of research and hundreds of studies, the connections between people's consumption of the mass media and their subsequent behaviour have remained persistently elusive. Indeed, researchers have enjoyed an unusual degree of patience from both their scholarly and more public audiences. But a time must come when we must take a step back from this murky lack of consensus and ask – why? Why are there no clear answers on media effects?

There is, as I see it, a choice of two conclusions which can be drawn from any detailed analysis of the research. The first is that if, after over 60 years of a considerable amount of research effort, direct effects of media upon behaviour have not been clearly identified, then we should conclude that they are simply *not there to be found*. Since I have argued this case, broadly speaking, elsewhere (Gauntlett 1995), I will here explore the second possibility: that the media effects research has quite consistently taken the *wrong approach* to the mass media, its audiences, and society in general. This misdirection has taken a number of forms;

for the purposes of this chapter, I will impose an unwarranted coherence upon the claims of all those who argue or purport to have found that the mass media will routinely have direct and reasonably predictable effects upon the behaviour of their fellow human beings, calling this body of thought, simply, the 'effects model'. Rather than taking apart each study individually, I will consider the mountain of studies – and the associated claims about media effects made by commentators as a whole – and outline ten fundamental flaws in their approach.

1 The effects model tackles social problems 'backwards'

To explain the problem of violence in society, researchers should begin with that social problem and seek to explain it with reference, quite obviously, to those who engage in it: their background, lifestyles, character profiles, and so on. The 'media effects' approach, in this sense, comes at the problem *backwards*, by starting with the media and then trying to lasso connections from there on to social beings, rather than the other way around.

This is an important distinction. Criminologists, in their professional attempts to explain crime and violence, consistently turn for explanations not to the mass media but to social factors such as poverty, unemployment, housing, and the behaviour of family and peers. In a study which *did* start at what I would recognise as the correct end – by interviewing 78 violent teenage offenders and then tracing their behaviour back towards media usage, in comparison with a group of over 500 'ordinary' school pupils of the same age – Hagell and Newburn (1994) found only that the young offenders watched *less* television and video than their counterparts, had less access to the technology in the first place, had no unusual interest in specifically violent programmes, and either enjoyed the same material as non-offending teenagers or were simply *uninterested*. This point was demonstrated very clearly when the offenders were asked, 'If you had the chance to be someone who appears on television, who would you choose to be?':

> The offenders felt particularly uncomfortable with this question and appeared to have difficulty in understanding why one might want to be such a person . . . In several interviews, the offenders had already stated that they watched little television, could not remember their favourite programmes and, consequently, could not think of anyone to be. In these cases, their obvious failure to identify with any television characters seemed to be part of a general lack of engagement with television.
>
> (Hagell and Newburn 1994: 30)

Thus we can see that studies which begin by looking at the perpetrators of actual violence, rather than at the media and its audiences, come to rather different conclusions (and there is certainly a need for more such research). The fact that effects studies take the media as their starting point, however, should not be

taken to suggest that they involve sensitive examinations of the mass media. As will be noted below, the studies have typically taken a stereotyped, almost parodic view of media content.

In more general terms, the 'backwards' approach involves the mistake of looking at individuals, rather than society, in relation to the mass media. The narrowly individualistic approach of some psychologists leads them to argue that, because of their belief that particular individuals at certain times in specific circumstances may be negatively affected by one bit of media, the removal of such media from society would be a positive step. This approach is rather like arguing that the solution to the number of road traffic accidents in Britain would be to lock away one famously poor driver from Cornwall; that is, a blinkered approach which tackles a real problem from the wrong end, involves cosmetic rather than relevant changes, and fails to look at the 'bigger picture'.

2 The effects model treats children as inadequate

The individualism of the psychological discipline has also had a significant impact on the way in which children are regarded in effects research. Whilst sociology in recent decades has typically regarded childhood as a social con-struction, demarcated by attitudes, traditions and rituals which vary between different societies and different time periods, the psychology of childhood – developmental psychology – has remained more tied to the idea of a universal individual who must develop through particular stages before reaching adult maturity, as established by Piaget. The developmental stages are arranged as a hierarchy, from incompetent childhood through to rational, logical adulthood, and progression through these stages is characterised by an 'achievement ethic'.

In psychology, then, children are often considered not so much in terms of what they *can* do, as what they (apparently) cannot. Negatively defined as non-adults, the research subjects are regarded as the 'other', a strange breed whose failure to match generally middle-class adult norms must be charted and discussed. Most laboratory studies of children and the media presume, for example, that their findings apply only to children, but fail to run parallel studies with adult groups to confirm this. We might speculate that this is because if adults were found to respond to laboratory pressures in the same way as children, the 'common sense' validity of the experiments would be undermined.

In her valuable examination of the way in which academic studies have constructed and maintained a particular perspective on childhood, Christine Griffin has recorded the ways in which studies produced by psychologists, in particular, have tended to 'blame the victim', to represent social problems as the consequence of the deficiencies or inadequacies of young people, and to 'psychologize inequalities, obscuring structural relations of domination behind a focus on individual "deficient" working-class young people and/or young people of colour, their families or cultural backgrounds' (Griffin 1993: 199). Problems such as unemployment and the failure of education systems are thereby traced to individual psychology traits. The same kinds of approach are readily observed in media effects studies, the production of which has undoubtedly been dominated by psychologically-oriented researchers, who – whilst, one imagines, having nothing other than benevolent intentions – have carefully exposed the full range of ways in which young media users can be seen as the inept victims of products which, whilst obviously puerile and transparent to adults, can trick children into all kinds of ill-advised behaviour.

This situation is clearly exposed by research which seeks to establish what children can and do understand about and from the mass media. Such projects have shown that children can talk intelligently and indeed cynically about the mass media, and that children as young as seven can make thoughtful, critical and 'media literate' video productions themselves.

3 Assumptions within the effects model are characterised by barely concealed conservative ideology

The systematic derision of children's resistant capacities can be seen as part of a broader conservative project to position the more contemporary and challenging aspects of the mass media, rather than other social factors, as the major threat to social stability today. Effects studies from the USA, in particular, tend to assume a level of television violence which is simply not applicable in Canada, Europe or elsewhere, and which is based on content analysis methods which count all kinds of 'aggression' seen in the media and come up with a correspondingly high number. George Gerbner's view, for example, that 'We are awash in a tide of violent representations unlike any the world has ever seen . . . drenching every home with graphic scenes of expertly choreographed brutality' (Gerbner 1994: 133), both reflects his hyperbolic view of the media in the US and the extent to which findings cannot be simplistically transferred across the Atlantic. Whilst it is certainly possible that gratuitous depictions of violence might reach a level in US screen media which could be seen as unpleasant and unnecessary, it cannot always be assumed that violence is shown for 'bad' reasons or in an uncritical light. Even the most obviously 'gratuitous' acts of violence, such as those committed by Beavis and Butt-Head in their eponymous MTV series, can be interpreted as rationally resistant reactions to an oppressive world which has little to offer them (see Gauntlett, 1997). The way in which media effects researchers talk about the *amount* of violence in the media encourages the view that it is not important to consider the *meaning* of the scenes involving violence which appear on screen.

Critics of screen violence, furthermore, often reveal themselves to be worried about challenges to the status quo which they feel that some movies present

(even though most European film critics see most popular Hollywood films as being ridiculously status quo-friendly). For example, Michael Medved, author of the successful *Hollywood vs. America: Popular Culture and the War on Traditional Values* (1992) finds worrying and potentially influential displays of 'disrespect for authority' and 'anti-patriotic attitudes' in films like *Top Gun* – a movie which others find embarrassingly jingoistic. The opportunistic mixing of concerns about the roots of violence with political reservations about the content of films represents an asinine trend in 'social concern' commentary. Media effects studies and TV violence content analyses help to sustain this approach by maintaining the notion that 'antisocial' behaviour is an objective category which can be measured, which is common to numerous programmes, and which will negatively affect those children who see it portrayed.

4 The effects model inadequately defines its own objects of study

The flaws numbered four to six in this list are more straightforwardly method-ological, although they are connected to the previous and subsequent points. The first of these is that effects studies have generally taken for granted the definitions of media material, such as 'antisocial' and 'prosocial' programming, as well as characterisations of behaviour in the real world, such as 'antisocial' and 'prosocial' action. The point has already been made that these can be ideological value judgements; throwing down a book in disgust, sabotaging a nuclear missile, or smashing cages to set animals free, will always be interpreted in effects studies as 'antisocial', not 'prosocial'.

Furthermore, actions such as verbal aggression or hitting an inanimate object are recorded as acts of violence, just as TV murders are, leading to terrifically (and irretrievably) murky data. It is usually impossible to discern whether very minor or extremely serious acts of 'violence' depicted in the media are being said to have led to quite severe or merely trivial acts in the real world. More significant, perhaps, is the fact that this is rarely seen as a problem: in the media effects field, dodgy 'findings' are accepted with an uncommon hospitality.

5 The effects model is often based on artificial elements and assumptions within studies

Since careful sociological studies of media effects require amounts of time and money which limit their abundance, they are heavily outnumbered by simpler studies which are usually characterised by elements of artificiality. Such studies typically take place in a laboratory, or in a 'natural' setting such as a classroom but where a researcher has conspicuously shown up and instigated activities, neither of which are typical environments. Instead of a full and naturally-viewed television diet, research subjects are likely to be shown selected or specially-recorded clips which lack the narrative meaning inherent in everyday TV productions. They may then be observed in simulations of real life presented to them as a game, in relation to inanimate objects such as Bandura's famous 'bobo' doll, or as they respond to questionnaires, all of which are unlike inter-personal interaction, cannot be equated with it, and are likely to be associated with the previous viewing experience in the mind of the subject, rendering the study invalid.

Such studies also rely on the idea that subjects will not alter their behaviour or stated attitudes as a response to being observed or questioned. This naive belief has been shown to be false by researchers such as Borden, who have demon-strated that the presence, appearance and gender of an observer can radically affect children's behaviour.

6 The effects model is often based on studies with misapplied methodology

Many of the studies which do not rely on an experimental method, and so may evade the flaws mentioned in the previous point, fall down instead by applying a methodological procedure wrongly, or by drawing inappropriate conclusions from particular methods. The widely-cited longitudinal panel study by Huesmann, Eron and colleagues, for example, has been less famously slated for failing to keep to the procedures, such as assessing aggressivity or TV viewing with the same measures at different points in time, which are necessary for their statistical findings to have any validity. The same researchers have also failed to adequately account for why the findings of this study and those of another of their own studies absolutely contradict each other, with the former concluding that the media has a marginal effect on boys but no effect on girls, and the latter arguing the exact opposite (no effect on boys, but a small effect for girls). They also seem to ignore that fact that their own follow-up of their original set of subjects 22 years later suggested that a number of biological, developmental and environmental factors contributed to levels of aggression, whilst the mass media was not even given a mention. These astounding inconsistencies, unapolo-getically presented by perhaps the best-known researchers in this area, must be cause for considerable unease about the effects model. More careful use of similar methods, such as in the three-year panel study involving over 3,000 young people conducted by Milavsky, Kessler, Stipp and Rubens has only indicated that significant media effects are not to be found.

Perhaps the most frequent and misleading abuse of methodology occurs when studies which are simply *unable* to show that one thing causes another are treated as if they have done so. Such is the case with correlation studies, which can easily find that a particular personality type is also the kind of person who enjoys a certain kind of media – for example, that violent people like to watch 'violent films' – but are quite unable to show that the media use has *produced* that character. Nevertheless psychologists such as Van Evra and Browne have assumed that this is probably the case. There is a logical coherence to the idea that children whose behaviour is antisocial and disruptional will also have a greater interest in the more violent and noisy television programmes, whereas the idea that the behaviour is a *consequence* of these programmes lacks both this rational consistency, and the support of the studies.

7 The effects model is selective in its criticisms of media depictions of violence

In addition to the point that 'antisocial' acts are ideologically defined in effects studies (as noted in item three above), we can also note that the media depictions of 'violence' which the effects model typically condemns are limited to fictional productions. The acts of violence which appear on a daily basis on news and serious factual programmes are seen as somehow exempt. The point here is not that depictions of violence in the news should necessarily be condemned in just the same, blinkered way, but rather to draw attention to another philosophical inconsistency which the model cannot account for. If the antisocial acts shown in drama series and films are expected to have an effect on the behaviour of viewers, even though such acts are almost always ultimately punished or have other negative consequences for the perpetrator, there is no obvious reason why the antisocial activities which are always in the news, and which frequently do *not* have such apparent consequences for their agents, should not have similar effects.

8 The effects model assumes superiority to the masses

Surveys typically show that whilst a certain proportion of the public feel that the media may cause other people to engage in antisocial behaviour, almost no-one ever says that they have been affected in that way themselves. This view is taken to extremes by researchers and campaigners whose work brings them into regular contact with the supposedly corrupting material, but who are unconcerned for their own well-being as they implicitly 'know' that the effects will only be on 'other people'. Insofar as these others are defined as children or 'unstable' individuals, their approach may seem not unreasonable; it is fair enough that such questions should be explored. Nonetheless, the idea that it is unruly 'others' who will be affected – the uneducated? the working class? – remains at the heart of the effects paradigm, and is reflected in its texts (as well, presumably, as in the researchers' overenthusiastic interpretation of weak or flawed data, as discussed above).

George Gerbner and his colleagues, for example, write about 'heavy' television viewers as if this media consumption has necessarily had the opposite effect on the weightiness of their brains. Such people are assumed to have no selectivity or critical skills, and their habits are explicitly contrasted with preferred activities: 'Most viewers watch by the clock and either do not know what they will watch when they turn on the set, or follow established routines rather than choose each program as they would choose a book, a movie or an article' (Gerbner *et al.* 1986: 19). This view, which knowingly makes inappropriate comparisons by ignoring the serial nature of many TV programmes, and which is unable to account for the widespread use of TV guides and VCRs with which audiences plan and arrange their viewing, reveals the kind of elitism and snobbishness which often seems to underpin such research. The point here is not that the content of the mass media must not be criticised, but rather that the mass audience themselves are not well served by studies which are willing to treat them as potential savages or actual fools.

9 The effects model makes no attempt to understand meanings of the media

A further fundamental flaw, hinted at in points three and four above, is that the effects model *necessarily* rests on a base of reductive assumptions and unjustified stereotypes regarding media content. To assert that, say, 'media violence' will bring negative consequences is not only to presume that depictions of violence in the media will always be promoting antisocial behaviour, and that such a category exists and makes sense, as noted above, but also assumes that the medium holds a singular message which will be carried unproblematically to the audience. The effects model therefore performs the double deception of presuming (a) that the media presents a singular and clear-cut 'message', and (b) that the proponents of the effects model are in a position to identify what that message is.

The meanings of media content are ignored in the simple sense that assumptions are made based on the appearance of elements removed from their context (for example, woman hitting man equals violence equals bad), and in the more sophisticated sense that even *in* context, the meanings may be different for different viewers (woman hitting man equals an unpleasant act of aggression, *or* appropriate self-defence, *or* a triumphant act of revenge, *or* a refreshing change, *or* is simply uninteresting, *or* any of many further alternative readings). In-depth qualitative studies have unsurprisingly given support to the view that media audiences routinely arrive at their own, often heterogeneous, interpretations of everyday media texts. Since the effects model rides roughshod over both the meanings that actions have for characters in dramas *and* the meanings which those depicted acts may have for the audience members, it can retain little credibility with those who consider popular entertainment to be more than just a set of very basic propaganda messages flashed at the audience in the simplest possible terms.

10 The effects model is not grounded in theory

Finally, and underlying many of the points made above, is the fundamental problem that the entire argument of the 'effects model' is substantiated with no theoretical reasoning beyond the bald assertion that particular kinds of effects *will* be produced by the media. The basic question of *why* the media should induce people to imitate its content has never been adequately tackled, beyond the simple idea that particular actions are 'glamorised'. (However, *antisocial* actions are shown really *positively* so infrequently that this is an inadequate explanation.) Similarly, the question of how merely seeing an activity in the media would be translated into an actual *motive* which would prompt an individual to behave in a particular way is just as unresolved. The lack of firm theory has led to the effects model being based in the variety of assumptions outlined above – that the media (rather than people) is the unproblematic starting-point for research; that children will be unable to 'cope' with the media; that the categories of 'violence' or 'antisocial behaviour' are clear and self-evident; that the model's predictions can be verified by scientific research; that screen fictions are of concern, whilst news pictures are not; that researchers have the unique capacity to observe and classify social behaviour and its meanings, but that those researchers need not attend to the various possible meanings which media content may have for the audience. Each of these very substantial problems has its roots in the failure of media effects commentators to found their model in any coherent theory.

So what future for research on media influences?

The effects model, we have seen, has remarkably little going for it as an explanation of human behaviour, or of the media in society. Whilst any challenging or apparently illogical theory or model reserves the right to demonstrate its validity through empirical data, the effects model has failed also in that respect. Its continued survival is indefensible and unfortunate. However, the failure of this particular *model* does not mean that the impact of the mass media can no longer be considered or investigated. Indeed, there are many fascinating questions to be explored about the influence of the media upon our perceptions, and ways of thinking and being in the world, which simply get ignored whilst the research funding and attention are going to shoddy effects studies.

It is worrying to note the numbers of psychologists (and others) who conduct research according to traditional methodological recipes, despite the many well-known flaws with those procedures, when it is so easy to imagine alternative research methods and processes. (In one case, I employed a method which equipped children to make videos themselves, as a way of exploring what they had got from the mass media (Gauntlett, 1997), and it is not hard to think of alternative methods. The discourses about 'media effects' from politicians and the popular press are often laughably simplistic. Needless to say, academics shouldn't encourage them.

D. Gauntlett, 'Ten Things Wrong with the Effects Theory', available at: www.theory.org.uk/effects.htm

A conversation. Four of us are out for a walk, two married couples in late spring, on the Mendips. Good friends for a long time, we're catching up on things we've each been doing. In the flow of exchanges, a film comes up: *Breaking The Waves* (1996). Our friends had been to see it, mainly at Simon's behest – Maureen had been pretty unsure about seeing it, bearing in mind what she had heard about it on 'Barry Norman' (as most British people, of course, affectionately call 'Film-whatever-year-it-is').

The film, they told me (I still haven't seen it), is set in Puritan Scotland, and concerns a woman, outsider to her own community, who marries a foreigner. After he becomes disabled, his only source of sexual gratification is to get his wife to have sex with other men, and then tell him about it. Unwillingly she agrees to this, and the film follows what happens to them and to their relationship as a result. I don't even know if this is an adequate description of the film, and as I recall the conversation, I am aware that I am probably filling bits in to make it make sense for what I am going to use it to illustrate – but then that's what people do.

As I hadn't seen the film, I could only listen, and ask, while they reswapped their very different reactions to it. Simon was enormously fascinated by it, and had particularly enjoyed the complexity of the interactions he felt it portrayed. Maureen was very uncomfortable. It was a 'good film', she granted, but she'd been really uneasy about the role the woman had taken on herself. She felt that the film had a 'message' she didn't like – something she couldn't quite articulate, but having to do with 'what a woman is expected to do for a man'.

Here was classic ordinary talk: people discussing in the way that people do, at many points in their lives, what they felt about a media experience – and in the very act of talking, working out what something meant to them. Here also were tangible 'media effects': complex and rich pleasures, unease provoking arguments about meanings, self-justifications, reinforcement of relationships via sharing experiences. Even (beloved of Hollywood) 'scuttlebutt', the everyday word-of-mouth publicity on which films heavily depend, and therefore much sought after. And it worked, because I shall now make a point of seeing the film. But here, also, were two very individuated responses, which I, as friend *and* analyst, can't help seeing as clothed and nuanced by all kinds of social processes. For example, the very evident gender-dimension to the difference: there's little point in denying that men are more likely than women to get an erotic charge out of this narrative, and that is one dimension of pleasure – but it would be cheap and easy to say that Simon 'put himself in the place of the men' in the film.

Harder to diagnose is Maureen's notion of a 'message' that she tried to hunt out, by talking out loud about the film. It's self-evident that the message that disturbed her didn't in fact 'reach' *her*. If it had, either she would be able to articulate it, or she wouldn't be able to see it *as a message* – it would just *be* the point of the film, and she would be agreeing. (In other words: Maureen, it seems to me, is working with a non-academic version of the encoding/decoding model of media power, and the implications of that bear thinking about . . .) But then, what does it mean to say that there *is* a message? For whom? What if it only 'exists' as a message for those who reject it? If it has to be 'hunted for', what does it mean to call it a message? The implications roll on, and importantly, for such reasoning (not in Maureen, but in many public arenas) readily participates in arguments for banning films with 'dangerous messages': *Kids*, recently, and *Crash*.

A real conversation with real individuals, showing real media processes and effects . . . as people indeed do. But these are not the kinds of 'individual', nor the kind of 'effect', that get much talked about in audience theory and research. Not because our friends are both teachers, and might be seen therefore to be 'protected' by having available to them some relatively self-conscious 'languages' for discussing their experiences. Rather, because when audience theory and research talks about 'the individual', it is not *actual* individuals, but an *idea* of an individual which is being debated. And the languages for description of this 'individual', the processes and problems attributed to this 'individual', are hardly recognisable for the *actual* individuals that I, for one, ever get to meet and talk with.

In principle, there is nothing wrong with that. Scientific theories do deal in concepts and terms which won't necessarily be recognized by those whom they seek to describe and explain – even, yes, when what are being examined are people's thoughts, experiences, responses, preferences, uses and needs. But there *is* a problem, I want to argue, when our scientific languages are so antithetical to those experiences etc., that they undermine the possible authority of the people being investigated. Then, issues become indissolubly scientific *and* political, with a vengeance.

Take a couple of the terms unreflectively used in some of the essays in this section: 'exposure', and 'consumption'. People are assessed for their 'exposure' to television, or for how much television they have 'consumed'. Our normal use of the term 'exposure' has to do with processes over which we have no control (may not have known about, were hit by unexpectedly), but want to control. If I am exposed to radiation, or to pesticides, the term 'exposure' sums up my attitude towards something I don't like. It refers to something I will try to avoid in future. Maureen could well have used the term to mark her reaction to some of the sex scenes in *Breaking The Waves* – she didn't know it was going to come at her like that, and she felt uneasy at best; *in extremis* she might have closed her eyes, or left.

But in our 'scientific' parlance, to say that someone has been 'exposed' to television or film is not to describe them – it is to impute vulnerability to them, and to measure the degree of likely 'harm' done, on an analogy with the impact of radiation or pesticides. And they are vulnerable precisely to the degree that they aren't able to recognize what is happening to them. The issue is in real senses prejudged. But this means that the normal uses of 'exposure' by actual audiences are the precise opposite of the 'scientific' uses applied to them: normally, audiences are 'hit' by something they don't want, and try to get away. I am 'exposed' to something that makes me squeamish, and don't like it (my worst are embarrassing situations in sitcoms). You don't like to be 'exposed', without warning, to horrific scenes in the news. Whatever. The point is the wholesale conflict between the directions of the two languages.

Or take 'consumption': not immediately such a negative term, but ultimately having some of the same force, rather like 'heavy viewing' vs. 'light viewing'. In the 'scientific' discourses, such terms suggest a rising intake of media calories, a digestive stuffing of the senses and mind. Yet again, these terms *are* in use among us ordinary folks. Whenever I go abroad, I take with me some novels, bought as cheaply as possible second-hand (so I can leave them behind) because I fear boredom. The novels all have one characteristic – they are fat enough (I buy by the inch thickness) and narratively driven enough, that I can 'consume' them at great and undemanding speed.

Every holiday I do this, and every year I have a problem – the manner of my consumption is such that I can't even remember their titles. I am in real danger of rebuying the same books – though it would hardly matter since I probably could re-read most of the book and not recall even that I had read it before, let alone how it went. To 'consume' in this sense is to retain as little as possible – again, the exact opposite of the implications behind talk of 'audience consumption' and 'heavy' media use. The whole *point* of my books is that being heavyweight in size means they can be lightweight in demand! Whereas in the 'scientific' discourse the 'heavy viewer' who 'consumes' all the time is understood to be accumulating deposits of message-fat . . .

'Exposure' and 'consumption' are of course the languages of residual behaviourism, for which media 'effects' are presumed to be cumulative. Our ordinary

languages presume almost exactly the opposite – that which has the least impact is the expected, the ritually returned to, the repeat experience. That which has the most impact is the unexpected, the startling, the first-time encounter. But it isn't only behaviourism which offends, in my view. Take, just as much, the concept of 'activity': central concept of the 'new audience research'. 'Activity' poses as the concept which distinguishes the new research, which sees audiences as responsive and as constructing meanings, from the old research which sees them/us as passive, malleable. My problems with this are hardly different.

When Simon and Maureen argued over *Breaking The Waves*, one of their prime disagreements was over a scene in which the woman masturbates a man she sits next to on a bus. Apparently most people in the cinema, Simon included, burst out laughing at the scene. Maureen was appalled – to her, to laugh was to join in the woman's denigration. She stayed silent, 'inactive'. Simon argued that the *way* the film presented the scene, was *meant* to be funny – and he laughed.

Which was the 'active' response? Simon was *influenced* by the film to laugh, actively. Maureen *resisted* the film, and therefore *refused* the proposed activity of laughing. Of course I accept that in other (mental) senses Maureen was active – indeed, angrily reactive – at that point. But I use the example to show the extraordinary looseness and imprecision of the notion of 'activity'. In other research I have been doing recently, I have talked with film audiences for whom the very point of going to the cinema is to achieve a state of planned passivity. Choosing a warm cinema with good seats into which one can slump, in which surround-sound will engulf, close enough to the screen to get maximum whomping impact from special effects: these are sought-after pleasures. Exactly: activity (choice of cinema, of film, knowledge of genre, following the 'hype') leads to welcome passivity (hit my senses hard with those special effects). 'Audience activity' is another concept requiring a deal of critical scrutiny, far more than I am giving in these gestural remarks.

M. Barker, 'Critique: Audiences 'Я' Us', in R. Dickinson, R. Harindranath and O. Linné (eds), *Approaches to Audiences: a Reader*, Arnold, 1998, pp. 184–7

Martin Barker's essay is a short and a simple return to basics in terms of the effects debate. Barker's work, including his book *Ill-Effects: the Media Violence Debate* (2001), questions the arguments surrounding 'media effects' and the way that various media forms – most frequently film, video and television, but increasingly the Internet – are 'demonised'. Barker questions the way in which the media is supposed to influence consumers and affect behaviour. He argues that we need to have a more developed and sophisticated under-standing of the ways in which people actually use and interact with media texts, in this case the film *Breaking the Waves*.

The essay reflects a much more accurate understanding of how we interact with texts like films; that there may be a variety of different opinions – that we all come to media texts with an individual set of values, ideas and backgrounds (our 'situated culture'), all of which will influence the way in which we interpret and make sense of particular texts. Barker is suggesting that the interaction between a viewer and the film itself is a complex process that crude effects-models are unable to explain.

ACTIVITIES

➤ Barker suggests that for many people the point of going to the cinema is 'to achieve a state planned passivity'. Do you think that this is correct? Consider your own reasons for going to the cinema. To what extent is getting lost in the visceral pleasure of the special-effects, the soundtrack, or the warm and dark of the cinema part of the pleasure that you get? Carry out a small-scale survey amongst your peers and try to identify the reasons why they see films in the cinema rather than on video or DVD at home or in a friend's house.

➤ You could compare the reactions of several people to one particular film, especially if it is a slightly 'controversial' film, perhaps because of its sexual content or the degree of violence portrayed.

➤ Choose a film that you have recently seen and consider how it might have 'affected' you or influenced your behaviour. How easy or difficult is it to make these judgements? What are the problems for researchers, like Martin Barker, who are trying to conduct similar research?

FURTHER READING

Barker, M. and Petley, J. (eds) (2001) *Ill Effects: The Media/Violence Debate*, Routledge, 2nd edn.
A series of articles that address some of the major debates concerning media 'effects'.

Casey, B., Casey, N., Calvert, B., French, L. and Lewis, J. (2002) *Television Studies. The Key Concepts*. Routledge.
A short and accessible attempt to provide an overview of the issues surrounding media effects.

Cohen, S. (1972) *Folk Devils and Moral Panics*. Routledge.
This is the original source of the term 'moral panic' and deals with the media coverage of the mod/rocker fights at various British seaside towns in the 1960s. It is a useful book when studying other more recent 'moral panics' such as asylum seekers or 'video nasties' as cited, incorrectly, in the Jamie Bulger case.

Gunter, B. (2000) 'Measuring Behavioural Impact of the Media' in *Media Research Methods: Measuring Audiences, Reactions and Impact*, Sage.
Includes a detailed breakdown of the various studies that have been undertaken into the measurement of media effects.

> ➤ Identify an ongoing example of a moral panic (this might be asylum seekers or teenage drug-taking) and start to collect material from newspapers, radio and television. When you have a sizeable collection of material, start to analyse it and try to identify the process of exaggeration and campaigning that Cohen claims goes on in the cases of moral panics. Are there particular newspapers or television programmes that are more strident than others? If so, why do you think this is?

▼ 7 AUDIENCE PARTICIPATION AND REALITY TV

Reality TV is a wide-ranging term that covers a variety of new and highly popular television genres which take as their subject matter 'ordinary people' and/or real-life situations and events. In *Freakshow: First Person Media and Factual Television* (2000), John Dovey argues that we live in a confessional society and describes the phenomenon of these new television genres as 'first person media' where subjectivity, the personal and the intimate become prioritised.

This section contains a series of essays and articles reflecting on the popularity and worth (or otherwise) of 'reality' television programmes where the public are, in one form or another, the stars of the show. These include programmes like *Big Brother* and *Survivor*, docu-soaps (*Driving School, Airport*), emergency and crime shows (*Rescue 911, Police Camera Action*) and confessional talk shows (*Rikki Lake, Trisha, Kilroy* and *Jerry Springer*).

REALITY TV: A DEARTH OF TALENT AND THE DEATH OF MORALITY

I've managed to miss out on reality TV until now. In spite of all the talk in Britain about nasty Nick and flighty Mel, and in America about the fat, naked bastard Richard manipulating his way to desert-island victory, I have somehow preserved my purity. I wouldn't recognise Nick or Mel if I passed them in the street, or Richard if he was standing in front of me unclothed.

Ask me where the Big Brother house is, or how to reach Temptation Island, and I have no answer. I do remember the American Survivor contestant who managed to fry his own hand so that the skin peeled away until his fingers looked like burst sausages, but that's because he got on to the main evening news. Otherwise, search me. Who won? Who lost? Who cares?

The subject of reality TV shows, however, has been impossible to avoid. Their success is the media story of the (new) century, along with the ratings triumph of the big-money game shows such as Who Wants to be a Millionaire? Success on this scale insists on being examined, because it tells us things about ourselves; or ought to.

And what tawdry narcissism is here revealed! The television set, once so idealistically thought of as our window on the world, has become a dime-store mirror instead. Who needs images of the world's rich otherness, when you can watch these half-familiar avatars of yourself – these half-attractive half-persons – enacting ordinary life under weird conditions? Who needs talent, when the unashamed self-display of the talentless is constantly on offer?

I've been watching Big Brother 2, which has achieved the improbable feat of taking over the tabloid front pages in the final stages of a general election campaign. This, according to the conventional wisdom, is because the show is more interesting than the election. The 'reality' may be even stranger. It may be that Big Brother is so popular because it's even more boring than the election. Because it is the most boring, and therefore most 'normal', way of becoming famous, and if you're lucky or smart, of getting rich as well.

'Famous' and 'rich' are now the two most important concepts in western society, and ethical questions are simply obliterated by the potency of their appeal. In order to be famous and rich, it's OK – it's actually 'good' – to be devious. It's 'good' to be exhibitionistic. It's 'good' to be bad. And what dulls the moral edge is boredom. It's impossible to maintain a sense of outrage about people being so trivially self-serving for so long.

Oh, the dullness! Here are people becoming famous for being asleep, for keeping a fire alight, for letting a fire go out, for videotaping their cliched thoughts, for flashing their breasts, for lounging around, for quarrelling, for bitching, for being unpopular, and (this is too interesting to happen often) for kissing! Here, in short, are people becoming famous for doing nothing much at all, but doing it where everyone can see them.

Add the contestants' exhibitionism to the viewers' voyeurism and you get a picture of a society sickly in thrall to what Saul Bellow called 'event glamour'. Such is the glamour of these banal but brilliantly spotlit events that anything resembling a real value – modesty, decency, intelligence, humour, selflessness; you can write your own list – is rendered redundant. In this inverted ethical

universe, worse is better. The show presents 'reality' as a prize fight, and suggests that in life, as on TV, anything goes, and the more deliciously contemptible it is, the more we'll like it. Winning isn't everything, as Charlie Brown once said, but losing isn't anything.

The problem with this kind of engineered realism is that, like all fads, it's likely to have a short shelf-life, unless it finds ways of renewing itself. The probability is that our voyeurism will become more demanding. It won't be enough to watch somebody being catty, or weeping when evicted from the house of hell, or 'revealing everything' on subsequent talk shows, as if they had anything left to reveal.

What is gradually being reinvented is the gladiatorial combat. The TV set is the Colosseum and the contestants are both gladiators and lions; their job is to eat one another until only one remains alive. But how long, in our jaded culture, before 'real' lions, actual dangers, are introduced to these various forms of fantasy island, to feed our hunger for more action, more pain, more vicarious thrills?

Here's a thought, prompted by the news that the redoubtable Gore Vidal has agreed to witness the execution by lethal injection of the Oklahoma bomber Timothy McVeigh. The witnesses at an execution watch the macabre proceedings through a glass window; a screen. This, too, is a kind of reality TV, and – to make a modest proposal – it may represent the future of such programmes. If we are willing to watch people stab one another in the back, might we not also be willing to actually watch them die?

In the world outside TV, our numbed senses already require increasing doses of titillation. One murder is barely enough; only the mass murderers make the front pages. You have to blow up a building full or people or machine-gun a whole royal family to get our attention. Soon, perhaps, you'll have to kill off a whole species of wildlife or unleash a virus that wipes out people by the thousand, or else you'll be small potatoes. You'll be on an inside page.

And as in reality, so on 'reality TV'. How long until the first TV death? How long until the second? By the end of Orwell's great novel *1984*, Winston Smith has been brainwashed. 'He loved Big Brother'. As, now, do we. We are the Winstons now.

S. Rushdie, 'Reality TV: a Dearth of Talent and the
Death of Morality', *Guardian*, 9 June 2001

WATCH WITH BROTHER

Watching Big Brother II is about as dignified as looking through the keyhole in your teenage child's bedroom door. To do it occasionally would be shameful; to get hooked on it is downright depraved. People who like watching torture will tune in regularly to see a table dancer, an air steward, a hairdresser, a medical rep and a website designer (inter alia) struggling with the contradictions inherent in having simultaneously to bond with and to betray perfect strangers. Then, if they're in the mood, they will flick over to ITV to watch an ex-footballer, a policewoman and a property developer and the rest of the *Survivor* castaways face absurd and potentially dangerous ordeals on a remote island in pursuit of a large amount of money.

More than 10 million people watch these shows now every week. They visit the websites and read about the participants daily in newspapers and magazines. What does this say about them – about us – and about our culture?

Pope John Paul II has denounced reality TV as incompatible with human dignity. But human dignity has taken worse knocks than this and the churches were conspicuously silent. Religions whose hierarchs ordered the torture and murder of dissidents have historically been more concerned with the dignity of God than the dignity of man, and their swift and savage judgments were in some ways violent ancestors of the voting-off procedure.

Reality television is not the end of civilisation as we know it; it is civilisation as we know it. It is popular culture at its most popular, soap opera come to life. The celebrities who risked the wreck of their pampered egos by humiliation on *Celebrity Big Brother* were bowing to the inevitable. Any day now the royal family will challenge the Royle family for top ratings by exposing itself in a special *Royal Big Brother*. The Tories should probably let the populace help them elect their new leader via a Tory *Big Brother*.

Five thousand people sent videos of themselves to the UK *Big Brother* production team; what they wanted was less the modest prize money of £70,000 for the one person who survives all the evictions than the chance to be watched by 37 cameras for nine weeks, to be seen 24 hours a day on the *Big Brother* website and 21 hours a day on C4's youth channel E4.

Once in the *Big Brother* house the successful candidates career from one bruising confrontation to another, because politeness, that most useful lubricant of difficult interactions, is unknown to them; anyone who spares the feelings of someone else by concealing his own will be exposed as two-faced. 'Why don't you like me?' moans one. 'You make me feel stupid,' whines another, while Davina McCall screams herself hoarse with simulated excitement about these 'tempestuous' and 'turbulent' weeks.

Reality television is not very real. The situations are contrived and the protagonists are handpicked. No one online or on TV sees everything that is seen by the cameras because what is streamed is already edited. The least real of all the reality shows must be *Survivor*. The middle-class middle-management types on Pulau Tiga recruited from the dead reaches of the urban middle class may be strong on strategies for people management but they are absurdly devoid of practical initiative. Watching them faff and flounder is less entertaining than irritating, especially as every viewer is aware that real ingenuity and industry are being deployed off-screen by the production crew, which must greatly outnumber the castaways, in building a spectacular tribal meeting house, outrigger canoes, rafts and wooden pinball games while facing the same kinds of logistical problems that afflict the castaways.

For it's always the case that although the people who volunteer for reality shows may all be exhibitionists, someone who is careful to remain unwatched is pulling their strings. The contestants may say what they please, but someone else will decide who, if anyone, can hear. This dilutes the voyeur's thrill, which is also dependent upon his victim's unawareness that he (more often, she) is being watched. And since the participants in reality TV have agreed to be watched, they cannot provide the same satisfaction.

In the 17 countries that have worked the *Big Brother* formula, the programmes have had besotted fans; though they may be sad and lonely, they are not voyeurs. They are worse than voyeurs, for the part they agree to play is not that of a helpless peeping Tom but that of Big Brother, Chief of the Thought Police. The viewers who vote for exclusions from the *Big Brother* house, and we are told that they are far more numerous than the people who voted for the present government, are happy to observe, evaluate and judge their fellow humans on capricious and partial evidence and condemn them to ostracism, one of the most powerful weapons in the human social armoury, just because they don't like them. In Spain, where libertarian anarchism once had a genuine chance, the denizens of the *Big Brother* house refused to evict anybody, but in carping, envious, class-bound Britain everyone bitched about everyone else. Not surprising then that a nonentity won at the first go-round, or that we have a nonentity government.

Reality television is nothing new. In 1968 I worked on one of the earliest examples of reality television. The programme, which was called *Nice Time*, was conceived as a corrective to the rather callow satire of the day. It was to be simply fun, and the fun was to be generated by ordinary people doing silly things. It was my job to persuade middle-aged ladies to slide down the banisters of the main staircase at Bury Town Hall, or retired gentlemen to tie hankies over their noses and play cowboys and Indians dodging round the displays in a department store, while we filmed them. One day I stood in Kensington High Street asking passers-by if I could kiss them. 'I think you're very rude!' spluttered a gentleman with majestic sideburns and a handlebar moustache. . . .

Nice Time came after *Candid Camera*. Jonathan Routh, who walked through Selfridge's with his hat on fire while a cameraman was walking behind him, filmed the reactions of shoppers, was one of my co-presenters. The other was the late, great Kenny Everett. The three of us made fools of ourselves as much as other people did, and never made fools of any but ourselves. No one was humiliated or hurt. We were aware that well-to-do people from the Home Counties were unlikely to join in our japes, and that children and pensioners understood best what it was we were trying to do. By the time we were winding up the last series, even their innocence was beginning to tarnish.

G. Greer, 'Watch with Brother', *Observer*, 24 June 2001

Both the articles by Germaine Greer and Salman Rushdie are critical of reality formatted game shows such as *Big Brother, Survivor* or *Temptation Island*. Both articles are critical of the audiences that watch these programmes – 'depraved' (Greer), 'numbed' voyeurs (Rushdie) – and of those who appear in them, 'talentless . . . tawdry' (Rushdie), 'two-faced . . . exhibitionists' (Greer) – and of the programme-makers themselves, suggesting that they are exploitative (Greer) and, according to Rushdie, on a par with the torturers and despots in George Orwell's *1984*.

Yet as John Plunkett's article 'Reality TV Shows Scoop Viewers' Choice Awards' (16 October 2002) shows, programmes like *Big Brother* and *Pop Idol* in the 'reality TV' genres are very popular. *Big Brother 3*, broadcast in 2002, attracted more viewers and voters than did either of the preceding series. Kate Lawler, the winner, received over 3 million votes and there were over 8 million votes cast during the final week alone. Despite warnings that the reality TV boom is over, there seem to be more and more programmes recycled into 'Celebrity' versions. It therefore seems undeniable that, despite the misgivings of highbrow social commentators like Germaine Greer and Salman Rushdie, these types of programmes offer something that continue to appeal to television viewers.

REALITY TV SHOWS SCOOP VIEWERS' CHOICE AWARDS

The new breed of reality television shows came of age last night, picking up a hat-trick of top prizes at the National TV Awards, the 'people's Oscars' of the television industry.

ITV's *Pop Idol* won most popular entertainment programme and its hosts, Ant and Dec, won the award for the most popular entertainment presenters. *Big Brother*, on Channel 4, which began the reality trend two years ago, picked up the prize for most popular factual programme. Nearly 25 million viewers tuned in for the finals of the two rival reality shows . . .

> The National TV Awards are the only awards of their kind voted for entirely by members of the public.
>
> J. Plunkett, 'Reality TV Shows Scoop Viewers' Choice Awards',
> *Guardian*, 16 October 2002

According to Dovey (2000), part of the appeal of these types of shows is their human interest stories where individuals triumph over adverse circumstances, overcome tremendous odds, or survive extreme situations. Some of these may be 'real' events and re-enacted for television (*Blues and Twos* or *Emergency 999* for example), which appear to offer 'real' versions of narratives we're used to seeing in fictional drama on television or in the cinema, while offering the reassurance of a successful outcome. They are also highly personalised first-person accounts and often presented by an established 'authoritative' presenter such as Michael Buerk.

Dovey argues that this increasing reliance on trivialised and emotional programming is a reaction to traditional intellectual and authoritative television programmes that are closer to public service broadcasting ideals but which came across to many viewers as boring and elitist. It may be that part of the popularity of these new genres is that they are perceived as more democratic, involving real situations and 'ordinary people', while also being emotionally engaging and fun. They are also cheap to produce and seem to guarantee television companies large numbers of viewers and, for commercial companies, good advertising revenues.

As Germaine Greer points out, making fools of the public as a form of cheap entertainment has been around for some time. *Candid Camera* was one of ITV's most popular shows in the 1960s and *Beadle's About* was a mainstay of ITV's Saturday night schedule for many years. The recent glut of these types of shows could be part of a wider fascination with seeing 'ordinary people' in extraordinary circumstances. As Dovey notes, Reality TV is subject to an increasing blurring of the distinctions between television genres. The recent popularity of docu-soaps can be explained in part by the way in which they combine conventions from soap operas (continuing storylines, a sense of emotional involvement with particular characters and the sense of particular communities or individuals under pressure or close scrutiny) with conventions of 'fly-on-the-wall' documentaries that give viewers the impression of watching something uncensored and 'authentic'.

Big Brother and *Survivor* are other competitions characterised as a mixture of quiz show (there can only be one winner), soap opera (we eavesdrop on how they cope with the stress and relationships of the situation) and documentary (the episodes are not scripted and thus unpredictable).

Peter Balzalgette is the creative director of Endemol, the company that produces *Big Brother*, and a director of Channel 4. He challenges some of the more common criticisms aimed at these types of shows and suggests that *Big Brother* is 'pure television'. He goes on, 'It uses all the industry's production techniques openly; it caters for participants who simply want to be on television; it satisfies viewers' eternal curiosity about the minutiae of others' characters and relationships; and it is wonderfully entertaining (perhaps the medium's most important function).'

'IT'S ONLY A GAMESHOW'

Ghastly, cynical, dissipated, distasteful, a new low, tedious, desperate, voyeuristic, seedy, a sham, pointless, sad and pathetic, creepy, inane, barrel-scraping, phoney, gross, tacky . . . all comments from national newspapers about *Big Brother*. Time to take up lettuce growing in the Scilly Isles? Certainly not. Particularly in view of last week's drama when Nick was finally rumbled and made his hasty exit.

But apparently we are definitely guilty of manipulation. Here's Paul Watson in this newspaper: 'It was phoney from the start . . . straight away I felt manipulated by others than those I was watching . . . The suspicion that somebody was manipulating them became more obvious. Why did the women go to the door to find the clay penis made by the men?' Watson is the justly celebrated director of *The Fishing Party*, *Sylvania Waters* and *The Dinner Party*. But when he accuses us of manipulation it feels like being attacked by Richard Branson for publicity-seeking. I think I know what is really bugging Watson and other moaners and groaners from the documentary freemasonry. *Big Brother* has put all the tricks of their trade on open display. We have Penn-and-Tellered them. Not for us the tongue-loosening wine supplied by the production behind the scenes, the discreet suggestion as to what they should talk about, the results shown as naturally occurring events. Not for us the traffic wardens, customs officers, driving instructors (delete where necessary) resolutely pretending they haven't got cameras pointing up their nostrils. *Big Brother* is unashamedly upfront.

There are the cameras on the wall (now nicknamed by the participants – 'Charlie' is their favourite). If *Big Brother* wants them to talk about their first love, you will hear it suggested. Call it manipulation if you like but it happens on camera and not behind the tapestry.

A Sunday newspaper journalist, hot on our trail, then accuses us of being selective because we televise only half an hour a day and edit out the rest. Yes, Lord Copper, that's how all TV gets made. We offer to show him our rushes – an offer gratefully accepted. But unfortunately this is a scoop open to everyone. He is simply directed to our website where our raw material is, uniquely, available 24 hours a day. I don't recall Watson offering the rushes of *The Fishing Party* or *The Dinner Party* for inspection. Now, what about the gross exhibitionism? 'A boring showcase for exhibitionists' (the *Independent*). 'They have that manic, 24-hour-auditioning, I'm-up-for-anything-me hysteria' (A.A. Gill, *Sunday Times*). Guilty as charged. There's certainly a lot of showing off. I remember a particularly mad schoolmaster who accused any boy who wanted to act in the school play of being a ghastly show-off and threatened to beat him. But no show-offs, no school play.

And it is not yet a crime to be an extrovert. Any television presenter, actor or bylined journalist has the same egotistical desire to project and be recognised. There's something unedifying about their pulling up the drawbridge after them once they have made it.

Big Brother highlights something fundamental about television. People want to be on it for their 15 minutes of fame. This is neither laudable nor reprehensible. It's just a fact. *Big Brother*, along with docu-soaps, game shows and the rest, offers that opportunity. Television creates cohorts of people who are famous for being famous. Not such a terrible thing. You can rail at it, but you might as well howl at the moon.

That's all very well, our critics say, but this is Peeping Tom television. Organised voyeurism. Er . . . no, I don't think so. The voyeur spies on people without their knowledge. The *Big Brother* inmates are there voluntarily with the cameras in full view. Anna (you know, the lesbian and former trainee nun) plays Supertramp's 'It's Raining Again' on her guitar. 'It's hard to pretend,' she sings. Precisely, Anna. You all know you are being watched and you admit it.

Finally there's the social experiment thingy: 'What rankles most about the whole seedy exercise is the pretence that it is some sort of genuine social investigation and not just a cynical drive for ratings and profits.' (Chris Dunkley, *Financial Times*). '*Big Brother* apparently pretends to be an experiment . . . Only the fluffiest of couch potatoes can have failed to see through its commercialism.' (Daniel Johnson, *Daily Telegraph*). Steady. We were careful to make no such claim. *Big Brother* is a challenge, a gameshow with a prizewinner, a piece of TV entertainment. True, we include psychologists in our Monday edition. But that is because we want them to analyse the behaviour of the competitors for viewers, not because we want them to publish a treatise. As it happens, they may do so – but that is not why we are making the programme.

If the academics do go into print, I hope they consider how revealing *Big Brother* has been about 20- and 30-somethings. They never talk about politics, though they are interested in ethics (witness their animated discussion of George Michael's arrest or their even more animated debate about Nick's illegal notes). They are more interested in New Age nostrums such as tarot cards and yoga than in traditional religion. They have few hang-ups about nudity and bodily functions and no hang-ups about so-called bad language. Perhaps Channel 4's presentation department could save time by forewarning us only when there are no naughty words in the nightly slot. How strong is 'strong language' when it is common parlance for this generation?

But back to that unkindest cut of all – that this is a commercial exercise, a drive for ratings and profits. Yes, that is precisely what it is. Journalists do not work for free and they quite like to attract readers. We're in business too. I know the British system of television content regulation means that we are frequently expected to claim higher motives in order to earn Brownie points. But some television is there to entertain and earn enough to enable more of the same. 'Cynical' is the only word I would baulk at. I prefer 'realist'.

Big Brother is pure television. It uses all the industry's production techniques openly; it caters for participants who simply want to be on television; it satisfies viewers' eternal curiosity about the minutiae of others' characters and relationships; and it is wonderfully entertaining (perhaps the medium's most important function). Disappointing, then, that we Brits can take no credit for it whatsoever. It was invented in the Netherlands by producers who come from an entertainment background. They were unconstrained by the petty deceits and intellectual pretensions that are the currency of the UK television industry. That is how they got closer to the core of what television can do than we are likely to. However, don't accuse me of hyperbole on top of everything else. *Big Brother* is not the greatest thing since sliced bread. But nor is it the end of civilisation as we know it. It's just a revealing and riveting piece of entertainment.

The press, of course, has not been unremittingly hostile. Two weeks ago the *Daily Telegraph* published a leader supporting the programme. That could destroy the street cred of Ruth Wrigley, Conrad Green and the rest of the *Big Brother* production team forever. Talk about power without responsibility.

P. Bazalgette, 'It's Only a Gameshow', *Guardian*, 6 September 2000

ACTIVITY

➤ Peter Bazalgette has made a lot of money out of the Reality TV types of programmes. To what extent do you think this motivates him to defend them, and to what extent do you think he believes in their integrity? Do you agree with Bazalgette when he describes the programme-makers as 'realist' rather than 'cynical'?

Confessional chat-shows, such as *The Oprah Winfrey Show* or *The Jerry Springer Show*, form a related genre that has also become increasingly popular. This confessional manner became particularly popular through programmes such as *Video Diaries* and *Video Nation*, where 'ordinary people' were given the technology (although not control of the editing process) to talk about their lives. Dovey suggests that we generally regard it as a 'good thing' to disclose personal problems to certain 'significant' others. Where this was once done confidentially, through an organisation such as the Samaritans, or a community religious figure, it is now increasingly done publicly on television.

➤ Consider Dovey's idea of a confessional society and undertake some research into the range of opportunities that exist for 'ordinary' people to confess aspects of their private lives. This may include problem pages in magazines and newspapers and radio phone-ins as well as television programmes or specialist websites. Can you identify any common characteristics about these shows and/or magazines and newspaper articles? Do you think that we have become increasingly 'confessional'? If so, why do you think this is?

➤ In television programmes such as *The Jerry Springer Show*, *Rikki Lake*, *Trisha* and *Esther*, members of the public are encouraged to use television as a confessional. Does this factor alone account for their popularity with British audiences? (AQA Unit, 4 January 2002)

➤ Discuss the proposition that television has become 'a paradise for Peeping Toms'. To what extent do you think that these types of programmes are 'exploitative spectacles' or 'participatory and democratic'?

➤ Consider the advertisement below that appeared in the *Guardian* in the summer of 2002. Discuss with others what type of show you think this might have been, on which channel it might have appeared and at what time of day/week?

TV DOCUMENTARY

Are you a group of outgoing girls who are up for a laugh?

Are you going on holiday before the end of August and will you be doing some hair removal before you go?

If so we'd love to hear from you. Call Ceri or Sarah on . . .

➤ How do you think the group of girls would have been selected and presented? In what ways do you think that this programme could be described as 'confessional'?

➤ To what extent do you agree with the views presented by Salman Rusdie and Germaine Greer? How would you challenge them?

FURTHER READING

Casey, B., Casey, N., Calvert, B., French, L. and Lewis, J. (2002) 'Reality Television' in *Television Studies. The Key Concepts*, Routledge.
A short but comprehensive overview of the main issues in relation to reality television.

▼ 8 GENDERED CONSUMPTION

The main focus of feminist audience research has been on genres and texts aimed at a female audience. Much important scholarship has been published exploring which aspects of media texts appeal to women. In 1982, Dorothy Hobson published a study of the soap opera *Crossroads*, while in 1991 Christine Geraghty produced a study of soap operas in which she identifies some of the common conventions that appeal to women. These include strong female characters and a focus on personal relationships set within the domestic sphere. Janice Radway explored the genre of the romantic novel in a study entited *Reading the Romance* (1991; 1st edn 1984).

A particularly important study of gendered media consumption is the work of Ien Ang, who looked at the popularity of *Dallas* among female viewers in her book *Watching Dallas* (1985). She advertised in a women's magazine asking about women's interest in the series, and the replies she received formed the basis of her study. She was able to identify three types of response:

- The ideology of mass culture suggested viewers liked the programme because it was successful and a high-profile piece of American popular television culture.
- The ironic or 'detached' position where viewers could watch it knowing it was 'bad' but wanting to see what it was other people were watching.
- The ideology of popularism which is based on people's 'everyday' routines and experiences and the 'pleasure' they get from watching *Dallas*, even though they may recognise that it is 'trash'.

Another key writer in the field of gender is Yvonne Tasker. In her book *Spectacular Bodies* (1993), she writes about the appeal of action heroines in Hollywood films. One of the key texts she examines is Ridley Scott's film *Thelma and Louise*. The significance of this film is the fact that it features two women as lead characters in a road movie, a genre previously identified as the preserve of men. The success of the film in the US and Europe created a lot of debate. Response to the film was diverse and in some cases quite negative, as Tasker points out: 'Far from being about empowering women, in this view the women with guns render the protagonist symbolically male.' In the extract that follows, Tasker explores some of the diverse responses to the film.

SEXUALITY, FEMINISM AND FILM

'This film is a con'. Thus ran the opening of *Spare Rib*'s review of Ridley Scott's *Alien* on its initial release back in 1979. With the exception of this film, in which Sigourney Weaver stars as Ripley, when feminist writers have addressed the action cinema at all during the 1980s, it has only been to dismiss the genre as macho and reactionary in familiar terms. However, the emergence of a series of

CONTINUED

MEDIA AUDIENCES

diverse action-based films centred on female protagonists has begun to generate a debate as to the political status of these films and their heroines. *Thelma and Louise*, a road movie also directed by Ridley Scott, was the surprise hit of the summer of 1991, both in America and in European countries such as Britain and France. The success of the film generated a series of articles, reviews and other commentaries which diversely praised, expressed concern or fascination at its 'gun-toting' heroines. Some saw *Thelma and Louise* as a feminist reworking of a male genre, the road movie, with women taking the place of the male buddies familiar to viewers of popular Hollywood cinema. For others, the film represented an interrogation of male myths about female sexuality, an admirable commentary on rape and sexual violence. I've already spoken of the way in which *Thelma and Louise* has been appropriated by some women as a 'lesbian film'. Elsewhere *Thelma and Louise* has been characterised as a betrayal, a narrative that cannot follow through on its own logic. Far from being about empowering women, in this view the image of women-with-guns is considered to be one which renders the protagonists *symbolically male*. Whatever view we take, *Thelma and Louise* and associated female heroines have generated, at the beginning of the 1990s, an academic and journalistic debate analogous to that sparked by the muscular male stars of the 1980s. The film has also been consumed in an historical moment marked by the public re-emergence of familiar questions to do with sexuality, violence and relations of power between men and women, in the publicity surrounding the nomination of judge Clarence Thomas to the Supreme Court and the Kennedy rape case in the United States.

Thelma and Louise follows the adventures of two white southern women in the United States who take off for a weekend of fun and end up on the run from the law. After an attempted rape leads to a fatal shooting and flight from the police, the theft of Louise's savings leads Thelma to armed robbery. With its outlaw heroines pushed beyond the point of no return, *Thelma and Louise* takes its place with a group of recent movies which put female protagonists at the centre of those action-based genres often reserved for men. A series of talked-about film performances from a variety of action sub-genres, all invoked the figure of the independent woman as heroine. Whilst films such as *Aliens* and *The Silence of the Lambs* and the performances of their female stars have caused much critical interest, an attendant suspicion can be detected that this type of role, indeed the appearance of women in the action cinema at all, is somehow inappropriate. Critical responses are never univocal, of course, but feminist critics have responded to these films with various combinations of pleasure and disgust, enthusiasm and suspicion. These films, it seems, whilst praised and enjoyed for their centring of women, are for some potentially tainted by exploitation. Such a sense of critical unease is certainly worth exploring. For if action movies centred on men have drawn condemnation for their supposed endorsement of a hyper-masculinity, how can the negative reaction to the emergence of female action heroines be contextualised and understood? The films themselves may well prove easier to understand when placed within the context of the popular cinema, and the tradition of the American action movie in particular, rather than in the context of a tradition of feminist film-making against which they are sometimes judged and, inevitably, found wanting.

Laura Mulvey concluded her well-known polemic essay of the 1970s, 'Visual Pleasure and Narrative Cinema', with the suggestion that women would have little or nothing to mourn in the passing of the Hollywood cinema. While recognising that the popular cinema of today is, in many ways, different from the popular cinema that Mulvey addresses, I want to raise a set of questions about the pleasure that both female and feminist spectators *do* take from mainstream movies, pleasures which are not dictated by any rules of same-sex identification or by heterosexual understandings of desire. The best way to express this might be in terms of a contradiction between what 'we' know and what 'we' enjoy, since the kinds of fantasy investments at work in the pleasures taken from the cinema cannot be controlled by conscious political positions in the way that some criticism seems to imply. A tension between the project of legitimating women's pleasures and the desire to assess representations politically informs a good deal of feminist criticism. It is ironic then that a critical disapproval of the 1980s' and 1990s' action heroine may stem in part from a feminist cultural criticism which has, in seeking to legitimise various pleasures and pastimes, classified popular forms and genres into male and female. The notion that some forms of activity and entertainment are more appropriate to men and some to women, that some genres can be called 'masculine' whilst others are labelled 'feminine', has a long history. Such a notion has its roots in commonsense understandings of appropriate male and female behaviour as well as in the categories set up by those who produce images and fictions – such as the 'woman's film'. Ironically a designation of 'inappropriate' images derived from a feminist critical tradition, coincides here with a more conventional sense of feminine decorum, a sense of knowing one's place within a gendered hierarchy. As much as anything, this critical trajectory reveals the operation within feminist criticism of a class-based, high-cultural, attitude towards the popular cinema, an attitude familiar from other forms of criticism. This is an important point since, as we have seen in previous chapters, class is a central term in the narratives of the popular action cinema.

Thelma and Louise charts the development of its two heroines as they move from the routines and confinement of everyday life to the freedom of the open road. In the process they move from the supposedly female space of the home to the freedom of the supposedly 'male' space that is the great outdoors. The martial-arts movie *China O'Brien* also follows this trajectory, with China resigning her job as a city cop to return to her home town, where she ultimately becomes sheriff. A montage sequence shows her driving through the countryside in an open-top car, images of her face in close-up intercut with her surroundings. Whilst there

is nothing particularly unusual in this, cinematically speaking, Rothrock here occupies the role of a 'figure in a landscape', the phrase Mulvey uses to describe the narrative control assigned to the male protagonist. The film seems to coyly acknowledge this shift, including a shot of a male gas-pump attendant, his chest exposed and hair blowing in the wind. The construction of this secondary male figure as spectacle provides a counterpoint to China's position as a dominating figure within the film. The road comes to signal a certain mythicised freedom.

At the outset of *Thelma and Louise*, Thelma (Geena Davies) is a shy, childlike woman, playing the role of meek housewife to husband Darryl's macho self-centredness. Louise (Susan Sarandon) is a waitress, capable and in control, balancing the demands of customers and workmates. The two set off for the weekend, Thelma's inability to decide *anything* resulting in a jokey sequence in which she packs just about everything she owns. This confusion is intercut with the neatness of Louise's apartment, everything cleaned and in its place. These images conjure up two recognisable extremes of an inability to cope, set against a calm efficiency. These comic extremes in turn set up the terms within which these characters will change and develop through the course of the narrative. I've already spoken of the ways in which a rites-of-passage narrative is a key feature of the Vietnam movie, a narrative in which the (white) hero 'finds himself' in the other space of Vietnam. These narratives build on a tradition of imperialist fictions within film and literature, in which Asia and Africa are constituted as exotic spaces for adventure. This structure is seen most explicitly in *Platoon* and is parodically, if rather viciously, drawn on in the 'Asia' of *Indiana Jones and the Temple of Doom*. The heroine of women's fiction is centred in a rather different rites-of-passage narrative, though one which nonetheless represents a coming to knowledge. Maria La Place discusses the operation of such a narrative trajectory in many women's novels and stories which 'centre on the heroine's process of self-discovery, on her progression from ignorance about herself (and about the world in general) to knowledge and some kind of strength'. Specifically referring to the 1940s' film and novel *Now Voyager*, La Place outlines the extent to which this transformation is both signalled and partly achieved through changes in the heroine's appearance – weight loss, new clothes, hairstyle and so on. This transformation is reminiscent of the narratives constructed around the male bodybuilder, whose physical transformation supposedly signals his changed status in the world. The rites-of-passage narrative that situates women in relation to health or body culture defines the heroine's transformation through the body. Such a transformation is enacted over the protagonists of *Thelma and Louise*, with their changing appearance seen by Kathleen Murphy as a literal shedding of skin when, in the final moments of the film, 'the Polaroid of two smiling girls on vacation that Louise shot so many miles ago blows away in the wind, as insubstantial as a snake's outgrown skin'. The end credit sequence continues this theme with a series of images of the two women, taken from different points in the narrative, which trace their transformation.

There is though a further sense in which the film's drama is enacted over the bodies of the two heroines. A drunken sexual assault on Thelma propels the two women on the road. Initially it is Louise who takes control, who rebukes and then shoots Harlan dead. Thelma's response is hysteria. 'What kind of world are you living in?' cries Louise on hearing Thelma's suggestion that they hand themselves over to the police. Later, when Louise's life savings have been stolen by JD (Brad Pitt), a young man Thelma has taken a liking to, it is Thelma who begins to take charge. She robs a convenience store, a performance we see through the flickering images, filmed by the store's surveillance video, as they are replayed by the police to an astounded Darryl. By the end of the movie both Thelma and Louise are armed, literally with a gun stolen from a state trooper, and metaphorically with a powerful sense of self and of the impossibility of a return to their earlier lives. They decide to head for Mexico since, as Thelma puts it, 'Something's crossed over in me. I can't go back – I just couldn't live'. Through these later scenes, the women are no longer just running, but enjoying the journey. The film offers a series of spectacular images, visual echoes of the women's changed perception. The two women shoot up a tanker, after its driver, who has plagued them at various points along the road, has refused to apologise for his behaviour. The truck explodes in a mass of flame. Driving through the desert landscape at night, their car is lit up from within – a surreal beacon. In this quiet moment they contemplate the night sky. Exhilarating and frustrating, the now notorious final image of the film has the two women driving off a precipice rather than give themselves up.

The narrative of transformation which structures *Thelma and Louise* is analogous to the developments in Linda Hamilton's character, Sarah Connor, in *The Terminator*. Like Louise, Sarah begins the film as a harassed waitress. Told by her lover and protector, Kyle Reese, that she is destined to become a legend to the rebels of a future society, she moans that she can't even balance a cheque book. By the end of the film she has acquired military discipline, becoming well-armed and self-sufficient. The militaristic iconography is continued in the sequel, *Terminator 2*, extended and literally embodied through Hamilton's muscular frame. A turning-point for Sarah Connor in *The Terminator* comes when Kyle is wounded and she must take control. At the very moment that he looks like giving up the fight, she screams at him to move. Addressing him as 'Soldier', she takes up the role of a commanding officer who harangues a tired platoon in order to save them, a role familiar from many Hollywood war movies. It is after this proof of her transformation, and Kyle's death which follows soon after, that Sarah finally terminates the Terminator. Kyle must die since, like the male hero, it seems that the action heroine cannot be in control of an adult sexuality. At the beginning of *Aliens* Ripley refuses the offer to accompany the military on an Alien-hunting mission, telling company man Carter Burke – 'I'm not a soldier'. She finally agrees to accompany the military platoon as an observer. Once there, however, despite her protestations, Ripley effectively takes control from the

CONTINUED

inexperienced military leader – like Sarah Connor she is transformed into a soldier.

It is perhaps the centrality of images of women with guns in all the films I've referred to thus far, that has caused the most concern amongst feminist critics. The phallic woman, that characters like Sarah Connor and Ripley represent, is seen as a male ruse, and a film like *Thelma and Louise* as 'little more than a masculine revenge fantasy' whose 'effect is perversely to reinforce the message that women cannot win'. Here we can see the obverse process of that critical move by which the suffering of the hero has been read as a testament to his, and consequently patriarchy's, invincibility. In turn the struggles of the female protagonist seem only to reinforce her passivity and secure her ultimate failure. Disruptive narrative or representational elements exist, within such a critical view, as little more than precursors to their ultimate hegemonic incorporation. Hence these images are taken to represent a double betrayal, holding out a promise that can never be fulfilled ('This film is a con'). . . . It might well be worth exploring further the kinds of masochistic fantasies at work in such critical moves. Alternatively, situating a film like *Thelma and Louise* within the tradition of popular cinema might, as I've argued, allow us to see it differently. Within many Hollywood action narratives, access to technologies such as cars and guns (traditional symbols of power) represents a means of empowerment. These technologies are also intimately bound up with images of the masculine. The female protagonists of the films discussed above operate within an image-world in which questions of gender identity are played out through, in particular, the masculinisation of the female body. Within *Thelma and Louise* the possession of guns and the possession of self are inextricably linked through the dilemmas that the film poses about freedom and self-respect. Drawing on a long history of representations of male self-sufficiency, the film traces the women's increasing ability to 'handle themselves', a tracing that follows their ability to handle a gun. Thelma can barely bring herself to handle her gun, a gift from husband Darryl, at the start of the film – picking it up with an expression of distaste, in a rather 'girlish' fashion. As the narrative progresses, she acquires both physical coordination, which denotes self-possession, and the ability to shoot straight. When the two women shoot out the tanker, they happily compliment each other on their aim.

Y. Tasker, 'Action Heroines in the 1980s', *Spectacular Bodies*, Routledge, 1993, pp. 134–9

Another perspective on gendered consumption is offered by Jacqui Gabb in her essay 'Consuming the Garden: Locating a feminine narrative with popular cultural texts and gendered genres'. Gabb's approach is through her own interest in the long-running programme *Gardeners' World*: 'I have used my own interest and viewing pleasures as a way into my analysis, and as a useful means of constructing a dialogue between myself and my informants.'

MEDIA STUDIES: THE ESSENTIAL RESOURCE

Gardeners' World in its time was the most popular programme of its genre, attracting an audience of around 5 million viewers. Using a similar methodology to Ang, Gabb placed an advertisement in the Hull *Daily Mail* asking fans why they watched the programme. The 30 replies she received were all from women. She selected eight of the respondents for in-depth interviewing.

A key figure in the programme was the presenter Geoff Hamilton who fronted the programme for 17 years up until his death in 1996. In the extract that follows, Gabb explains the complex nature of the appeal of this male presenter to a female audience, suggesting that he represented 'a complex blend of patriarchal authority and feminine (maternal) power'.

In the extract that follows, Gabb points out that she is at pains to steer clear of a purely text-based analysis in favour of a more expansive approach to locate female viewing pleasures.

The viewer is not seen as a product of the (feminine) text, but is posited as a social subject, whose gendered identities are composite and contingent. *Gardeners' World* ably addresses this fluidity. It explicitly employs the conventions that are associated with the most popular women's genres, incorporating the broader (domestic) context of most women's lives within its feminine narrative. With its open structure, multiplicity of 'storylines', and lack of narrative closure, *Gardeners' World* appropriates soap opera conventions and reproduces them within its own unique 'herbaceous' narrative. The centrality of nature's cyclic process, the ongoing saga of the 'television garden' project, and the familiarity and ordinariness of the presenters' faces, are all characteristics of traditional soap opera. It serves up a familiar blend of education and entertainment: a formula that 'educates (with a very small "e")'. Enabling an identification with the storylines and characters alongside an escapist narrative, it takes the spectator outside the mundanity of 'her' domesticity. It both facilitates fantasy while analogously reproducing the concerns of many women's lives.

Members of the female audience of *Gardeners' World* feel passionately that the programme is their own; it is specifically and individually, tailor-made for them. 'Just sitting down in the evening, feeling that the programme was mine . . . it was my programme. I could just sit there and it used to absorb me completely' (Rosie M). Using the feminine language associated with 'mother' nature, it slips almost seamlessly into the television genres traditionally associated with the female audience. Characteristics traditionally denoted as feminine, such as fertility, nurturing and beauty, are all celebrated within the television garden, in a rare and spectacular representation of maternal plenitude. The audience is implored to look after their tender (dependent) seedlings. Many female names and garden flora are interchangeable, for example Rose, Poppy and Lily. And gendered adjectives are the descriptors of feminine and horticultural beauty alike. Indeed

the language of the garden, in all its representations, is so heavily gendered that gardening and plants become 'marked' as female, signifying a femininity which sutures the programme (with its male presenters) and the female subject. Masculinity is largely absent from this arena, being pushed to the margins of manual labour and/or hard landscaping, or discreetly contained within the garden shed alongside all the (technical) garden machinery.

The garden and its flowers represent and symbolize femininity The female viewer thereby feels comfortable within the narrative of the garden as it offers her an expression of her own (constructed) maternalism. 'It's like being a mother again. Watching your little plants, nurturing them and feeling sad if they die. All these maternal instincts come into it really' (Rosie M). Irrespective of their own maternal and/or familial status – not all fans of gardening programmes are mothers! – the audience is implored to 'give' their love, affection and time to the garden and its plants, on the promise of reciprocity. 'Gardening is like no other leisure activity because we gardeners actually create hundreds, perhaps thousands, of new lives each season' (Geoff Hamilton). Unlike the emotional investments tied up within the family, these attentions are supposedly 'guaranteed' to give you something back in return. 'Give them a bit of encouragement to show them that you love them, giving them a feed . . . then they'll reward you with their very best display of colour' (Hamilton). Thus, under the aegis of Geoff Hamilton, *Gardeners' World* evoked the *myth* of the garden, the role of 'Mother Nature', the precariousness of life, and the ever-present need for the virtues of nurturing and growth to secure its loyal female following.

The television garden represents the female viewer's (domestic) subjectivities and thus privileges her viewing pleasure. The inanimate routine of gardening 'chores' become conflated with the 'living' needs more usually assigned to her family members. It is not only her children and/or partner who need to be cared for, the garden also needs to be nurtured and looked after or it too might fall into disrepair, and she be deemed negligent, inadequately equipped to deal with her familial responsibilities. Tania Modleski's 'ideal mother' is figuratively identifiable within this *living* scenario. The domestic (familial) routine that constructed Modleski's maternal subject is embedded within the daily needs of the garden. The female spectator not only provides the central support mechanism upon which her family depends, she is also the 'mother' to all her plants. It is only through her skills, dexterity and loving attention, coupled with those of her ally 'mother nature', that her family and garden will flourish. The fictional 'ideal mother' becomes identifiable and realized within this living context.

AUTHORITY AND THE ANCHOR-MAN

Once the female audience inhabits this domain of the 'ideal mother', then Geoff Hamilton may appear to appropriate the role of the (symbolic) 'father':

'Geoff was the Governor and always will be' (Tony C). 'I cannot imagine doing anything in the garden without first thinking what Geoff would advise' (Maggie F) (*Radio Times*, 24 August 1996). Hamilton presented *Gardeners' World* from 1979 until his death in 1996, being known both inside and outside the gardening industry as 'the grand old man of the garden'. His popularity had risen in line with the ratings of the programme itself. With his amiable manner, and informal dress code, he was instantly recognizable, and was duly adored by millions of gardening fans. But while his direct address to the female viewer may appear to characterize him as the absolute patriarch of the gardening world, such interpretation would exclude many of the feminine pleasures that are present within the text. I wish to posit that Geoff Hamilton was so popular with the female audience precisely because he signified something greater than (masculine) expertise. As I will show, Hamilton represented a complex blend of patriarchal authority and feminine (maternal) power, singularly embodied within a male physique.

Traditionally the presenter signifies the ultimate authority: articulating the producers' voice, 'he' controls the gaze. Yet while most other 'famous' television gardeners apparently relish the mantle of (patriarchal) expert, Geoff Hamilton endeavoured to rebuff this title. He subverted the direct address of the anchor-man, successfully overturning the authoritarian relationship between the television expert and 'his' audience. By describing his own expertise as the result of experience he placed it within the audience's grasp. He constantly addressed the audience – 'we gardeners' – bringing himself down from the echelons of stardom to within our reach; he was one of us. 'I think he just came over as such a simple person. That was his appeal really, he was so simple and down to earth . . . [He] made you feel "we can do that"' (Rosie M). Hamilton encouraged his armchair gardeners rather than give them instruction. He addressed 'his' viewing public as knowledgeable friends, an identification that was further enhanced by his body language. The (subservient) gesture, kneeling before us, represented *his* identification with us: he was our equal, open and vulnerable like any 'ordinary' gardener.

Geoff Hamilton established a contract between the viewer and himself, drawn up by mutual agreement. Like other presenters of his kind, he cajoled the viewer into an illusory dialogue, an intimacy that made us feel special, uniquely identified. The (female) audience of *Gardeners' World* believed his credible performance and invested heavily in his character. The responses to his death illustrated the extent of such affections and how deeply embedded he was within their 'real' lives. 'We are richer than we could have possibly imagined thanks to this gentle, lovely man. We shall miss him – very, very much' (Daphne W). 'The death of Geoff Hamilton will leave a huge gap in the lives of gardeners everywhere. Geoff sowed seeds not only in the soil but in the heart' (Dorothy B) (*Radio Times*, 24 August 1996).

J. Gabb, 'Consuming the Garden: Locating a Feminine Narrative', in J. Stokes and A. Reading (eds), *The Media in Britain: Current Debates and Developments*, Macmillan, 1999, pp. 257–60

> ➤ Choose a text that you feel is targeted primarily at a female audience and try to identify what appeal it offers for women.
> ➤ Consider how you feel this gendered approach has contributed to the study of media audiences. Do you feel that a similar approach to audience study from the perspective of different minority might be valuable?

FURTHER READING

Geraghty, C. (1991) *Women and Soap Opera*, Polity Press.
A useful entry point to the topic

Livingstone, S. (1990) *Making Sense of Television*, Routledge.
Uses soap opera as the basis of a case study into audience reception.

Mumford, L. S. (1998) 'Feminist Theory and Television Studies', in C. Geraghty and D. Lusted (eds),. *The Television Studies Book*, Arnold.
A broad-ranging analysis of the topic.

Radway, J. (1991) *Reading the Romance: Women, Patriarchy, and Popular Literature*, 2nd edn, University of North Carolina Press.
Exploration of the genre of the romantic novel.

Tasker, Y. (1998) *Working Girls: Gender and Sexuality in Popular Cinema*, Routledge.
An engaging and accessible exploration of Hollywood genres and representation.

▼ 9 *BUFFY* AND HER FANS

Fandom is an increasingly popular area of audience study. Although fanzines have been around since the 1940s, it is only with the development of cheaper technology and the development of a new wave of fanzines such as those associated with the punk movement and football (such as the fanzine *When Saturday Comes*), that the idea of fans as something worthy of critical study has taken hold. Many early ideas about fans saw them as 'obsessives', 'anoraks' or 'geeks', whose obsessive interest in a particular cultural object was cultivated to hide or make up for their social inadequacy.

According to Casey *et.al.* in *Television Studies – The Key Concepts*, fans were initially thought of as 'socially inadequate and ineffectual people who are enticed and deluded by a popular culture, in particular the media, which offers them synthetic fulfilment and escape from their pitiable lives' (Casey*et al.* 2002: 91).

Casey and colleagues go on to look at how we are often both fascinated and repelled by this representation of fans

> Repelled, because the obsessive fan appears to have been 'taken over' by the text in a way that 'we' have not, or has wilfully submitted to a zealousness that, in the extreme, can manifest itself in the pathological behaviour of the stalker. In focussing on those individuals or groups whose practices we, the 'non-fan' or 'ordinary' audience member, consider peculiar, we construct our own position as 'normal' set squarely against the activities of the fan as a deviant and dangerous 'other'. Despite the fact that we may enjoy the same texts, 'they' are somehow different to 'us' and we are content to keep the boundaries between us clearly demarcated.
>
> (Casey *et.al.* 2002: 90)

Recently this representation of fandom has changed, and fans are no longer seen in such a negative light. This is partly because of the recognition that nearly all of us are, in one way or another, 'fans' of something, whether it is a particular programme, *Big Brother*, personalities such as Ant and Dec, or a pop star such as Kylie. Although we may not be obsessive, we recognise that we will probably take more interest in our favourite programme/personality/pop star than in others and we may access specialist websites or buy specialist products such as books, magazines or videos that focus on these interests. We may also share our enthusiasm with others of similar taste – so in effect we are acting like 'fans'.

Henry Jenkins' *Textual Poachers* (1992) is an influential study in the development of the idea of fandom as something positive and empowering. He suggests that fandom is a way in which audiences can become active and participate in the creation of a text's meaning.

> Rather than being a sign of misguided psychological compensation, their closeness to particular texts demonstrates a desire to negotiate with the media in an active and creative way, in order to make its products relevant to the material and cultural conditions in which the fan, or fan community, is located.
>
> (Casey *et al.* 2002: 93)

Jenkins suggests that fandom allows people to 'take apart and assemble television's artefacts according to their own wants and desires' in what he calls a 'cutural bricolage' (Casey *et al.* 2002: 93).

The Internet has played a significant part in facilitating fans' communication with one another, and is increasingly replacing fanzines and fan conventions as the means of exchanging ideas, gossip and information. Dedicated websites provide an opportunity for fans to express their views, views that were often previously ignored by mainstream 'official' culture, as well as sharing 'inside' gossip and speculating on future narrative developments. These manifestations of fandom generate a sense of fellowship and support for fans who may otherwise feel isolated and/or misunderstood.

➤ Using your own media consumption, try to identify those texts that you are a 'fan' of. To what extent do you think you fit with Jenkins's notion of what fans do with particular texts?

➤ Explain in your own words what the term 'bricolage' means. What do you think Jenkins means by the term 'cultural bricolage'?

BUFFY THE VAMPIRE SLAYER

With the articulate dialogue and playful irony characteristic of 1990s teen dramas such as *Dawson's Creek* (Warner Bros., 1998) and *Clueless* (UPN, 1996–9), *Buffy the Vampire Slayer* (Fox/Kuzui/Sandollar/Mutant Enemy, 1997–) depicts its eponymous heroine as she struggles to juggle her sacred birthright as a demon-slayer and the everyday demands of adolescent life. Assisted by her friends Willow (Alyson Hannigan) and Xander (Nicholas Brendan), and Giles (Anthony Stewart Head), her 'Watcher', Buffy (Sarah Michelle Gellar) encounters a different demonic foe each week, defeating them with a combination of archaic investigation, high-school savvy and impressive fighting skills. These single episode storylines act as metaphors for the 'real' anxieties of *Buffy*'s teen protagonists, and are integrated into a continuous narrative that follows them from high school to college (in the fourth season) as they gain sexual awareness and increasing freedom from parental and institutional authority.

A spin-off from the film of the same title (Fran Rubel Kuzui, 1992) *Buffy the Vampire Slayer* was produced as part of the Warner Bros. network's move into prime-time hour-long drama, helping to solidify its signature as the 'family' network with a strong teen appeal. As such it reflects the American networks' growing interest over the 1990s in the adolescent market as a valuable niche demographic. This appeal to a teen audience is combined with the high production values associated with quality prime-time television. The series' sophisticated scripts address with wit and sincerity the enormity of growing up in contemporary America, complemented by a glossy visual style, fluid camera-work and artistically choreographed fight sequences.

Much of the series' drama (and comedy) stems from the incongruity of Buffy's position, as she wisecracks her way through fights with vampires twice her size while dressed in heels and a party dress. Her concern that she will ruin her hair or break a nail is combined with a painful awareness of the responsibilities and dangers of her powerful position. As such, *Buffy the Vampire Slayer* combines the female address of earlier series such as *Bewitched* (ABC, 1964–72) and *I Dream of Jeannie* (NBC, 1965–70) that attempted to explore the social contradictions for 'powerful' women through the introduction of fantasy into the domestic sphere, with the potentially titillating representations of highly feminised action heroes in series like *Charlie's Angels* (ABC, 1976–81) and *Wonder Woman* (ABC, 1976–7; CBS, 1977–9).

While *Buffy* provides men with a position from which they 'can safely indulge the male fantasy of the dominatrix and combine it with the Lolita fixation' (Forest, 1998, p. 6), it also 'offers transgressive possibilities for re-imagining gendered relations and modernist American ideologies' (Owen, 1999, p. 24). Broadly post-feminist in its address, the series attempts to create spaces in which women can be powerful, vulnerable and feminine, and to explore the consequences of this regendering for traditional masculine roles. In its self-conscious and playful inversion of the conventions of the horror genre, *Buffy the Vampire Slayer* engages with a perceived crisis both in gendered relationships and in the place of the adolescent in contemporary American society.

C. Johnson, 'Buffy the Vampire Slayer' in G. Creeber (ed.),
The Television Genre Book, BFI, 2001, p. 45

The American television programme *Buffy the Vampire Slayer* and its follow-up series *Angel* have both attracted a lot of 'fan' attention as well as the interest of many academics. In Britain, *Buffy the Vampire Slayer* regularly achieves audience figures of over 70,000 viewers per episode on Sky One and over 4 million on BBC2, comparable with other BBC2 programmes such as *The Naked Chef* and *Gardeners' World*. Johnson offers explanations for its popularity, including the fact that it has won several awards, and that the script is 'witty and sophisticated'. *Buffy* also offers progressive and 'enlightened' representations of adolescent sexuality – an increasingly important niche demographic for American and British television companies – as well as a progressive representation of the female heroine, although as Johnson points out, it follows in a tradition that includes *Bewitched* and *I Dream of Jeannie*.

DECONSTRUCTING BUFFY

It used to be that a vampire was easy to deal with: you ate plenty of garlic, you waved a crucifix at it, you stuck a stake in it – if you wanted to be fussy about it you could go the whole hog and cut its head off and scatter millet over the corpse, so that if it should happen to reawaken for some reason, it would have to count all the grains before it came after you. These days, though, nobody does anything as straightforward as just killing a vampire: they have to go and deconstruct it too.

Specifically, they go and deconstruct *Buffy the Vampire Slayer*, the American television series created by Joss Whedon. In October this year [2002], the School

CONTINUED

of English & American Studies, and the School of Language, Linguistics and Translation Studies at the University of East Anglia will be playing joint host to a two-day conference entitled 'Blood, Text and Fears: Reading Around *Buffy the Vampire Slayer*' (it was originally planned as a one-day conference but, apparently, interest from academics in Europe and the US was so intense that it had to be extended). Last year saw the publication of *Reading the Vampire Slayer*, a collection of essays edited by the critic Roz Kaveney, with such titles as 'Entropy as Demon: Buffy in Southern California', 'Vampire dialectics: Knowledge, institutions and labour', and '"They always mistake me for the character I play!": Transformation, identity and role-playing in the Buffyverse (and a defence of fine acting)'. You can find out more about these things at Slayage, 'the online international journal of Buffy studies' (www.slayage.tv), where you will also be invited to submit contributions for a planned new collection, *Monsters and Metaphors: Essays on Buffy the Vampire Slayer*. The renowned orientalist Robert Irwin is a fan; so is the anti-science polemicist Bryan Appleyard.

There's nothing new, now, about academics treating popular culture with a slightly absurd seriousness: large swathes of North America have been defor-ested to provide paper for theses called 'Meep! Meep! – Roadrunner, Wile E Coyote and the Auditory Dynamic of Despair', and suchlike. But nothing has generated the quantity of commentary that *Buffy* has, and in a comparatively short time (the first episode was broadcast in early 1997).

A little essential background: Buffy is Buffy Summers, a pretty, fluffy-headed Californian teenager who discovers that she is the Chosen One, the Slayer – latest in a long line of young women endowed with preternatural strength and fighting skills and charged with the task of slaying mankind's supernatural enemies – chiefly vampires. The town where Buffy lives, Sunnydale, is inconveniently sited over a Hellmouth, a portal to other dimensions which acts as a magnet to all kinds of demon. She is assisted by her schoolfriends Willow (a computer whizz and, later, trainee witch) and Xander (whose main qualities are a gift for snappy one-liners and dogged loyalty); by Rupert Giles, her English-born 'Watcher', appointed to guide her with his knowledge of the occult; and by a variety of friends, lovers and allies of convenience – notably Angel, a 'good' vampire who is the love of Buffy's life, and has been rewarded with his own spin-off series.

Many people are put off by the fact that *Buffy* is genre fiction. Some *Buffy* fans complain that this is snobbery, but I think it is quite understandable: genres are defined by a set of expectations, and knowing what to expect is a dubious pleasure. But *Buffy* rarely settles for satisfying expectations. The scripts regularly add ingenious twists; the expectations are absorbed and transformed. For example, in 'Buffy *vs* Dracula', the first episode of the fifth series (the most recent series on terrestrial television in Britain), Buffy found herself unable to resist the Count's wiles – seduced less by his saturnine good looks and his ability to control minds than by his sheer celebrity. Knowing what to expect from a Dracula story became the programme's subject.

Tried and trusted tropes of the horror genre crop up on a regular basis: were-wolves, fish-men, murderous mummies, human sacrifices; but they are integrated into a larger drama of characters and relationships. Often, the supernatural subplot serves as a neat metonym for the wider drama: when Xander and a group of louder, rougher kids were turned into human hyenas while on a trip to the zoo, a comment was being made on the pack mentality of adolescent boys, the need to get in with the in-crowd. When Oz, Willow's cerebral boyfriend, struggled with lycanthropy, wasn't that just the universal struggle with physical urges writ large?

It's not all just adolescent sex, though. In recent episodes, Buffy's 'darker side' has become a focus of attention – a sense of kinship with the monsters she combats, and also an underlying desire to have done with the fighting and killing, an urge for oblivion that culminated, at the end of series five, with her (temporary) death: the tombstone read 'She saved the world. A lot'. To begin with, the series rested on the contrast between Buffy's night-time life as teenage girl, worrying about boys and clothes and school. But now what is at stake – the pun isn't easy to avoid – are the larger questions of what makes us human, how to be good and why we should bother, and why we should stay alive at all. The bleakness of the themes puts the series closer to Philip Roth, even Samuel Beckett, than to Anne Rice.

All this makes it sound pretentious and heavy-going. But the other point to make about *Buffy* is that it is deliciously competent. More than 100 episodes have now been broadcast, plus 50 or so of *Angel* (which is somewhat inferior): that's over 100 hours of screentime now. Over that time, the dialogue has been unvaryingly slick and witty, often up there with the best Hollywood screwball comedies; the story-lines have been brilliantly laid out, within episodes but also over long spans of time. And the characters have grown in ways that are recognisable from life, while wholly unfamiliar to television – Xander has developed from classroom clown to believable builder; shy Willow, who used to worship Xander, has turned out confident and gay.

This is what attracts the intellectuals: the fact that *Buffy the Vampire Slayer* allows you to choose whether you are going to wallow in mindless, soapy action, or indulge yourself in the luxury of thought. Either way, it is wonderful.

Well, maybe not always wonderful. But four or five episodes of *Buffy* would be on my list of the 10 best pieces of television drama ever made: 'The Zeppo', in which Buffy, Willow and Giles save the world from apocalypse in the background, while in the foreground a neglected, self-pitying Xander is thrown into a maelstrom of demon-slaying and sexual experience; 'Hush', in which demons steal everybody's voices, and most of the dialogue is conducted in mime; 'Superstar', in which

a local nerd bribes a demon to transform reality, turning him into a fearless vampire-slayer and all-round sex-god; and 'The Body', which followed the aftermath of the death of Buffy's mother – slow-moving cameras, oddly miked sound and long silences made for the most acute portrayal of the isolation of grief I've ever seen. At its best, the intelligence and compassion on display in Buffy can make you glad to be alive. Or at any rate, undead.

R. Hanks, 'Deconstructing Buffy', *Independent*, 1 July 2002

According to Robert Hanks, *Buffy the Vampire Slayer* is part of a particular genre. 'Tried and tested tropes of the horror genre crop up on a regular basis: werewolves, fish-men, murderous mummies, human sacrifices', and although Hanks suggests that 'genres are defined by a set of expectations, and knowing what to expect is a dubious pleasure', he argues that *Buffy* 'rarely settles for satisfying expectations.' Instead he suggests that the scriptwriters add 'ingenious twists', for example *Buffy* falling for Dracula.

However, Hanks argues that there are larger representations at work.

Often the supernatural plot serves as a neat metonym for the wider drama: when Xander and a group of louder, rougher kids were turned into human hyenas while on a trip to the zoo, a comment was being made on the pack mentality of adolescent boys, the need to get in with the in-crowd.

Hanks suggests that the later series of *Buffy the Vampire Slayer* deal with grand issues: 'now what is at stake . . . are the larger questions of what makes us human, how to be good and why we should bother, and why we should stay alive at all.' For Hanks, *Buffy*'s appeal is that it offers the viewers a choice 'to wallow in mindless, soapy action' or 'indulge . . . in the luxury of thought'.

ACTIVITY

➤ Identify the ways in which Buffy the Vampire Slayer conforms to genre expectations. What does 'metonym' mean? What does Hank mean by his example?

The article is from the online journal *Intensities: the Journal of Cult Media* (www.cult-media.com) produced by the School of Journalism, Media and Cultural Studies at Cardiff University. The article discusses the scheduling of *Buffy* and *Angel*, the censorship and editing of the series, and how scenes and even entire episodes have been cut by UK broadcasters to conform to taste and decency guidelines . It also looks at the way in which fans of *Buffy* and *Angel* use websites.

Fans seek out explicitly British websites in order to participate in fan message boards and discussions because it gives them a forum to express grievances, share information and validate their fan status. The experience of being a *Buffy* or *Angel* fan in the UK highlights culturally specific fan activity. (p. 1.)

There is a long discussion on the scheduling of *Buffy* and *Angel*. Hill and Calcutt suggest that the ideal channel for watching US cult television is Sky One. This is because Sky One broadcasts both *Buffy* and *Angel* uncut during their evening prime-time schedules and the episodes are only a few weeks behind the US screenings. In contrast, BBC2 who broadcast *Buffy*, and Channel 4, who broadcast *Angel*, both broadcast the shows during the early evening, seeing the shows as children's programming. This means that the shows have to be 'adjusted' to fit into a family viewing slot. The Broadcasting Standards Commission (BSC) upheld complaints about a 'sexually charged' scene in 'Harsh Light of Day' shown on BBC2 at 6.45 pm in October 2000 and the BBC cut scenes from 'Where the Wild Things Are' in which sex scenes between Buffy and Riley were shortened.

According to Hill and Calcutt

> As *Buffy* is made for a niche US audience watching after eight o'clock in the evening, adjustments must be made to fit the programme in a family slot. Although 'the BBC will try to ensure that editing interferes as little as possible with the original intentions of the film maker' in the case of *Buffy*, substantial editing occurs in order for it to be shown in the UK. Channel 4 must adhere to the ITC programme codes which mirror the BBC in terms of the nine o'clock watershed. The ITC's Family Viewing Policy 'assumes a progressive decline throughout the evening in the proportion of children viewing, matched by a progression towards material more suitable for adults'. Thus Channel 4's decision to show *Angel* in early prime-time ensured that it had to edit the series to fit the timeslot . . . By classifying *Buffy* and *Angel* as children's programming UK terrestrial TV is unable to respond to the expectation of fans, who are predominantly 16–35-year-old prime-time viewers.
>
> (Hill and Calcutt 2001: 3)

Hill and Calcutt (2001) discuss the way in which members of the BBC online *Buffy* message board posted messages criticising BBC2 for the way in which it was promoting the series as a children's programme. The BBC replied that 'as a public service broadcaster we have to try and cater for the varied interests of our diverse audience . . . therefore it is not possible to please all our viewers'. According to Hill and Calcutt this type of response illustrates the point made by Jenkins that 'fan response is assumed to be unrepresentative of general public sentiment and therefore unreliable as a basis for decisions' (Jenkins 1992: 279).

Henry Jenkins's argument that 'fandom constitutes a basis for consumer activism' is particularly applicable to the circumstances of *Buffy* and *Angel* in the UK. As Jenkins notes, 'network executives and producers are often indifferent, if not overtly hostile, to fan opinion' (1992: 278–9); in the UK this indifference has created an online community which is primarily a forum for complaints, and for sharing information on the availability of the shows across all media. Thus, the UK treatment of *Buffy* and *Angel* has led to an

online fan community which specifically seeks out other UK fans. The sites offer UK fans an opportunity to talk about the experience of watching *Buffy* and *Angel* in the UK, an experience which on the one hand emphasises the negative side to cult TV fandom, and at the same time celebrates being a fan. The network treatment of both series in the UK does little to contradict the misconception that *Buffy* is not 'mature, quality programming', and fans seek to validate their status by participating in message boards and discussion which celebrates rather than denigrates being a *Buffy/Angel* fan.

Fans' postings on websites

There are several sites available for the UK-based *Buffy/Angel* fan, some of which are TV industry sites (BBC.co.uk/Buffy, Skyone.com or Channel4.com), others fan-based sites (www.slayage.tv, www.unofficiallybuffy.uk, www.Slayed.co.uk or www.BuffyUK.org), although some of these sites may have moved or closed down since publication of this book. (You can use the Google search engine to look for new sites. Enter 'Buffy+UK' for specific UK sites.) The industry sites tend to be more anonymous and fans generally access the sites created by other fans. One exception is the BBC's Online Cult TV website which has a message board as well as profiles of key characters and information about episodes.

Hill and Calcutt (2001) argue that sites like these are typical of the ways in which fandom operates. By using websites to create a sense of community, fans are also constructing particular identifies for themselves and actively participating in the creation of certain types of meaning for popular cultural texts. Fan-based websites offer a distinctive way of engaging with popular media texts, whether it is through expressing one's own personal views, giving information, or entering into discussion with other fans. Through these websites fans can come together and create alternative social communities.

Below are two examples of fans' postings on *Buffy/Angel* websites.

Some postings are just requests for information:

QUERY??? willow_the_wiccan – 7th post – 3 Jul 2002 14:51

does anyone know when season 6 is coming to bbc2?? Because i missed one of the episodes and i reeeeeeaaaaaaaaaallllllllllyyyyyyyy want to see it!!!!! PLease tell me if you know [reply]

www.bbc.co.uk/cult/buffy/index.shtml

Others reflect an individual's interpretation of a particular episode and ask for other fans to comment and share in this interpretation. This is the approach in the message posted by one fan, revealed below.

I *Will Remember You* is without a doubt one of the most important chapters in the Angel–Buffy story. It is a beacon to many B/A fans. Here's my tribute to the forgotten day . . .

I Will Remember You

Poignancy runs hand in hand with the Angel–Buffy relationship. When there is pleasure, it follows that not long after there is pain. It is in this frame that 'I Will Remember You' (IWRY) lies, as do many of the most heart-rending Angel–Buffy centred episodes such as 'Innocence' and 'Becoming II'. Yet it seems that IWRY is the most gut-wrenchingly-emotionally-devastating one of the lot. Why? What makes it such a heartbreaker?

Perhaps one of the factors in the episode's impact is the sacrifice that Angel makes. He gives up his mortality, so precious to him, for Buffy's life. For so long, he has been a creature of the night, unable to walk in the sunshine, watch the sunset, experience the full joy and tenderness of love or the pangs of hunger which can be satisfied by rich cookie dough fudge mint chip!! For Angel, those things are all encapsulated in the one person: Buffy. The something he really wants.

As a mortal, he was subject to 'all the pleasures and pains' of this kind of experience, something which Angel, a vampire with a soul, must yearn for more than anything. With his humanity restored to him through the curse, he wants those things, yet cannot have them, because he is not human. It is only as a mortal that the full range of the human experience becomes available to him. Yet he relinquishes this, proving that he is 'not a lower being'. He has the misfortune of being distinct from the humanity that flows within him, a strange mixture which cannot succumb to the 'simple matter of love', instead forcing him to forgo happiness for the sake of humanity. It's here that a most powerful point becomes clear: Angel's love for Buffy is deeper than any human's could ever be. He who yearns for humanity knows humanity better than any other: he feels her soul. Yet, he would surrender this all for her.

This leads to the way that the theme of duty over personal wishes and desires pervades the glowing light of optimism and love in this episode. The whole gig is so fatalistic: there is no way to escape the ever-imminent conclusions. The view that seems to claim mastery over everything else is the one expressed by Cordy, that '[Buffy] can't save the world and have Angel'. It is such an inflexible, rigid and indomitable attitude, pervasive throughout the fictional and real world of the show: it seems that the Powers That Be (PTB) have more than a little in common with Joss Whedon . . .

Yet why is this so? The Mohra demon itself stated that 'together [Angel and Buffy] were strong', a point on which it was more than qualified to comment (considering it pretty much had its ass whipped by them). So this begs the question of why they are apart. Surely this episode demonstrated more solidly than any other that as warriors to the cause they are more effective together and happy, than when they are severed and in pain?

Angel himself admits in IWRY that 'Buffy will always be a part of [him]. That will never change.' They are two sides of the same coin that complement each other. They have a deep, instinctive soul-bond that can be felt 'inside' by both of them. Only when they are together are they at full fighting strength: their dependency is mutual.

For example, in 'Amends', Buffy persuades Angel to carry on as they stay 'strong' by fighting, a point later echoed by Angel in Graduation Day I: 'I was wrong. I need [Buffy].' Likewise, if it wasn't for Angel, Buffy would never have resumed her slayer duties fully: and in times of trouble, her 'first instinct is to run to Angel'. Thus, this all exemplifies their reciprocal need. '*How can I go on with my life, knowing what we had, what we could have had . . .*' Buffy, 'I Will Remember You'.

So 'what' exactly is it that Angel and Buffy have that makes our chins quibble whenever we see the closing seconds of Angel and Buffy's 'day' together? Certainly there's the sizzling chemistry and the obvious attraction that is present right from when Buffy makes her rather upset and angry entrance into Angel's office. Yet there are many other much deeper things that make their relationship unique, even spellbinding: that is their total and utter love for one another. Buffy accepts Angel, vampire and all, including his darker, more evil nature. Here are two people who would do anything for one another, even give their lives; this is not a kind of love which you find easily.

However, the fly in the ointment, as ever, is Angel's perpetual guilt and need to redeem himself: a part of him that will never go away. This overrides everything, even his most cherished personal wishes and desires. He still misguidedly believes that unless he is mortal, a relationship with Buffy is not possible. He doesn't realise that without her, he's less effective: only 'together [are they] strong'. Sadly, Angel hasn't yet realised the perfect solution: Buffy and he fighting together, so that he is redeeming himself and experiencing the love he craves. Alas, for now, it is not to be. In IWRY Angel and Buffy are so close, yet so far from having a life together. It's cruel, very cruel and poignant.

W. Dootson, www.immortalbliss.co.uk/lca/

On the home page it says: 'This is a B/A shipper site and nothing else. If you're not interested in Angel and Buffy being together, this site isn't for you.' The website had over 12,700 hits by September 2002.

FURTHER READING

Casey, B., Casey, N., Calvert, B., French, L. and Lewis, J. (2002) 'Fans', in *Television Studies. The Key Concepts*, Routledge.
Comprehensive and accessible overview of the changing perception of fans.

Hill, A. and Calcutt, I. (2001) 'Vampire Hunters: the Scheduling and Reception of *Buffy the Vampire Slayer* and *Angel* in the UK', *Intensities – the Journal of Cult Media*, Issue 1, Spring/Summer 2001. Accessed at www.cult-media.com/issue1/Ahill.htm
Provides accessible information about viewing figures, censorship issues and scheduling for *Buffy* and *Angel*. It also provides an analysis of the various *Buffy the Vampire Slayer* and *Angel* fan-based websites.

Jenkins, H. (1992) *Textual Poachers: Television Fans and Participatory Everyday Life*, Routledge.
A key text in theorising about fans and fandom.

Kaveney, R. (ed.) (2002) *Reading the Vampire Slayer. An Unofficial Critical Companion to Buffy and Angel*, Tauris Parke Paperbacks.
A series of essays that explore the themes and narratives of *Buffy* and *Angel*. Also includes a short episode guide to the first five seasons of *Buffy*.

O'Sullivan, T., Dutton, B. and Rayner, P. (1998) 'Football fanzines', in *Studying the Media*, Arnold.

Pullen, K. (2000) 'I-love-Xena.com: Creating Online Fan Communities' in D. Gauntlett (ed.) *Web Studies: Rewiring Media Studies for the Digital Age*, Arnold.
An interesting, sometimes provocative set of essays dealing with 'new media'. Pullen uses *Xena: Warrior Princess* as a case study on the way in which fans use the World Wide Web to create 'fan communities'.

▼   **1 INTRODUCTION**

For many students the role of media institutions is considered less important than more 'glamorous' considerations in Media Studies, such as textual analysis, ideology or representation. However, analysis and critical review of how our media are owned, structured, staffed and regulated are an important aspect of understanding how and why the media operate in the way they do on local, national and international levels.

All media texts are the result of a complex set of determinants and it is important to have some knowledge and understanding of the political, social, historical and economic factors that help shape media texts. These may include changing ideas about the place and function of broadcasting in Britain in the twenty-first century and the changing economic climate within which it is produced, or the effects on developing countries of the increasing proliferation of western-style media technology, texts, personalities and codes and conventions. It is impossible to come to a deeper understanding of the implications and meanings of any given media text without taking into consideration the ways in which political, ideological, social and commercial institutions have shaped its production, distribution, consumption and interpretation.

Increasingly, the study of media institutions can be undertaken as a purely fact-finding exercise; it is easy to determine which media conglomerates own which newspapers, magazines, television channels and film studios through most industry-based websites. However, there are often implicit *ideological* assumptions that underpin much of the institutional organisation and structure of the media. This section will examine a wide range of issues that shape how texts are produced, distributed and consumed. These include the relationship between the State and the media; why some areas of broadcasting such as television news and public service broadcasting are given a more 'respectable' status; and the ways in which the media and their audiences are affected by current changes in terms of globalisation and the development of new media technology.

▼ 2 REGULATION AND THE PRESS

One of the key characteristics of the media in Britain is the Government's involvement in the control or regulation of media organisations, their activities and products. The relationship between the State, which has ultimate control and responsibility for the media, and organisations responsible for media production is a complicated one. As a democracy, Britain supports the idea of freedom of speech and of the press, while also needing to exercise some sort of regulatory control over the media. Much of the British media sector is commercially owned, rather than State owned, which means that many media organisations are businesses run for the profit of directors and shareholders. There is therefore a complicated set of factors at work in the relationship between the Government and the media; while the Government does not own all media organisations, it is able to impose rules and laws which may contradict the commercial aims of these organisations. This is a particularly British tension; in other parts of the world the influence of the Government on the media is very different. In some countries the media is completely under the control of the State, while in others commercial pressures or market forces govern the media, and State regulation is minimal.

As Julian Petley (1999) points out in 'The Regulation of Media Content' the dominant view that Britain enjoys a largely free media is contradicted by the fact that there are over 50 pieces of legislation in place to restrict media freedom. These include the Contempt of Court Act, the Obscene Publications Act and the European Convention on Human Rights. Amongst the most commonly invoked are the law of libel and issues of personal privacy. There have been many famous cases in recent years involving Jeffrey Archer (against the *News of the World* and the *Star*), Elton John (against the *Sun*) and Naomi Campbell (against the *Daily Mirror*). Petley argues that unlike in the United States, in Britain,

> there has never been any domestically created, statutory, legally enforceable right to freedom of expression . . . In law, journalists are not regarded as society's watchdogs . . . Similarly, newspapers and broadcasters are treated . . . in exactly the same way as any other commercial organisation.
>
> (Petley 1999: 144)

In Britain there is a wide variety of organisations, some governmental (Independent Television Commission, Broadcasting Standards Commission), some industry-based (Press Complaints Commission, Advertising Standards Authority and British Board of Film Classification) and some consumer-based (Mediawatch-UK, Voice of the Listener and Viewer). All of these organisations have varying degrees of control or influence over the media industries that they are supposed to regulate. Government-based regulatory bodies can inflict severe penalties on media organisations they find to be in contravention of their regulations. The ITC, for example, is able to fine a television company or revoke its licence, and has recently put considerable pressure on ITV and Channel 5 about which slot in their programming schedules the main evening news bulletin should occupy. Similarly, in March 2002, the Radio Authority fined Virgin Radio £75,000 for a serious breach of 'the rules on taste, decency and offence to public feeling'. According to the Radio Authority Report,

> The broadcast concerned an on-air competition called 'Swear word hangman', at just before midnight on 18 January. The broadcast involved a 9-year-old child taking part by phone in a live on-air feature competition in which callers guess the letters of a sexually explicit phrase that uses swear words. The resulting programme was highly offensive, and inappropriate even in the context of adult alternative comedy.
> (www.radioauthority.org.uk/index.html)

In contrast, consumer-based pressure groups like the Campaign for Press and Broadcasting Freedom (www.cpbf.org.uk/), the Voice of the Listener and Viewer (www.vlv.org.uk) or Mediawatch-UK (www.mediawatchuk.com) (which used to be known as the National Viewers and Listeners Association) have limited powers, and rely on lobbying media organisations and government bodies in an attempt to influence regulation decisions.

Ofcom

In 2002 a new communications 'super-regulator', Ofcom, was set up. This organisation replaced the ITC, Radio Authority, BSC, the Radio Communications Agency and Oftel. It was established to recognise the 'synergy' that has come into being between the broadcasting and telephony industries. In an age where we may listen to web-only radio stations through our mobile phones or watch subscription video feeds of *Big Brother* on our PCs, it was felt that a regulatory body was needed with a wider, more integrated remit; one that was not restricted to one particular kind of media or broadcasting, like the ITC or Oftel.

Ofcom will be different to previous regulators in that it will regulate both content (in terms of programmes) and commercial matters, as it will be authorised to decide which companies can merge or buy out a competitor. However, according to Government ministers, Ofcom will have a 'light touch' approach to regulation and has been criticised for having only partial authority over the BBC. For example, while Ofcom will be able to fine the BBC on grounds of taste and decency, it will have no jurisdiction over wider day-to-day issues of the BBC. According to many media commentators, there is also a danger that Ofcom, being only one organisation instead of five, may operate with a more limited, predominantly business-oriented range of concerns, and that it will view regulation in a narrow economic way rather than stimulate wider research and discussion on the role of television in general, as the ITC and BSC have done in the past.

For a concise précis of the main points of the 2002 Communications Bill, see 'Masterplan for the media' in the *Guardian*, 21 November 2002, available online at media.guardian. co.uk/whitepaper/story/0,7521,844341,00.html.

For a detailed criticism of the Communications Bill, see 'Why the Communications Bill is bad news', produced by the Campaign for Press and Broadcasting Freedom (www.cpbf.org.uk/).

Most of the organisations that regulate or control the media have websites where you can access information about their remit and membership as well as access their codes of conduct and study details of their adjudications:

www.asa.co.uk (Advertising Standards Association)
www.bbfc.co.uk ((British Board of Film Classification)
www.bsc.org.uk (Broadcasting Standards Commission)
www.itc.org.uk (Independent Television Commission)
www.ofcom.gov.uk/ (Office of Communications)
www.pcc.org.uk (Press Complaints Commission)
www.radioauthority.org.uk (Radio Authority)

ACTIVITIES

➤ Look up the various organisations' websites and examine their membership. How representative of their readers, listeners and viewers do you think these organisations' members are? To what extent do they reflect what Petley calls 'the great and the good'?
➤ Look through their adjudications and note what proportion of these are upheld. Petley suggests that the PCC only upholds 1.15 per cent of the total complaints that it receives. Do the other organisations have a similar degree of resolution? If so, why do you think that is?
➤ Write an article of 1,000 words describing the work of the BSC. At the end you may wish to consider how effective you feel this organisation is.

▼ 3 SELF-REGULATION AND THE PRESS

The Press Complaints Commission (PCC) was set up in 1991 to replace the Press Council, itself introduced in 1951 as a means of curbing the then perceived power of press barons like Lord Beaverbrook. The Press Complaints Commission, like its predecessor, is a self-regulatory organisation; in other words it has been set up by the newspaper industry itself and has no legal powers. It has a code of practice to which newspaper owners, editors and reporters (in theory) adhere. However, if a newspaper flouts this code of practice, the PCC has only limited ways of punishing it. If the PCC upholds a complaint, it will ask the newspaper to print the adjudication or an apology. When the *Daily Mirror* was criticised in 1993 over photographs it published of the Princess of Wales in a gym, it threatened to

MEDIA STUDIES: THE ESSENTIAL RESOURCE

withdraw from the PCC rather than face any punishment. This would have seriously weakened the authority of the PCC and so rather than let that happen, the PCC toned down much of its criticism of the *Daily Mirror*.

Lord Wakeham, until recently Chairman of the PCC, claimed that the PCC:

> delivers to ordinary members of the public and high-profile figures alike a Rolls-Royce complaints handling service. Unencumbered by the red tape of statute and legal regulation, and working with the unerring good will of editors whose own Code we administer, we are able to get most problems sorted out quickly and effectively. Mindful that justice delayed is justice denied, we deliver swift redress without cost to those aggrieved. No statutory or legal system could match that.

ACTIVITY

➤ Why do you think Lord Wakeham does not want any legal powers or status for the PCC? Access the PCC website at www.pcc.org.uk/about/benefits.htm where you can find more information regarding its history, purpose and adjudications.

In 2002 Lord Wakeham resigned as a result of the collapse of Enron in the United States. This resulted in much analysis and criticism of the role of the PCC and reopened the debate surrounding the self-regulation of the press in Britain. The newspaper industry is keen to avoid the introduction of a 'proper' regulatory body with legal powers to impose fines. They argue that this would represent a threat to the freedom of the press and so would ultimately be anti-democratic. The Government will probably be unwilling to take on the newspapers by trying to impose such a regulatory body, as Governments need the support of national newspapers, especially in the run-up to elections. It seems likely therefore that the current situation of newspaper self-regulation will remain in place. However, as the article by David Lister suggests, there are many problems with the status quo and the effectiveness of the PCC.

WHY WE SHOULD BE COMPLAINING ABOUT THE PCC

Let us for a moment consider the state of the Press Complaints Commission and newspaper self-regulation from the perspective of a concerned newspaper reader. She – many of the PCC's recent adversaries, from Anna Ford to Sara Cox to Vanessa Feltz, have been female, so grammatical positive discrimination is not amiss – may have listened to *Today* on Radio 4 yesterday.

There she will have heard Stuart Kuttner, the managing editor of the *News of the World*, agree with his paper's description of Charles Moore, the editor of the *Daily Telegraph*, as "Lord Snooty" and "the hypocrite of Fleet Street". Charles Moore then likened being insulted by the *News of the World* to a "lunatic coming up to you on the Tube".

She will have heard Mr Moore repeat the point I made here a couple of weeks ago – that it was wrong for the director of the PCC and his partner to holiday with the editor of the *News of the World* and her partner, as there must be seen to be distance between the PCC and editors.

Our newspaper reader would doubtless agree with that. If she had time on her hands she might then study the papers from yesterday and the weekend, and note internecine hostility and vitriol. There was the *News of the World* editorial describing the *Daily Telegraph* as a "struggling, dreary newspaper [which] repeatedly breaches PCC press guidelines". Our reader would be as puzzled by this as by the *News of the World* describing Guy Black as the "distinguished" PCC director. Thoughtful he certainly is, but it's a bit early in his career for him to be distinguished.

Our reader may not care about the rights and wrongs of all this, but it would be her right to conclude that if the papers distrust each other's integrity, why should she trust them to be regulators? Thus inspired to ponder on the shortcomings of the PCC and the current state of self-regulation, she would give passing thought to the following random episodes, much rehearsed in the press in recent days.

First, the ruling of the PCC, defended by Lord Wakeham only last month, that Anna Ford and her family had no right to privacy on a public beach in Mallorca. If the PCC had wished to advocate a new class system where celebrities only holiday on private beaches, it could hardly have done better.

Second, the Prince Harry drink and drugs story, where a behind-the-scenes deal between palace and PCC has been alleged.

Third, the "Sophiegate" tapes where the PCC was again alleged to have gone behind the scenes with Royal aides to stop a *News of the World* scoop by helping to secure an interview for the newspaper with the Countess of Wessex. Only those with a ludicrously naïve understanding of the press would have believed that this would have buried the tapes.

Our newspaper reader would surely begin to wonder why the PCC was not more transparent and consistent in its operations.

Transparent it is certainly not. When I phoned last week to check that Lord Wakeham earned £156,000 a year for his three-day week, a PCC spokesman replied: "I've seen that figure quoted, but I don't know if it's right and I'm not interested." There speaks the body that regulates part of the communications industry.

Our reader might wonder, too, what actually goes on at PCC meetings. She couldn't be blamed for thinking the unthinkable. Are editors really sufficiently disinterested and above reproach to be a key part of this self-regulation? The editor of the *Sunday People*, estimable chap that he is, is soon to be cited by the Radio 1 presenter Sara Cox under human rights legislation over his paper's pictures of her naked on a private holiday. Yet he is on the PCC's panel. Is it comfortable for the editor of the *Sunday Telegraph*, who is on the panel, to be involved in censuring the editor of *The Daily Telegraph*, who is not? Worse, might it be too comfortable?

Why is there a need for the director or chairman to attempt secret behind-the-scenes deals? The PCC exists to adjudicate and urge good practice, not to broker compromises. Why indeed wait for a complaint in the first place? One important change the PCC could make is for it to become proactive and speak out on abuses before the formality of a complaint.

Bill Norris of the pressure group Presswise make the very fair point that a proactive PCC is particularly important in cases of racial or ethnic slurs, which at present can be ignored because of the commissioner's refusal to accept "third party" complaints. Damian Tambini, senior research fellow at the Institute for Public Policy Research, makes the crucial point that the much used and mush abused term "the public interest" needs to be properly publicly defined by the PCC.

Among editors there is no such consensus. Charles Moore says there is "a lack of fairness in the relationships between the PCC and newspapers. The public must be assured that it works."

Roger Alton of the *Observer* adds: "There is probably an issue around quite how close editors should be to the PCC administration. I'm a fan of self-regulation, but the behind-the-scenes deals must stop."

However, Piers Morgan, the editor of the *Mirror*, tells me: "It is facile for broadsheets to claim the PCC hasn't worked when it so patently has. We have to be very careful in light of Lord Wakeham's departure that we don't allow broadsheet editors with embarrassingly small circulations to put one of their cronies in to dictate how mass-market, dare I say *popular*, newspapers go about our successful businesses. I say we have cleaned up our act enormously in the last decade. Self-regulation, despite all the predictably miserable bleatings from my broadsheet pals, has worked very well. So much so that public figures now have more to fear from the likes of Charles Moore and his dumbed-down *Telegraph* than me."

Of course, one could argue that any cronyism at the moment is between PCC and tabloids rather than broadsheets. But, with a more transparent PCC all such insinuations would be redundant.

No one in the newspaper industry wants regulation by government. The temptation for any government to confuse the public interest with its own interest would be overwhelming.

The courts are another option. The argument against the courts ruling on intrusion of privacy were reinforced by Lord Wakeham just before his departure. He contrasted "the quick and effective procedures of self-regulation" with "the more cumbersome, time-consuming and costly procedures of the law". But why should a lengthy procedure be worse than a quick fix if the lengthy procedure established a precedent that would inform all future newspaper practice?

Today a meeting of Pressbof, the inelegant sounding body that funds the PCC, will decide what long-term measure to take over Lord Wakeham's decision to stand down temporarily as chairman while the Enron investigations continue. There is a likelihood that the newspaper managing directors and other senior executives who make up Pressbof will decide that Lord Wakeham's absence should not be temporary, but permanent. The PCC, after all, needs stability and consistency.

But it needs more than that. It needs transparency and accountability. Unless it moves quickly to secure public and newspaper confidence, it is possible that by the time the Enron investigations are complete, there may not be a PCC for Lord Wakeham, or anyone, to chair.

D. Lister, 'Why we should be complaining about the PCC,'
Independent, 5 February 2002

David Lister questions whether newspaper editors and owners are 'sufficiently disinterested and above reproach' to be able to regulate their own and their competitors' newspapers. As the article points out, there is a small group of national editors who work closely with the PCC and one, Neil Wallis, editor of the *People*, is on both the PCC panel and is also the subject of a complaint to the PCC by the BBC Radio 1 presenter Sara Cox. Lister suggests that there are serious problems in terms of accountability and that the term used by the PCC, 'public interest', as a justification for the printing of many stories and photographs, needs to be much more clearly defined. Finally David Lister suggests that for the PCC to survive, it needs to introduce 'transparency and accountability'.

Defending the current system, Piers Morgan, editor of the *Mirror*, is quoted as saying that 'self-regulation . . . has worked very well' and he makes the point that it is often the broadsheet newspapers that criticise the PCC partly, he suggests, because they are envious of the tabloids' readership. In the popular tabloid press, Piers Morgan argues there are no complaints over the way in which the PCC's self-regulation works. Piers Morgan is suggesting that the readers of tabloid newspapers are therefore happy with the content of their newspapers and it is only 'the predictably miserable bleatings from . . . broadsheet pals' who are critical of tabloid newspapers and their stories.

MEDIA STUDIES: THE ESSENTIAL RESOURCE

➤ How fair do you think is John Tulloch's assertion that the PCC is 'more like the customer complaints department of a commercial organization'?

THE PRESS IS CANTANKEROUS, CYNICAL AND ESSENTIAL

This service will, I suspect, create ironies for some of us – and perhaps not least for St Bride's itself. For when *The Daily Courant* was launched in 1702, its main competition was held not to be that of other forms of the then media – books and pamphlets – but the power of the sermon. Not newspaper *vs* newspaper, but press *vs* pulpit. I am glad you are both still here 300 years on, as strong and as robust as ever – and glad, too, that this church still stands as a wonderful haven in which we can come together today to celebrate three hundred years of newspapers, and of press freedom.

That St Bride's has such a special place in the soul of the British press is a testimony to the dedicated work of many newspapermen and women and many incumbents of the church over the generations. There is no doubt also an irony inherent in my presence here today. After all, we both represent longstanding institutions – mine admittedly rather older – and we have both over the centuries endured a degree of criticism and opprobrium.

I would make one more point about our two different institutions – that from time to time we are probably both a bit hard on each other, exaggerating the downsides and ignoring the good points in each.

I want to do my best to redress the balance – and to pay tribute to the very real good that newspapers and magazines do – *pro bono publico*.

Yes, from time to time you get things wrong: everyone does. But most of the time you are seeking to keep the public informed about developments in society, to scrutinise those who hold or seek positions of influence, to uncover wrongdoing at a national level, in business or in local communities, to prick the pomposity of the overbearing, and – a point sometimes forgotten – to entertain us.

There is, of course, a careful balance to be struck in all this. For three centuries, the press has in that process been awkward, cantankerous, cynical, bloody-minded, at time intrusive, at times inaccurate and at times deeply unfair and harmful to individuals and to institutions. However, there is a great deal in what Thomas Jefferson said: those faults are the 'reality of our liberty', and the underpinning of a just balance in our society. Virtues and vices rolled into one, and long may it be so.

CONTINUED

For those of you expecting a large 'but' at the end of that paragraph, there is indeed one coming – though you will have to wait a moment for it. Before I reach it, I do want – as I have done in the past – to underline my own very real gratitude and, indeed, surprise for the manner in which all newspapers have sought to give my two sons – William and Harry – as much privacy as possible in their position.

And, now, very briefly, to the 'but' – which is this. Is it not the case that in the legitimate pursuit of news, in the desire to make information available to the public, in the desire to hold public bodies and public figures to account, and in its desire to entertain, the media in all its forms sometimes becomes too cynical, too ready to assume the worst, and to construct the general out of the particular? And is not the result that important parts of British life have become damaged because of the failings not of the institutions themselves, but of individuals within them? Of course, scrutiny and exposure of wrongdoing are important. But so is the good that we so often overlook and take for granted.

Travelling abroad, I see a very different view of Britain from that I sometimes see here: their view is of a vibrant, energetic, innovative and, yes, still proud and civilised land with timeless values rooted in our rich history. Perhaps all of us need at the time of this coincidence of anniversaries – your 300th and the Queen's 50th – to wonder what more each of us can do to correct the genuine ills in our society and create a climate which leads to ever more of us feeling that Britain is a great country to which we can give our love and loyalty.

Speech by Prince Charles, printed in the *Independent*, 12 March 2002.

It is worth reading this speech by Prince Charles closely and noting how much of the speech deals with newspapers and their 300-year history and how much deals, either directly or obliquely, with criticisms of the monarchy both as an institution and vis-à-vis its individual members.

ACTIVITIES

➤ To what extent is this speech offering praise to British newspapers and to what extent is it critical of the newspapers? How accurately does the headline 'The Press is . . . ' reflect the tone and content of the speech?

➤ Thomas Jefferson once suggested that the 'faults' of the press are a necessary price to pay for the 'reality of our liberty'. In other words, Prince Charles suggests that we have to put up with the type of press that we have today because it is an important part of our democratic process. Would you agree with this statement? Can you explain exactly how newspapers like the *Sun* and the *Daily Express* are important parts of our democratic process?

➤ Re-read the last paragraph of the speech by Prince Charles. What does it suggest about Britain as a country? About newspapers? And about the monarchy?

Like most newspaper cartoons this one by Steve Bell (*Guardian*, 12 March 2002) works on various levels of understanding and humour.

Consider what prior knowledge the cartoonist expects us to have. For example, we are presumably expected to recognise the character of Prince Charles, who like many public figures is caricatured in a way that quickly becomes recognisable; he has been identified in part by his large ears, and we share in this understanding. Rupert Murdoch may not be so easily identified until we read his speech-bubble which then clearly anchors the caricature. The other two figures kneeling with their backs to the reader are also identifiable but the reader would need to be able to unpick the clues, i.e. the names of the two newspapers on their backs and the brief glimpses we see of their appearances: the bald head that identifies David Yelland, the editor of the *Sun* and the hat and glasses that identify Richard Desmond, owner of the *Daily Express* and *Star*. It might also help us to understand the cartoon if we know that Prince Charles's speech was delivered in a church, St Bride's in Fleet Street, a church traditionally associated with the press.

To understand the humour of the cartoon we also need to have knowledge of both the speech that the Prince of Wales made regarding the press and the contents of the various newspapers identified. We would also have to acknowledge that some newspapers rely on pictures of topless models to attract readers.

ACTIVITIES

> ➤ Prince Charles, in defending the important role the press plays in society, said that part of that role was to 'keep the public informed of developments in society'. How do you think this relates to the newspapers identified in the cartoon?
>
> ➤ Another layer of meaning, and humour, is represented by the speech-bubble from Prince Charles which refers to what many perceived as his lack of a significant role and purpose. To what extent might this tie in with views on the monarchy held by many *Guardian* readers?
>
> ➤ Part of the humour of the cartoon works because of a particular view of the Prince of Wales. However, not everyone shares that view and so many people might find it offensive. How likely are these people to be *Guardian* readers?
>
> ➤ With broadsheet cartoons these layers of meaning and humour can be quite complex and are aimed at reflecting the characteristics of the newspaper's readership. For example, would this cartoon seem humorous to a reader of the *Sun* or the *Daily Express*? Give reasons for your answer.

The press, as with other branches of the media in Britain, is an important part of our democracy and in theory the principle of free speech should be protected to allow journalists to call to account those in positions of power and authority. For this to work, however, the press needs to maintain standards of accuracy and to respect individual privacy. This is a delicate balancing act that requires considerable finesse but in the case of the newspaper industry, Petley argues, the PCC with its creed of self-regulation offers nothing more than 'the newspapers' insurance policy against the threat of statute law'.

FURTHER READING

Engel, M. (1996) *Tickle the Public. One Hundred Years of the Popular Press*, Gollancz.
A readable and humorous history of the popular press written by a *Guardian* journalist. Particularly relevant are the last two sections on the *Sun* and the popular press.

Franklin, B. (2001) (ed.) *British Television Policy: A Reader*, Routledge.
Contains a large selection of original documents relating to television policy in Britain since the publication of the Peacock Report in 1986. Part Four of the book deals with key issues in three areas: programme content, media ownership and digital convergence.

Petley, J. (1999) 'The Regulation of Media Content' in J. Stokes and A. Reading (eds), *The Media in Britain: Current Debates and Developments*, Macmillan.
A concise and detailed overview of the regulatory bodies, both broadcasting and press, in Britain. Petley argues that Britain's media is highly regulated and is critical of many of the regulatory bodies that are responsible for overseeing Britain's media.

MEDIA STUDIES: THE ESSENTIAL RESOURCE

▼ 4 NEWS SELECTION AND PRESENTATION

News, whether it is on television, online, on the radio or in newspapers, is one of the key areas of media analysis. Research conducted on behalf of the Independent Television Commission in 1993 found that over 70 per cent of adults in Britain get their news from television (see Gunter *et al.* 1994). This means that it is television news that is generally the focus of analysis by media commentators and academics. Newspaper journalism is also seen as important but this is perhaps due to the role that news-carrying newspapers had in the first and second half of the last century rather than their importance today as a source of news. Popular newspapers today are largely concerned with celebrity gossip and entertainment and it is only the broadsheets, with their smaller readerships, that tend to focus on 'hard' news.

Generally the debates surrounding news have concentrated on the accuracy and impartiality of the news produced. This is particularly the case for television news where licences to broadcast are granted on the condition that the news reporting will be impartial and balanced. Research by groups such as the Glasgow University Media Group (1985; Eldridge 1995) has shown that this impartiality claimed by many news organisations is increasingly problematic and that the ideal of objective truth is largely untenable. Recent research has also focused on the way in which television news should be seen as part of the 'television flow' and has to fit within television schedules that are based largely around entertainment and popularity. This may mean that television news bulletins follow on from family situation comedies and are followed by gritty drama series, or, in the case particularly of ITN's *News at Ten*, are bracketed on either side by a major Hollywood film.

Because news is part of our daily and hourly television consumption, news bulletins have increasingly had to adopt many of the characteristics of other television codes and conventions whilst at the same time trying to remain distinctive and somehow more serious.

Apparent across the range of the different BBC and ITV newscasts under consideration are several shared features:

- **Interruption**: the opening sequence, usually composed of a 15–20 second segment of brightly coloured computer-animated graphics, rapidly unfolds to a sharply ascending piece of theme music (the use of trumpets is typical). Its appearance announces the interruption of the flow of entertainment programming by signalling the imminent threat of potentially distressing information (most news, after all, is 'bad news').
- **Liveness**: the opening sequence helps to establish a sense of urgency and, in this way, anchors a declaration of immediacy for the newscast's larger

claim to authoritativeness. The news is coming directly to you 'live'; its coverage of 'breaking news' is happening now (even though most of the content to follow will have been pre-recorded).

- **Time-space**: each of these segments privileges specific formulations of temporality (ticking clocks are used by both the BBC and ITN, which signal the up-to-the-minuteness of the news coverage) conjoined with those of spatiality (images of revolving globes spin to foreground an image of the British nation as defined by geography, in the case of the BBC; while for ITN's *News at Ten*, a London cityscape at night is slowly panned until the camera rests on a close-up of the clockface of the main parliamentary building, the apparent seat of political power).
- **Comprehensiveness**: implicit to this progressively narrowing focal dynamic time–space is an assertion of the comprehensiveness of the news coverage. The news, having been monitored from around the world, is being presented to 'us' from 'our' national perspective. That is, we are located as an audience within the 'imagined community' (B. Anderson 1991) of the British nation.
- **Professionalism**: the final shot in the succession of graphic sequences (ostensibly sounded by the gong of Big Ben in the case of ITN) brings 'us' into the televisual studio, a pristine place of hard, polished surfaces (connotations of efficiency and objectivity) devoid of everyday, human (subjective) features. A central paradox of broadcast news, as Crisell (1986: 90–1) writes, 'is that if there is one thing more vital to it than a sense of authenticity, of proximity to the events themselves, it is a sense of clear-sighted detachment from them – of this authenticity being mediated through the remote, sterile atmosphere of the studio.'

The camera smoothly glides across the studio floor while, in the case of the ITN *Lunchtime News*, a male voice-over sternly intones: 'From the studios of ITN (.) the news (.) with Nicholas Owen and Julia Somerville.' Both newsreaders are situated behind a shared desk, calmly organizing their scripts. Serving as a backdrop for them is what appears to be a dimly lit (in cool blue light) newsroom, empty of people but complete with desks, computer equipment, and so forth. Similarly, for the News at Ten, as the male voice-over declares: 'From ITN (.) News at Ten (.) with Trevor McDonald', the newsreader appears in shot seated behind a desk, typing on an invisible keyboard with one hand as he collects a loose sheaf of papers with his other one (which is also holding a pen). Whether it is ITN or the BBC, it is the institution behind the newsreader which is responsible for producing the news; it is the very 'impersonality' of the institution which, in ideological terms, is to be preserved and reaffirmed by the 'personality' of the newsreader.

As a result, the mode of address utilized by the respective newsreaders at the outset of the newscast needs to appear to be 'dialogic' in its formal appeal to the viewer's attention. This dialogic strategy of co-presence is to be achieved, in part, through the use of direct eye-contact with the camera (and thus with the imagined viewer being discursively inscribed). As Morse (1986: 62) observes, 'the impression of presence is created through the construction of a shared space, the impression of shared time, and signs that the speaking subject is speaking for himself [or herself], sincerely'. The impersonally professional space of the studio is, in this way, personalized in the form of the newsreader who, using a language which establishes these temporal and spatial relations of co-presence with the viewer, reaffirms a sense of shared participation.

Nevertheless, these dialogic relations of co-presence are hierarchically structured. The *direct* address speech of the newsreader (note that the 'accessed voices' will be restricted to *indirect* speech and eye contact) represents the 'news voice' of the network: the newsreader stands in for an institution charged with the responsibility of serving a public interest through the impartiality of its reporting. For this reason, these relations of co-presence need to be organized so as to underwrite the signifiers of facticity and journalistic prestige, as well as those of timeliness and immediacy.

In addition to the steady gaze of expressive eye contact, the visual display of the newsreader's authority is further individualized in terms of 'personality' (white males still predominate), as well as with regard to factors such as clothing (formal) and body language (brisk and measured). This conventionalized appeal to credibility is further enhanced through aural codes of a 'proper' accent (almost always received pronunciation) and tone (solemn and resolute). Such factors, then, not only may help to create the impression of personal integrity and trustworthiness, but also may ratify the authenticity of the newsreader's own commitment to upholding the truth value of the newscast as being representative of her or his own experience and reliability. Personalized terms of address, such as 'good afternoon' or 'good evening', may similarly work to underscore the human embodiment of news values by newsreaders as they seemingly engage in a conversational discourse with the viewers.

The newsreader or 'news anchor', as Morse (1998: 42) observes, 'is a special kind of star supported by subdued sartorial and acting codes that convey "sincerity".' Taken to an extreme, this can lead to 'Ken and Barbie journalism' where, as van Zoonen (1998) argues, the charge is made that physical attractiveness of the 'anchor team' is taking precedence over their competence as journalists. Also at issue here is the related trend, particularly pronounced in local news, of 'happy talk'. 'As the name suggests,' van Zoonen (1998: 40) writes, 'these are merry little dialogues between the anchors showing how much they like each other and how much they love their audiences.' The main purpose behind 'happy talk', according to her interviews with newsworkers, is 'to "people-ize" the news, as one news editor has put it, and to suggest that journalists and audiences are one big happy family.'

The immediacy of the implied discursive exchange is thus constrained by the need to project a sense of dialogue where there is only the decisive, if inclusionary, voice of the newsreader. As Stam writes:

> The newscaster's art consists of evoking the cool authority and faultless articulation of the written or memorised text while simultaneously 'naturalising' the written word to restore the appearance of spontaneous communication. Most of the newscast, in fact, consists of this scripted spontaneity: newscasters reading from teleprompters, correspondents reciting hastily-memorised notes, politicians delivering prepared speeches, commercial actors representing their roles. In each case, the appearance of fluency elicits respect while the trappings of spontaneity generate a feeling of unmediated communication.
>
> (Stam 1983: 28)

In play are a range of deictic features which anchor the articulation of time ('now', 'at this moment', 'currently', 'as we are speaking', 'ongoing' or 'today') to that of space ('here', 'this is where' or 'at Westminster this morning') such that the hierarchical relationship of identification for the intended viewer is further accentuated.

Contingent upon these relations of co-presence is what has been characterized as the regime of the 'fictive We'. That is, the mode of address employed by the newsreader, by emphasizing the individual and the familiar, encourages the viewer's complicity in upholding the hegemonic frame. To the extent that the newsreader is seen to speak not only 'to us', but also 'for us' ('we' are all part of the 'consensus'), then 'we' are defined in opposition to 'them', namely those voices which do not share 'our' interests and thus are transgressive of the codified limits of common sense. As Stam (1983: 29) points out, there needs to be a certain 'calculated ambiguity of expression' if a diverse range of viewers are to identify with the truth-claims on offer: 'The rhetoric of network diplomacy, consequently, favours a kind of oracular understatement, cultivating ambiguity, triggering patent but deniable meanings, encouraging the most diverse groups, with contradictory ideologies and aspirations, to believe that the newscasters are not far from their own beliefs. As a result, in attempting to authorize a preferred reading of the news event for 'us', the newsreader aims to frame the initial terms by which it is to be interpreted.

S. Allan, 'The Textuality of Television News',
News Culture, Open University Press, 2000, pp. 99–102

Stuart Allan's extract explores how the audience is positioned and directed towards particular preferred readings of television news bulletins. Looking at their mode of address and the way in which they 'codify' reality, Allan undertakes an analysis of the role of the news presenter(s) and the sounds and images of the opening sequences of the BBC's

Nine o'clock News and ITN's *News at Ten*. Allan identifies several features that are shared by a range of BBC and ITN newscasts.

Allen points out the way in which the newscasters address the viewer seemingly individually, simulating direct eye contact by looking straight into the camera. The newsreader seems to be addressing us personally, reaffirming 'a sense of shared participation' in today's news stories. Allan goes on to highlight the way in which these newsreaders represent the 'authority' and 'impartiality' of the news organizations: through the types of personalities who present the news, their clothing, body language, accent and enunciation they reinforce a 'sense of personal integrity and trustworthiness'. Moreover, through their continued familiar presence on our screens, they offer a sense of reassurance. According to Allan, newsreaders 'ratify the authenticity of the newsreader's own commitment to upholding the truth value of the newscast as being representative of her or his own experience and reliability'.

ACTIVITIES

➤ Allan suggests that the newsreader is a 'special kind of star'. To what extent do you think this is true? Consider, for example, the activities of newsreaders such as Trevor MacDonald, Michael Buerk or Mary Nightingale outside of their news reading. What other types of programmes are they involved in? Perhaps more importantly, what types of programmes do they *not* appear in? What are the reasons for this?

➤ Compare the opening sequences of the BBC and ITV new bulletins with those from other channels. Channel 5, for example claimed when launched in 1997, that it would offer a new type of news bulletin. In what way is its presentation of news different?

➤ If you have access to satellite or digital channels, look at American channels such as CNN or Fox News, as well as Arabic and other non-western news channels such as Al Jazeera or Star News. To what extent do American, British and the other channels share the same characteristics and conventions in the way that they present the news? Why do you think this is?

TV WATCHDOG ATTACKS NEWS BUDGET CUTS

Britain's most senior television regulator has called for the power to set a minimum budget for ITV's news coverage, following concerns about the substantial cut in the value of ITN's contract.

Patricia Hodgson, chief executive of the Independent Television Commission, said the BBC and Sky should not be allowed to dominate the journalistic marketplace.

CONTINUED

And she took a swipe at the BBC for its tendency to eschew creativity in the search for ratings. 'Beating ITV with *Blue Planet* is a triumph; beating it with *Celebrity Sleepover* is a tragedy,' she said in a speech last night.

There have been concerns about the level of investment in ITN after it was forced last year to shave almost £10m from its £45m contract to supply ITV's news bulletins, to see off a rival bid from a consortium that included Sky News. Abut 100 jobs were lost through the cuts, but ITN's contract is now secure for the next six years.

Jon Snow, the Channel 4 News presenter, has been the most senior internal critic of the move, pointing out last year that guidance from the ITC in the early 1990s suggested a reasonable level for the contract would be £55m to £60m a year.

There have been concerns that cuts threaten the long-term viability of ITN. In the Royal Television Society's annual Fleming lecture last night, Ms Hodgson said it was important to preserve a diverse range of voices in broadcast news. 'Not even the BBC's outstanding news machine can be relied on to reflect every sensitivity or to get the balance right every time. Sky offers an excellent alternative, drawing on the global resources of New International. But, in a complex world, are two news agendas really enough?'

Ms Hodgson called on the government to allow the proposed new communications regulator, Ofcom, to set a minimum level of investment for the ITV news contract when a draft broadcasting bill is published this spring. 'The bill should require proper investment in news,' she said. The ITC, whose responsibilities will be incorporated into Ofcom, only has the power to set the minimum level of foreign bureaux to be maintained by the ITV news contract holder.

Research reveals politics and business to be the subjects that least interest the viewers, but Ms Hodgson warned against gimmicks to re-engage them.

'The ingenuity and drive of today's journalists is more than capable of finding new ways to connect with public concerns – and not just by a few one-offs, however worthy, amongst a daily news agenda of crime, football and pop personalities,' she said. This was seen as an implied criticism of the BBC's NHS Day last month, when programmes were devoted to examining the state of the health service.

A more substantial strategy was needed: Channel 4 had managed to build its audience from 800,000 to more than 1 million in three years, Channel 5's news audience had increased from 400,000 to 1 million, and Radio 4's *Today* programme had put on 1 million listeners, she said.

Elsewhere in her speech, Ms Hodgson raised concerns about Channel 4, which has been criticised for steering away from its statutory obligations to provide diversity in broadcasting by investing in loss-making ventures such as Film Four and E4.

'It's trying to build a multi-channel presence with purely commercial channels. But maybe we should think about how to strengthen its public service offerings as well,' said Ms Hodgson.

M. Wells, 'TV Watchdog Attacks News Budget Cuts,' Guardian, 6 March 2002

The article by Matt Wells addresses some of the concerns that the ITC (and its replacement Ofcom) has concerning the 'quality' of ITN's news broadcasts. It is interesting to consider this article in conjunction with the tables below showing how the amount of both 'quality' news and foreign news has changed on both BBC and ITN in the last 25 years. There has also been a decline in factual programming about developing countries across the two networks, 28 per cent decline for the BBC; 74 per cent for ITV.

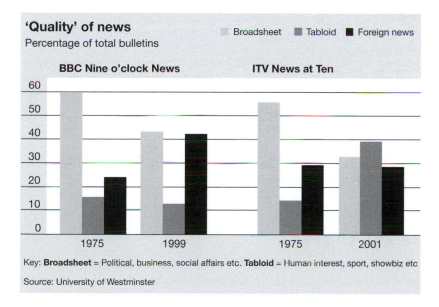

'Quality' of news
Percentage of total bulletins

Key: **Broadsheet** = Political, business, social affairs etc. **Tabloid** = Human interest, sport, showbiz etc

Source: University of Westminster

ACTIVITY

➤ Why do you think that foreign news has declined slightly for ITN but increased quite considerably for the BBC?

It is apparent from the table that the BBC's percentage of 'broadsheet' news (politics, business, social affairs, etc.) has also declined quite considerably although it is not criticised in the same way that ITN is.

It is also worth considering the extent to which viewers may not actually want 'broadsheet' news but prefer the human interest, sports and showbiz items that make up 'tabloid' news. If this is the case, how is it decided that politics and business, although of least interest to the majority of viewers, should be included in news bulletins?

ACTIVITIES

➤ Why do you think that the BBC escapes the types of criticism that ITN receives?
➤ The article quotes Patricia Hodge, who said it was 'important to preserve a diverse range of voices in broadcast news'. Why do think she says this? Do you think that a diverse range of voices exists? If so, what is the range of these voices? Can you think of any others that are currently excluded? Why do you think they are excluded?
➤ Do you think that it is right that Ofcom (the new media regulator) should have the power to 'set the minimum level of foreign bureaux to be maintained by the ITV news contractor'? Will Ofcom have the same powers over the BBC?
➤ Carry out a contents analysis of the commercial television channel's news bulletins. Consider the balance between hard news and soft news/entertainment-led stories. In what ways are the bulletins the same and/or different? The article says that both Channel 4 and Channel 5 had increased their audiences for their news bulletins. How do you think they have achieved this?

You could also look at the latest viewing figures from BARB either published in *Broadcast* each week or accessed via www.barb.co.uk.

DUMB AND DUMBER?

Information is more easily accessed than ever before; as mobile phones, the internet and e-mail become part of the everyday fabric of our society, we expect information at the touch of a button and, most importantly, at our convenience. As an information service provider, television news can't afford to be left behind in the digital revolution, and so it continues to adapt and respond to new challenges and audiences.

For many years, news presentation on British television involved a newscaster with a face the public could trust, sombrely facing the camera from behind a desk, recounting events. The set was serious, the atmosphere heavy with import. Regional magazine programmes aside, the news was never entertainment.

Satellite changed all this: if live images can be beamed from round the world 24 hours a day, why make people wait for a scheduled news bulletin? Rolling news, begun in the US by CNN (Cable News Network), was launched in the UK by Sky (then BSkyB), followed more recently by BBC News 24. Though Sky News makes no profit and the BBC's version has cost vast sums, more digital 24-hour news channels are planned.

Certainly during a major international crisis, such as the Gulf War, or a huge British story, like the death of Princess Diana, rolling news comes into its own. People want to catch events as they happen, whenever they can spare the time to turn on. The reason we don't tune in every day, perhaps, is that our appetite for such unmediated reporting is rather less when there's only today's catfight in Parliament to report. To hold an audience on a slow news day, the rolling news channels liberally pepper their headlines with showbiz news, sports reports and endless live interviews with 'experts'. 'Infotainment' is the new news, its delivery as important as its content.

Terrestrial news has also been embroiled in a ratings war, culminating in major makeovers: spruced-up, colourful sets, personality presenters, and hi-tech graphics have all played their part. Kirsty Young perched on the corner of a desk on Channel 5, and soon everyone from Jon Snow (Channel 4) to Jeremy Paxman (BBC2's *Newsnight*) was up on their feet or leaning on the furniture. News anchors have turned from a safe pair of hands into part of the identity of the channel they work for. Jon Snow's avant-garde neckties are as much a mark of C4's pride in its nonconformism as Michael Buerk's serious dismeanour is representative of the BBC's respect for tradition. Nor can one imagine ITV's paternalistic Trevor McDonald going for a politician's jugular, as we now expect *Newsnight*'s Jeremy Paxman to. But personalities are only a part of the change. There have been accusations that television news is 'dumbing down', lowering its standards and journalistic integrity in favour of sensationalism and 'easier' stories. There is concern that international news takes second place to homegrown human interest stories, and that considered analysis is being squeezed out.

The battle over *News at Ten* brought this to the fore. Warring with the BBC over percentage audience share, ITV decided it needed greater flexibility in scheduling popular dramas and feature films at the 9pm watershed, with no need to break for the news. It could then steal viewers from the 9 o'clock BBC bulletin and keep them all evening. Though it is a commercial organisation, ITV is obliged to broadcast a certain amount of serious programming, and MPs have lobbied for *News at Ten*'s reinstatement. The new 11pm bulletin has achieved a greater audience share (since less people watch *any* television at that time of night), but attracts fewer people than the old 10pm programme. Nevertheless, ITV has increased the audience of its early evening report by extending it, and moving it from 5.40pm to 6.30pm. BBC1's regional news now vies with

ITV's main evening bulletin; this increase in competition fuels concerns over dumbing down.

After criticism about the end of News at Ten, the ITC, which regulates independent terrestrial television, issued a directive in July to each of the ITV franchise holders, that the nightly news move to a more accessible time. ITV response was quick: it sought a judicial review of the ruling; ITV, it seems, is determined to stick to its guns.

Hard news is ever harder to sell. Reports on conflict and political upheaval around the world are now more likely to be illustrated by the lived experience of one or two local people than via historical and socio-economic analysis. We are rarely offered the big picture. This bias towards requiring the audience to respond to complex situations emotionally rather than intellectually is also shown in the evolving perspective of the foreign correspondent – perhaps best illustrated by the belief of Martin Bell, former senior BBC journalist turned MP, in a 'journalism of attachment'. This unapologetically opinionated method results in the reporter, in the midst of undeniable horror, demanding we be affected, and take sides. The brave news gatherer is no longer bringing back footage and facts for us to judge and form an opinion but saying: 'Look at this. It is terrible, it is unacceptable. We must act.' There is a place for first-person responses to tragedy – but not necessarily in a national news bulletin. Except when we are at war, we expect the news we receive to strive for objectivity or impartiality. As this news is distilled, so as to accommodate the needs of those tapping into it on the run, a balance between the extremes of uncontextualised, bald headlines and eye-catching, impassioned accounts must be found.

F. Morrow, 'Dumb and Dumber?', MediaWatch 2000, BFI Sight and Sound, 2000, p. 22

Fiona Morrow's article 'Dumb and Dumber' places this criticism of ITN's News at Ten within the context of the increasing range of news sources now available to us. Increasingly, organisations are using their websites to provide up-to-date news information. This is most often offered free of charge, although sometimes, for example in the case of financial news whose value lies in its being up to date, there is a charge to access the sites. As the article points out, mobile phone companies are also trying to encourage us to use their phone services by offering additional services such as news updates, although again we will have to pay to receive them.

The major change in terms of our consumption of televisions news, however, is the proliferation of rolling news channels such as BBC News 24, Sky News and the various American channels like CNN. As the author points out, 'If live images can be beamed from round the world 24 hours a day, why make people wait for a scheduled news bulletin?' The article goes on to discuss the way in which increasingly we use rolling news stations in the event of major stories such as the Gulf War, the death of Princess Diana or a major train crash 'People want to catch events as they happen, whenever they can spare the time to turn on.'

In the Morrow article, some of the suggested disadvantages include the way in which news is increasingly packaged as 'infotainment' and that the news anchor-people have become 'personalities' as the programmes compete with one another. The article also suggests that there has been a dumbing-down or a lowering of 'standards and journalistic integrity in favour of sensationalism and easier stories'. The article discusses the problems faced by *News at Ten* and suggest that 'hard news' is increasingly being eroded for more personalised and sensationalist reporting.

ACTIVITIES

- ➤ The events of September 11, 2001 were the biggest news story in recent memory. Can you recollect how, where and when you first heard of and then followed the news story? It would be interesting to carry out a small survey to see how many people switched on their television sets to watch these events as soon as they heard about them and, if they did, what channels they tuned to.
- ➤ What do you think are the main advantages of the rolling news services? Do you think that they have any disadvantages?
- ➤ How have terrestrial broadcast news programmes responded to the impact of digital news services? (AQA Unit, 4 January 2002)

News values are a daily – indeed, an hourly – concern for journalists. They are the air we breathe. And, like air, they tend to be invisible, taken for granted. Trainee journalists soon pick up a working knowledge of whether a story will make it or not, developing their nose for news in the process. But occasionally something happens that divides the pack and raises questions about the dominant news values of the day.

One such event took place last month when so many of the UK national newspapers decided to splash on the acquittal of Michael Duberry in the ill-fated Leeds United trial at Hull Crown Court. With the exception of the *Daily Telegraph*, our nationals relegated to below-the-fold or inside pages the story of Perry Wacker being found guilty of manslaughter for the deaths of 58 Chinese immigrants who suffocated in the back of his lorry.

What sort of news values would rate the verdict on a footballer charged with conspiring to pervert the course of justice – or the latest twist in the Sophiegate saga – as more important than one of the biggest mass killings in British history? This is an intriguing question which, as part of a wider debate about what news is, requires news values to be made visible and subjected to a critical gaze.

If newsworthiness is naturally a concern of journalists, new values are also an area of scrutiny for the growing band of researchers who study the media in general and journalism in particular. It was only when, after 20 years as a journalist, I set foot inside the world of academia to help train the next generation that I realised the extent to which so many academics had been tolling away in libraries trying to understand our craft.

The names Galtung and Ruge meant nothing to me at first, but I quickly discovered that this pair of Norwegian academics had come up with the 'classic' list of news values, published in the early Sixties. They identified 12 factors as being particularly important in the selection of news: frequency; threshold; unambiguity; meaningfulness; consonance; unexpectedness; continuity; composition; reference to elite nations; reference to elite people; reference to persons; reference to something negative.

Their names were soon as familiar to me as Posh and Becks because, in the academic equivalent of the cuttings job, their study was regurgitated – usually uncritically – in book after book, even though it was almost 40 years old, had been conducted in Norway, and had focused on foreign news. Dissatisfied, my colleague Deirdre O'Neill and I decided to put them to the test, and the results are published this month in the journal *Journalism Studies*.

We attempted to identify Galtung and Ruge's 12 news values in more than a thousand page-lead news stories published over a month in three major newspapers (the *Sun*, the *Daily Mail* and the *Daily Telegraph*). The most commonly identified factor was 'unambiguity', which raised more questions than answers. As journalists are trained to write news stories in an unambiguous way, is the unambiguity of any particular story inherent in the event itself or merely in the journalist's treatment of it. 'Reference to elite people' ranked just behind unambiguity at the top of the table, but as the elite people in question ranged from pop stars to politicians or religious leaders, it proved a less than useful category.

Around a third of the stories contained 'reference to something negative', but this was also problematic because a piece of ostensibly bad news might be good news for someone else.

At the same time as chipping away at the tablet of stone containing such news values, we began to notice stories that did not seem to fit any of the categories. Giving the lie to the old chestnut about the only good news being bad news, we found a large number of 'good news' stories featuring prize winners, miracle cures and unlikely rescues – not to mention the large number of 'lucky' pets who seem to fall off cliffs or tall buildings only to emerge unscathed in time for a smiling photograph and a punning headline.

Probably the most significant gap in Galtung and Ruge's list of news values is the concept of entertainment. A large and increasing proportion of news stories deal with entertainment in its broadest sense – either with the entertainment industry's ever-changing roll call of celebs or with stories and pictures apparently designed to entertain rather than inform readers. We noted: 'Certain combinations of news values appear almost to guarantee coverage in the press. For example, a story with a good picture or picture opportunity combined with any reference to an A-list celebrity, royalty, sex, TV or a cuddly animal appears to make a heady brew that news editors find almost impossible to resist.'

Based on our findings, we concluded that, although there will be exceptions, news stories must generally satisfy one or more of the following requirements to be selected for publication in the UK national press:

1 **The power elite:** stories concerning powerful individuals, organisations or institutions.
2 **Celebrity:** stories concerning people who are already famous.
3 **Entertainment:** stories concerning sex, showbusiness, human interest, animals, an unfolding drama, or offering opportunities for humorous treatment, entertaining photographs or witty headlines.
4 **Surprise:** stories that have an element of surprise and/or contrast.
5 **Bad news:** stories with particularly negative overtones, such as conflict or tragedy.
6 **Good news:** stories with particularly positive overtones, such as rescues and cures.
7 **Magnitude:** stories that are perceived as sufficiently significant either in the numbers of people involved or in potential impact.
8 **Relevance:** stories about issues, groups and nations perceived to be relevant to the audience.
9 **Follow-ups:** stories about subjects already in the news.
10 **Newspaper agenda:** stories which set or fit the news organisation's own agenda.

Taking such factors into consideration, it becomes easier to see why the Michael Duberry case won hands down over the Chinese immigrants when it came to front-page coverage. While the latter had the tragedy, magnitude and follow-up factors going for it, the footballer had celebrity and greater 'relevance' to readers, plus the drama of his courtroom evidence and photographs of him emerging victorious from the court.

Of course, these news values are based on an analysis of what actually appears in our papers. Whether they are the news values we should aspire to is, as they say, another story.

T. Harcup, 'What Is News? Galtung and Ruge Revisited', UK *Press Gazette*, 4 May 2001

MEDIA INSTITUTIONS

Tony Harcup's article attempts to update Galtung and Ruge's influential list of news values in the light of the increasing entertainment role that news, in both newspapers and on television, is increasingly taken on. This drive towards entertainment is partly due to the need of the commercial television stations like Channel 3, Channel 4 and Channel 5 to sell airtime to advertisers during the commercial breaks before, after and during news bulletins. The price of this airtime will partly depend upon the demographic of the viewing audience but will also be influenced by how many viewers are watching. These channels might not want to run the risk of jeopardising their ratings by broadcasting news that could be considered too serious, 'hard' or gloomy. The BBC seeks high ratings for its news bulletins partly as a justification for its licence fee and to show that it is adhering to its public service remit and is managing to combine information and entertainment.

FURTHER READING

Cottle, S. (1999) 'Ethnic Minorities and the British News Media: Explaining (Mis)Representation' in J. Stokes and A. Reading, (eds), *The Media in Britain: Current Debates and Developments*, Macmillan.
An examination of the way racism affects media representations of ethnic groups. This article also contains some interesting analyses of journalistic training and practices, news values and news genres.

Glasgow University Media Group (1985) *War and Peace News*, Routledge.
One in a range of studies of the ideology underpinning of the way in which 'balanced' television news is presented.

Hartley, J. (1982) *Understanding News*, Routledge.
A good basic introduction to the key issues surrounding both newspaper and television news production and presentation, although the examples may appear a little dated.

ACTIVITIES

➤ Look at the news values listed in the Harcup article: are these news values relevant to you? If you could select what stories went into the television news bulletins, what kinds of stories would you select and why?

➤ Carry out an analysis of several news stories taken from a range of media and try to identify Harcup's categories. How effective is his list in terms of explaining why these stories have been selected and presented as 'news'?

➤ Using the work of Allan and Harcup plus some of your own examples, consider how important visual criteria are to television news values.

➤ Using a range of television news bulletins describe and account for the balance between news and entertainment.

▼ 5 PROFESSIONAL PRACTICE

The construction of media texts is influenced by a wide range of economic, political, social and cultural factors. This section focuses on how the ideology, ideas and values of the 'professional' media worker contribute to the production and dissemination of media texts. An air of respectability, integrity, or glamour is often conferred upon media workers as a result of their particular knowledge or skills.

According to Tunstall, 'professionalism'

> typically stresses presentation techniques, the ability to select, to balance, to give 'both sides' of a story; it implies autonomy – independence from either political or commercial direction – with the communicator depending upon his [*sic*] 'professional' judgement to make decisions. Claims for 'professional' status in any occupation involve both technical and ideological elements. As compared with, say, doctors of medicine, the technical skills of professional communicators are uncertain and unstandardized; the ideological element is especially salient, then, in the communicator's 'professional' claim – although this ideology is expressed as value neutrality.
>
> (Tunstall 1977:214).

Tunstall maintains that there are particular 'professional' organisations or groups of people that will only admit new entrants once they have 'proved' their specialist skills or knowledge. Some examples of these are trade unions like Equity, the National Union of Journalists and the Directors' Guild of Great Britain. (For more information on these organisations, what they do, who belongs to them and how they might influence the media industry see the various websites: www.equity.org.uk, www.nuj.org.uk and www.dggb.co.uk). Often this sense of professionalism is used to justify particular working practices, the need for 'professional standards', and/or to exclude certain people.

ACTIVITY

➤ In the box below are some of the results of a survey of journalists. What do the results tell us about the type of people who become journalists? Does it matter that journalists seem to be recruited from such a small social demographic? If so, why? Why do you think it is mainly people from certain types of backgrounds that become journalists? What measures could be put in place to make it easier to recruit people from a wider social and racial background?

JOURNALISTS AT WORK

The results of an ambitious survey of journalists by the Journalism Training Forum have just been published in *Journalists At Work* [August 2002]. The forum is an advisory body funded by the two national training organisations, the Publishing National Training Organisation (newspapers, magazines, etc.) and Skillset (broadcasting).

The forum comprised editors, union leaders, accredited training bodies, publishers and broadcasters.

The survey has some interesting facts:

- There are roughly 70,000 journalists, and there will be a further 20,000 by 2010
- Over half of journalists work in London or the South East
- Journalists are mostly white (96 per cent)
- Salaries vary hugely and the average is £22,500. One in ten journalists earns less than £12,500 a year and women's pay lags behind men's by £5,000 a year
- Journalists are almost exclusively children of middle-class, professional homes. Only 3 per cent of new entrants have parents with semi-skilled or unskilled jobs.

'Journalist at Work', Campaign for Press and Broadcasting
Freedom (CPBF) website: www.cpbf.org.uk

THE LAST BASTION: HOW WOMEN BECOME MUSIC PRESENTERS IN UK RADIO

BBC Radio 1 presenters like Sara Cox and Jo Whiley have high national media profiles. On most commercial radio stations however, it is difficult to find more than one female music radio presenter, let alone one with a high profile. More often than not, the female commercial radio DJ is relegated to a weekend slot or to being the sidekick for a male anchor.

This chapter reports on the first stage of research across the UK radio industry (commercial and community sectors) which surveyed employment patterns and practices relating to female presenters and radio. Our research takes a snapshot of employment of female presenters in the UK; it looks at how women working as presenters are resisting the 'flexible sexism' identified by Gill (1993) and how radio managers are responding to the problem of recruiting women into presentation.

Researching DJs

When Annie Nightingale first applied to the BBC national youth station Radio 1 in 1967, she was told that they did not intend to take on female presenters because the male DJs functioned as 'husband substitutes' to the identified female listeners. From this idea, both BBC and commercial radio DJs built up a culture where it seemed the art of presentation was to flirt with the female listener who was characterised as 'Doreen' the housewife. Women seemed to be invisible as 'makers' of music radio until the 1980s. This is partly explained by the background roles that they performed 'off air', particularly as producers – including producing male DJs. This job is far from a secondary role (some would argue it is the key to good radio production), however it was not the *audible* role that listeners could identify with, and thus it could not act as a role model for women entering the profession. Until the early 1990s, women were almost completely absent from presentation roles in UK music radio, which meant that a symbolic and actual absence of female identity developed on the airwaves. [. . .]

In Ireland there was a similar story. Some female DJs presented a show jointly with a man – often as an assisting 'sidekick' rather than an equal, or presented a programme outside peak listening times. There was a similar pattern in pirate radio. The only station where there was 'gender parity' was the Irish language station 'Raidio na Life' (a community station) where women presented all types of music shows and at all times . More recent research [1997] in the commercial and community radio sectors in Ireland commissioned by Women On Air reflects a general trend: within programme making, men 'overwhelmingly' dominate in presentation or DJ work and technical areas, while women work mainly in research.

What are the reasons that help to explain this gender imbalance? Gill's survey of attitudes of commercial radio programme controllers (PCs) has gone some way to exploring the reasons for this inequality (Gill 1993). She used critical discourse analysis of their many explanations of the inequality to look at the ideological framework in which they interpreted the reasons for a lack of female DJs. She highlighted six different accounts of what she termed 'flexible sexism':

- Women do not apply to become DJs
- Women interested in broadcasting become journalists rather than presenters
- Audience objections: Listeners prefer male presenters
- Women's voices are not suited to radio presentation
- Women lack the skills necessary for radio presentation
- Male DJs are necessary to serve the predominantly female ('housewife') audience

(Gill 1993: 77–89)

She concluded that PCs use these methods to avoid responsibility for the lack of female DJs and at the same time to deflect accusations of sexism (Gill 1993: 90).

How women became music radio presenters in the 1990s

In order to start answering the question of why there were so few women radio presenters, we wanted to map out where and how women were employed as presenters in the BBC and commercial radio. (Although the research mainly focuses on the commercial and community sectors the BBC was surveyed to give a comparison as well as a whole view of the industry.) We surveyed station web pages to find out the number of women presenters and where they existed in the schedules. Although this method has its downfalls (occasionally programme names hide the gender of the presenter, or web pages are out of date) it is an effective way of collecting recent data. We also interviewed female radio presenters from the commercial and community sectors. The interviews were informal, carried out over the telephone or in radio stations using a structured pattern based on Gill's (1993) analysis of six accounts given by male programme controllers for the lack of women radio presenters (see above). Finally we sent a questionnaire to a small sample of community and commercial radio station managers particularly focusing on employment and recruitment methods.

A snapshot of the industry

We surveyed 225 web sites for BBC and commercial national local and regional radio stations. Stations employed between 1 and 23 presenters, with an average of 9 presenters per station. The sample comprised 98 per cent of all BBC stations – 40 stations in all (405 presenters) and 78 per cent of commercial radio stations – 185 stations in all (1583 presenters). We found:

- 26 per cent of BBC presenters are women
- 7.5 per cent of BBC stations have no female presenters
- 11.6 per cent of commercial presenters are women
- 38 per cent of commercial stations have no female presenters.

If one combines the BBC and commercial sectors to get a picture of mainstream UK radio, 14.6 per cent of presenters are female and 32 per cent of stations have no female presenters at all. Commercial stations aiming at the over 40s were particularly poor and stations promoting particular genres of music (for instance dance or gold) employed mainly men.

We made an attempt to break down which time slots and roles women are undertaking. Of the 11.6 per cent female presenters in commercial radio:

- 60 per cent are co-presenters
- 22 per cent are weekenders/specialist music presenters
- 18 per cent are solo/self-driving.

The majority of women were working as co-presenters on breakfast. Within this there seems to be a continuum ranging from genuine co-presenters sharing the work of the programme, through to 'sidekicks' reading weather and traffic, to an individual or posse member represented by a 'giggle' or comment, 'off mic.' at the back of the studio.

Of the 26 per cent of female presenters within the BBC:

- 23 per cent are co-presenters
- 33 per cent are weekend/specialist music presenters
- 44 per cent are solo/self-driving.

BBC local stations, which over the past decade have favoured news-based programming, have a better representation of female presenters compared with commercial or BBC national stations. In BBC Radio 1 where presenters have a high media profile, under a quarter of their presentation staff are women.

Our interview-based research used Gill's six categories of explanation as a thematic and methodological base to supplement information provided by the web sites.

'Women do not apply to become DJs'

In our questionnaire 66 per cent of managers said that they would like to employ women presenters but claimed they could not find them, again repeating claims made by Gill's research subjects in 1993. However, one interview respondent had moved on from blaming women themselves to looking at possible solutions:

> Recruitment is our industry's biggest problem . . . there are not enough female presenters . . . there are no proper formal routes to get into presentation and this needs addressing.
>
> (Female managing director, commercial radio)

> I have encountered negative discrimination from the ridiculous grey suit brigade . . . one said . . . 'you women all you do is have babies . . . I wouldn't employ any woman between the ages of 23 and 30'.
>
> (Female managing director, commercial radio)

It is likely that both of the above problems remain in the radio industry today. We were also interested in what routes into music presentation there are and how women use them.

The survey showed that in commercial radio most presenters were recruited through the informal contacts of programme controllers, within and outside their station or group of companies. This is supported in stations by the culture of volunteers working for free and hanging out at stations and then stepping in when a presenter is ill or on holiday. One woman we interviewed had left a further education course in Media Studies in order to 'hang around' a local station and gain the necessary experience. She made the tea and taught herself various jobs in an order to become 'invaluable' and felt that this was a better way 'in' than through training. She says:

> I've had more experience in however many years of radio than most people get in a lifetime, and so by saying no to the diploma . . . And actually going in and getting the practical experience, I'm more well versed in the ways that the media actually works and therefore more valuable to prospective employers.
>
> (Local commercial station, weekend presenter)

We found that community stations use a wide range of methods to positively attract women into presenting. Fem FM used local and national publicity to encourage women to put themselves forward. They ran workshops on how to put together demonstration tapes, and held a competition in conjunction with local commercial station group GWR. A North East community radio project, 107 The Bridge, trained a group of 30 women in radio techniques and put them to air for a week during International Women's Week. This gave them both training and experience in radio which could be carried forward into the industry.

'Women who want to be broadcasters become journalists not DJs'

The myth that women do not want to, or are just not able to, become presenters has long been perpetuated by programme controllers. All the women we interviewed were conscious of a lack of role models as they were growing up, and acknowledged the importance of women in radio becoming role models and mentors:

> I just thought women can't be DJs. It wasn't until I went to a party and there was a female DJ doing the disco – and she was good – that I realised that women could do it. I thought only men could – 'cos of their egos and their willingness to perform.
>
> (Community radio presenter)

> Just because you're little or whatever and particularly because you're female as well, they think there's some really silly reason why you want to do it.

Someone said – 'Did you have a troubled childhood?' to me! . . . and 'What makes you so aggressive that makes you want to present rock music?' It's really because so many people didn't agree to women doing it that sparked me off.

(Community radio presenter)

The 'DJ' job is often perceived as relating to 'club culture' and might shed a negative light on the role of the radio presenter (also known as a DJ) compared to the status of, say, a journalist's role in the radio industry. One interviewee from a regional commercial station highlighted how employed positions such as radio reporters provided more stable prospects for women who had family commitments and needed a regular wage.

'Audience objections – listeners prefer male presenters'

The way audience research is carried out might account for the supposed audience objections to female presenters. The sexualisation of the DJ's relationship with the female listener – constructing himself as replacing the absent husband in the women's life – extends to fantasising about a relationship with the female listener. Gill shows how this shift is understood by a commercial DJ she interviewed:

I think mid morning radio has always been considered 'housewife radio'. It isn't to the same extent now. Actually in some parts of the morning you have more men listening than women. But I think you still go for a female audience. I mean you flirt with them – that's exactly what you do for three hours. But what you've not got to do, is do it to the extent that it annoys the men listening.

(Gill 1993: 333)

Most of our female DJ interviewees said that they had been told that research showed that listeners, male and female, wanted to hear male voices: this was a perceived 'truth', based on research carried out by an unknown source. A community radio presenter talking about listening to women's voices said: 'women *like* to listen to women – look at how much we like the daytime chat shows hosted by women . . .' (her emphasis). One respondent had encountered identical attitudes that Gill (1993) identified:

He basically said it's proven, research has shown that people don't like to listen to women's voices on radio because they are high pitched and scatty and this that and the other . . . I just thought, you haven't got a clue pal. There are as many women who like to . . . listen to women's voices as they do like to listen to men's voices. It's not just a sex/girl thing, they like to relate as well,

but also on the other hand . . . women like to hear men's voices because of the sex appeal thing. I'm sure men like to hear women's voices. I would hope so.

(Community radio presenter)

One late night regional radio presenter said that she had worked in the industry for more than ten years and had only recently heard that 'audiences preferred male presenters'. She questioned the idea and wondered how old the research was.

Could it be that the lack of serious female presenters, those in other than 'giggling girl' slots, is preventing female listeners from taking women DJs seriously? This is answered by another interviewee: 'Women should like listening to women but they don't because there aren't the "right" women' (London commercial station, weekend DJ).

This argument is countered by managers who look to both cater for neglected audiences and to bring in new listeners. BBC Radio 1 Programme Controller Andy Parfitt brought in children's television presenter Zoë Ball as a 'sidekick' for a male presenter and ended up using her to front the BBC Radio 1 Breakfast show. She was brought in with the intention to: 'coax more young female listeners as part of a "girlification" strategy to redress the balance after the Steve Wright and Mike Read years' (O'Rorke 1999: 2).

The programme's share of listeners has risen since Ball's appointment. A victory for Parfitt and Ball and a useful point to those who doubt the audience pull of female broadcasters. It is interesting then that a large number of commercial stations use a female at breakfast only as a 'token' figure co-presenter, representing the female 'voice' and only a few 'solo' presenters are on the smaller local stations. As one presenter said:

Once there are a few more women presenting radio, the audience will not even notice whether they are listening to a male or a female, and then maybe we will have more than one woman per day shift, which in turn will encourage more women to enter to the industry because there are more interesting jobs to be had.

(Community radio presenter)

Cramer argues that a critical mass of women on air will lead to a change in on air representation. She cites two women who worked in US radio in 1992:

There are just too many women in radio for women's voices to be an issue any more . . . There are no problems any more with women's voices being too high. There are standards for both men and women.

(Cramer 1993: 165)

'Women's voices are not suited to radio presentation'

Gill's interviewees said that they believed the audience did not want to listen to a woman's voice, and yet our questionnaire found that a 'good voice' with 'warmth' were the most important features. Women's voices are often said to be too high pitched and yet only a sixth in our survey said this mattered. Other features of a good presentation voice were cited as clarity and tone. A large number said that 'personality' and 'suitability to the station style' were important. The latter is problematic because if a station style is based on what is generally heard, and what is heard has usually been a male presenter, then the station's style is based on a premise which excludes women.

Historically, women have trained their voices to fit in with a style needed for particular genres (e.g. lower pitch for presentation). What is worth discussion is women's ability to be adaptable. They do this by altering and training their voices to be more like their male counterparts' or bubbly 'ladettes' to get onto breakfast shows or developing their 'sexy' voices to get late night slots. The latter is usually in response to the programme controller wanting a sexy late night female voice because it's perceived that more men listen at night.

One female presenter said when asked what was the most important thing for a presenter to have: 'I think rather sadly in terms of the industry it's probably voice . . . most women who have made it are there because they have a really horny voice' (London commercial station, weekend presenter).

One regional commercial radio presenter said that she had never heard of any problems with the female voice. She said that it is a variety of voices that make listening interesting and that the idea that radio voices need to be deep and authoritative went out decades ago. However we may conclude that women's voices are being accepted only if they are adaptable. How much this is in a limited/gendered range of options ('sexy', 'horny', 'ladette', 'sidekick') needs more research.

'Women do not have the necessary skills for radio'

Women's level of production skills and their technical ability have long been thought to exclude them from radio work. Interestingly the BBC has traditionally had a reasonable number of women working as technical operators because they are trained from scratch through their studio manager's scheme. However women who enter as a DJ often have to learn desk operations 'on the job' and this may be more daunting. Computer and IT skills are deemed particularly important in contemporary radio where digital production is the norm. Most male and female solo presenters in our survey could 'drive' a desk and do digital editing. However most female co-presenters who do travel and weather work did not have these skills nor were required to learn them.

When we asked how skills were gained, three interviewees felt that being taught by men was a barrier to women learning radio technology: 'I think the only problem for women on the technical side is men telling them there is a problem' (community radio leader). One breakfast show presenter felt that any mistakes she made were judged as being because she is a woman and not because she is a human being:

> You can't get away from the fact that if you're a woman in radio, you're gonna get propositioned a lot . . . you're going to get people saying that your mistakes are because you're a woman but at the end of the day, that doesn't make you who you are.
>
> (Local commercial station, breakfast show presenter)

Another said the reason why there are so few women DJs in radio is because:

> I still think there are few [women] to choose from because some are put off by the technical stuff . . . Because they're being taught by men and they think 'this bloke's gonna think I'm really crap if I don't learn this straight away', if they were taught by women, they would quickly learn the technical stuff and make it a career instead of a hobby.
>
> (London commercial station presenter)

The community radio sector has been addressing this training issue for some time and there is evidence of women-only and women-taught courses in several stations.

Discussion and conclusions

Female newsreaders are now accepted as normal rather than the exception in all sectors of UK radio. Our research shows that women are now making inroads into music presentation in a number of different ways and some managers are beginning to address the issue of a lack of female presenters without blaming women themselves. The presence of more female presenters in a high-profile station like BBC Radio 1 may mean that an increase in role models should contribute to changes in representation on UK radio as a whole.

There is still a dearth of women in music presentation, particularly in commercial radio. Some commercial radio stations, even whole groups, have long stretches of their schedules (sometimes the whole 24 hours) with no female presenters at all. In the last ten years there has been a significant shift, however, in the perception within and outside the industry towards women entering it. Because of the high media profile of national presenters like Zoë Ball and Jo Whiley, the public perception of women as presenters is positive. Women are gaining skills and confidence through courses and by volunteering at commercial and community radio stations.

In our questionnaire two-thirds of PCs said that they would like to employ women presenters but claimed they could not find them. Some radio managers have moved from the position of 'Women don't apply' to 'How can we get more women to apply?' Some of the myths about women's voices being 'wrong' for radio and disliked by audiences are fading and women are adapting their voices to suit different time slots and station styles. Radio managers are becoming more interested in how they can attract new sectors of male and female listeners – witness Andy Parfitt's call for the 'girlification' of BBC Radio 1.

Women themselves are using a range of strategies to get on air. Some of these – like 'hanging out' at stations until a shift becomes available, getting as many practical skills and voluntary experience as possible – involve appropriating tried and tested methods of entering the industry up to now mainly used by men. In addition they are entering the on air space in new roles – in particular the role of breakfast 'sidekick'. Arguably this is an inferior role in relation to the male 'anchor', however it could be interpreted as being used to gain experience and 'visibility' on the most high-profile timeslot in any radio station. It can also be used to negotiate further skills training, for instance in how to drive the desk.

In the new millennium we have to ask whether female listeners constructed as housewives and/or pseudo sexual relationship objects, is still a hegemonic force in radio and whether new stereotypes (for instance the husky late night female voice chatting up men in the small hours) are emerging. The political economy of radio advertising related to female audiences, and a study of the symbolic level of representation in this area and new ways of defining audiences as part of audience research needs further study. The case of the short lived Viva! radio, and other stations that target female listeners, could shed light on some of these areas.

The combination of factors influencing managers and presenters explored through Gill's categories (1993) shows that 'flexible sexism' is multi-layered. The women we spoke to felt that competition for potential presenter jobs was made more difficult by there being only a possible number of shifts available for women:

> There is a feeling that there is only one on-air shift for a female going and that's wrong . . . at the moment they're either the late night show or the bimbo co-presenter on breakfast.
>
> (London commercial station presenter).

Could this added competition put off potential women presenters? Those who feel that maybe they do not fit into either category of 'bubbly girlie' or 'sexy late

night siren'? Could it also be that women who try for other shifts (in traditionally male areas) and who fail decide to move to other professions instead of compromising themselves? One woman had been offered a position as part of a 'posse' in a commercial station but had turned it down because she wanted her own show:

> It's just the nature of the company . . . I don't think it's because they didn't think I was good enough, they just don't put women in their own shows.

> (Potential London commercial station presenter)

Clearly women are offered a limited number of role models on air. Personal accounts and research suggest it is difficult for women to enter the profession and that a contributing factor could be a patriarchal institutional culture (and contributing individual attitudes) in the workplace. This is reflected in national/celebrity representations of female DJs, for instance Chris Evans talking about Jo Whiley 'The DJ most likely to give you the horn'.

What needs further exploration is the gendered nature of DJ/presenter culture, particularly how it is experienced within radio stations. It could be said that working in a male dominated environment could be difficult for all but the strongest of women. One woman from a London station talked about how you need 'personal character to survive'. She said that a belief in oneself was essential in order to overcome any gender 'knocking' that might take place within the workplace. Another local radio presenter said:

> I would say that the women I've met in radio are more confident than the men . . . They're not arrogant . . . there are some men who perhaps let their egos drive them, they say 'wow, I'm on the radio, I've made it' and I don't think you get the same thing from women.

> (Local commercial station, breakfast presenter)

So what does it take to work in radio presentation? Does it take a large amount of ego or assertiveness to work in the industry and how much room is there for acknowledging vulnerability? A community radio respondent said: 'Women are always so keen to get involved but they're always so scared as well, you can feel they're wary about their level of capability'.

Zilliacus-Tikkanen (1997) found in her study of gender and news in Scandinavia, that the proportion of women in an organisation and whether the organisational culture is flexible or rigid are important factors. A higher proportion of women and flexibility makes it easier for women to work in news organisations and promote a gender oriented journalistic culture.

So as we enter the new millennium and the world of digital and Internet radio, which will undoubtedly alter the face of what we now call radio, will institutional and cultural ideas about a woman's role in music radio alter? How do we continue to improve the numbers of women working as DJs in music radio? Can women get equal air-time, with equal shifts and access to both male and female audiences? How can female radio presenters define (and redefine) their roles?

K. Michaels and C. Mitchell, 'The Last Bastion: How Women Become Music Presenters in UK Radio', in C. Mitchell (ed.), *Women and Radio*, Routledge, 2000, pp. 238–48

The article by Kim Michaels and Caroline Mitchell looks at how difficult it has been for women to become radio presenters, especially in commercial pop-music radio. Based on research carried out among a variety of radio stations they conclude that, despite the high profiles of people like Zoë Ball and Sara Cox, this situation is partly due to the lack of positive role models for women DJs.

This is a difficult cycle to break: in order for more women to become radio DJs or presenters, there need to be more women on the airwaves as role models, in order to make a career in radio seem attainable for would-be female DJs. The continuing prevalence of the men on the radio protects aspiring and working male presenters and implicitly excludes women. As Michaels and Mitchell point out, this situation has often been justified by radio programme controllers or station managers in their claims that 'women don't apply to become DJs', or 'women do not have the skills necessary for radio presentation', or 'women's voices are not suited to radio presentation'. Michaels and Mitchell use the term 'flexible sexism' to describe the way in which the exclusion of women is justified.

ACTIVITY

➤ Read the article and then carry out a survey of the radio stations in your area and see to what extent your findings confirm or challenge Michaels and Mitchell's research. To what extent have things changed (for the better or worse?) since they wrote this article in 2000?

Recently, substantial changes in print, but in particular in television journalism, show that the gender of journalists is relatively unimportant for the way the news looks. What I will argue is that news and journalism at present, with its increase of 'human interest' topics and angles, is becoming more and more 'feminine'

CONTINUED

despite the ongoing minority position of women in journalism. I will also argue that it is exactly those changes that may open up journalism as a profession for women. Thus I will turn around the debate some 180 degrees: I will not discuss the question of whether an increase in the number of female journalists will change the news, but will instead show how changes in the news genre allow for more female journalists to enter the profession.

'FEMININE' VALUES IN JOURNALISM

Of course we cannot objectively define what is meant by male and 'the masculine.' Nevertheless, we can have a look at how journalists themselves perceive the gender of their profession, taking into account that some elements of journalism are not specifically gendered, like deadlines, space or broadcast hours. Survey and interview data from various Western countries suggest that it is in the definition of newsworthiness, particular angles and styles, professional norms and values that the masculine nature of journalism expresses itself . . . Female journalists often criticize the selection of newsworthy topics, claiming that topics that are relevant to women are often neglected in the press or relegated to marginal sections. The examples often mentioned are 'human interest' news, consumer news, culture, education and upbringing, and social policy. A Dutch female journalist, for instance, said: 'My colleagues and I used to fantasize about an alternative little paper that would appear besides the real one and which would only contain news we would really want to read: Funny events, unusual people that have interesting stories to tell, the ones you find in every little village; readers love that. Nobody is interested in this excess of political facts . . . The fetishization of facts and factuality is indeed another common concern of female journalists who would appreciate more emphasis on causes and impacts, instead of another accumulation of new facts. In addition, many of them despise the search for scoops and sensationalism which may take on very blatant forms, as in crime reporting, but which can also express itself in the horse-race character of political reporting.

The masculine character of the news is also recognized in the choice of sources and spokespersons who are overwhelmingly male, despite the growing numbers of female politicians, public officials and other professionals. The choice of sources and spokespersons is seen as reflecting the personal networks of male journalists rather than being a representation of actual gender divisions among sources. Again, the expressions of journalists as 'boys' comes up when female journalists observe the existence of what they call 'old boys' networks'. Another element of masculinity in the news lies in male worldviews which underlie the actual reporting. Many female journalists mentioned the issue of unemployment as an example in which they would also focus on the impact of unemployment on family life, whereas their male colleagues supposedly would look at general employment patterns and the immediate victims only. Another interesting case to consider here is the reporting on senior citizens. In most countries they are primarily women; nevertheless reporting usually focuses on the older man, questioning whether he can still be an active citizen, for instance. Finally, many female journalists claim that they hold a set of ethical values different to that of their male colleagues. Female journalists feel they show more respect to their readers and their readers' needs than do their male colleagues. They also scorn the detachment and insensitivity in many of their male colleagues, believing they are hiding behind the idea of objectivity to exclude all compassion and humanity that one should bring to journalism.

The gendered nature of journalism then – as many female journalists throughout the world perceive it – can be summarized as follows:

	Masculine	Feminine
Topics	politics	'human interest'
	crime	consumer news
	finance	culture
	education and upbringing	social policy
Angle	facts	backgrounds and effects
	sensation	compassion
	male	general
Sources	men	women
Ethics	detached	audience needs

Although male journalists interviewed in the research projects mentioned are less outspoken about the gendered nature of journalism, and certainly not critical of it, many of them also feel that female journalists do have another approach to news. This is demonstrated, of course, because part of these feelings are expressed in stereotypical views on what female journalists should do: cover fashion, babies and cooking, and in stereotypical views on what they cannot do: write tough stories on rising crime. Male journalists also assume that women are better at and more interested in 'human interest' stories, or in caring about audience needs.

Research results reveal what female and male journalists think and feel about their own professional values and conduct, what they think they do or would like to be doing. Whereas it may also seem that the data tell something about differences between women and men in journalism, they actually tell something about self-perceptions and self-images, which interestingly enough border on the stereotypical. Information on self-images, however, does not tell much about actual professional conduct. In fact, research on professional practices has found very little evidence of women performing differently from men in journalism, with

the exception of women looking for female spokespersons. In addition, large-scale surveys found only one – albeit quite a revealing one – significant difference in role conceptions: women are indeed more oriented to audience needs than men.

Yet, when the perception of female and male journalists regarding their profession is so profoundly gendered, what does that mean for working conditions and professional performance? Obviously, it may and does result in discriminatory attitudes toward women. While 'femininity' and what is considered professional journalism are not inherently at odds with each other, the current definitions of femininity and the historically specific requirements of journalism produce tensions which – while expressed in different forms – are felt by many female journalists. Women, for instance, often get very stereotypical assignments which relegate them to marginal areas of journalism. They also have to live up to a double requirement: they have to show in their daily performance that they are good journalists as well as 'real' women. In the Netherlands, many female journalists feel that they are primarily judged as women; they are subject to ongoing comments on their looks and they have to regularly confront friendly heterosexual invitations or unfriendly sexual harassment. Playing the game of heterosexual romance means that women will lose their prestige as professional journalists. But women who ignore it – or worse, criticize it – will not be accepted by their male colleagues as real women; instead they are seen as bitches, viragos or – the worst – 'feminists'. From a country as vastly different as Senegal similar tensions between what is considered appropriate for women and professional journalism have been reported: Senegalese female journalists are accused by their colleagues and their environment of having lost their femininity because their jobs require them to be away from home and 'neglect' their husband and children.

Given such very strong social prescriptions and restrictions on femininity, and by omission on masculinity, the almost stereotypical self-perceptions of female and male journalists make more sense. Apart from reflecting their ideas about journalism, female views may also be seen as efforts to show that despite their professionalism they are still very much 'true' women. This does produce a very awkward situation, of course, because the other way around, they also have to prove that despite their femininity they are good professional journalists. Since masculinity as it is currently defined in Western societies accords so much better with journalism's values, men's professional identities are much less fragmented and problematic than those of women in journalism. This, then, is the predicament in which female journalists have found themselves. It is the result of the minority position of women and the particular professional values of journalism. There are, however, a number of structural developments in journalism that suggest that the situation may change in the decades to come.

MARKET-DRIVEN JOURNALISM

To begin with, the number of women in journalism is steadily rising: according to a recent [1995] UNESCO report on employment patterns in the media, women now make up the majority of journalism students, especially in Europe and the Americas. In my own department of Communication Studies in Amsterdam, some 65 percent of the students are female; in the Netherlands as a whole this figure is 50 percent. In Norway, 55 percent of journalism and communication students are women, in the UK this figure is about 52 percent and in the USA it is 49 percent, to mention some arbitrary examples. This does not mean of course that these female students all end up in news journalism. Almost to the contrary, it seems there are still many barriers between having graduated from journalism school and becoming a news journalist. Recent European figures on the employment of women in television and print news confirm this.

	Press reporter/editor	TV journalist
Netherlands	26%	20%
Sweden	*	44%
Finland	*	44%
Denmark	24%	29%
UK	23%	25%
USA	34%	25%

Source: Gallagher 1995.
Note: * indicates figures not available

L. van Zoonen, 'One of the Girls? The Changing Gender of Journalism', in C. Carter, G. Branston and S. Allen (eds), *News, Gender and Power*, Routledge, 2000, pp. 35–8

The second extract is from an article entitled 'One of the Girls? The Changing Gender of Journalism' by Liesbet van Zoonen. The extract considers the way in which news is 'gendered' in terms of soft and hard news. Van Zoonen argues that there is an increasing 'feminisation' of news, resulting in the growth of human interest stories, consumer news and social policy at the expense of more traditional 'hard' news that deals with typically 'masculine' domains of crime, politics or finance. Van Zoonen suggests that the 'male character' of news is implied by mainly quoting men as sources for news stories, as spokespeople, or as presenters. Van Zoonen argues that this gendering of news means women journalists often get 'very stereotypical assignments which relegate them to marginal areas of journalism'. The extract concludes with Van Zoonen highlighting the tension that women journalists often face in having to 'be like men' in terms of carrying out their professional roles but are also required to meet certain (male) expectations of women's interests, talents and behaviour.

➤ What does van Zoonen mean by the 'fetishization of facts and factuality'? Try to find some examples of this in your newspapers.

➤ Carry out research amongst the journalists on your local newspaper(s). How many of the journalists are male and how many are female? Are different journalists responsible for different types of stories? If so, is there any evidence, as Van Zoonen suggests, that female reporters are expected to deal with a particular set of 'feminine' news stories? How easy or difficult is it to access this kind of information? Are newspaper editors open about the way in which journalists are allocated responsibility for different types of stories? You could also look through various editions of newspapers checking the by-lines on stories to see what types of stories have by-lines from male journalists and what type of stories have by-lines from female journalists.

➤ Carry out a small contents analysis exercise to test the accuracy of Van Zoonen's suggestion that the majority of spokespersons and/or sources quoted are male. What explanation does Van Zoonen offer for this?

The third article, by Tim O'Sullivan, Brian Dutton and Philip Rayner, offers a different view of professionalism by exposing the way in which Kelvin MacKenzie, when editor of the *Sun* newspaper, instilled a certain set of male attitudes and behaviour as 'normal' amongst his staff. The article points out that unless MacKenzie's fellow male workers acted in the way he wanted, they were excluded and as a consequence lost status within the organisation and may have found it difficult to progress in their careers there.

PROFESSIONAL AUTONOMY

Although ownership of media companies makes possible power over production from the point of view of allocating resources (capital investment, budgets, etc.), the day-to-day management of media organisations in the operational sense lies with media professionals. Of course, in small-scale enterprises the owners and controllers of production may well be the same people, but most organisations require a division of labour based on specialised areas of skill and technical expertise.

Such skills and expertise are often elevated to an occupational ideal, making it possible to lay claim to professionalism. Most media organisations require new recruits to undertake considerable in-house training on top of any formal qualifications already obtained. The ethos of the organisation – what it stands for and how it goes about things, together with the 'house style' of production – are central to the process of occupational socialisation. The ensuing collective thinking and practice provide a degree of solidarity from which external threats (owners, the government, the public, etc.) can be resisted. This also has implications for the boundaries of creative freedom within media production. The 'correct' or conventional way of doing something becomes enshrined in professional practice until, and if, someone is bold or strong enough to break or question the 'rules'.

The freedom to deviate from the accepted codes and conventions will very much depend on a previous hierarchical position. In cinema and television, producers and directors exercise the greatest control over the content and style of films and programmes. Some film directors have been seen as *auteurs* or artistic authors, able to imbue their films with a personal vision or look: e.g. Orson Welles, Alfred Hitchcock and David Lynch. However, media production, not least film, is essentially a cooperative venture, necessitating considerable mutual assistance and interdependence.

In newspapers and magazines, editors are in the strongest position to influence the shape and direction of the publication. Some individual editors have made a recognisable impression on their newspaper or magazine's identity: the *Sun* under the editorship of Kelvin MacKenzie is one example:

> But it was in the afternoon, as the paper built up to its creative climax of going to press, that the real performance would begin. MacKenzie would burst through the door after lunch with his cry of 'Whaddya got for me?' and the heat would be on. He had total control – not just over the front page but over every page lead going right through the paper. Shrimsley was remembered as a fast and furious corrector of proofs, but MacKenzie was even faster, drawing up layouts, plucking headline after headline out of the air, and all the time driving towards the motto he hammered into them all: 'Shock and amaze on every page.' [. . .]
>
> True to the code of sarff London MacKenzie also wanted to be surrounded by 'made men', who had proved themselves by pulling off some outrageous stunt at the expense of the opposition. One way of becoming a made man was to phone the *Mirror* and ask for the 'stone' where the final versions of pages were assembled for the presses. The trick was to imitate another member of the *Mirror* staff to fool the stone sub into revealing the front-page splash. One features exec became a made man by walking across Fleet Street into the *Express* and stealing some crucial pictures from the library. Hacks refusing to get involved in this sort of behaviour were suspect – falling into the category of those who were not fully with him, and could therefore be presumed to be against him.

Chippendale and Horrie 1990
T. O'Sullivan, B. Dutton and P. Rayner (eds) 'Professional Autonomy' in *Studying the Media*, Arnold, 1998, pp. 168–9

> ➤ What is meant by 'made men'? Do you think that it is possible in MacKenzie's opinion to have 'made women'? To what extent do you think this behaviour excludes women journalists? Do you think this is exclusion is deliberate? How does this view of a newsroom fit with, or contradict van Zoonen's ideas?

FURTHER READING

Casey, B., Casey, N,. Calvert, B., French, L. and Lewis, J. (2002) 'Women in Television', *Television Studies. The Key Concepts*. Routledge.
An interesting entry on the dominance of (white) men in British and American television, speculating on some of the reasons for this apparent discrimination.

Cottle, S. (1999) 'Ethnic Minorities and the British News Media: Explaining (Mis)Representation' in J. Stokes and A. Reading (eds), *The Media in Britain: Current Debates and Developments*, MacMillan Press.
An analysis of how racism affects media representations of ethnic groups. This article also examines the dominance of white, male, middle-class attitudes in news practices, news values and news genres.

Tunstall, J. (1977) *The Media are American*, Constable.
Although a little dated now, the book outlines some of the earliest concerns about the domination of American media texts and practices in an increasingly global media world, and provides a good early introduction to the concept of media imperialism.

> ➤ Consider the comment below by an employer of media students. To what extent does this reinforce some of the stereotypical views that have been discussed above?

'What I'd love is a Media Studies graduate who not only has a knowledge of the business, but looks gorgeous, happens to have design ability as well, because of doing a mixed degree, and could take over presenting a DIY programme.'
(Media employer quoted in Media Employability Project)

▼ 6 PUBLIC SERVICE BROADCASTING (PSB)

The concept of public service broadcasting (PSB) has been central to the idea of broadcasting in Britain since its very earliest days. The concept developed by the BBC's first Director General, John Reith, has served as a model for both radio and television broadcasting in Britain, and in many other parts of the world. Central to the concept of public service broadcasting in Britain is the notion of the Government licensing not just broadcasters, but also listeners and viewers, through the television licence fee payable by everyone who owns a television set.

When radio broadcasting became a possibility after the First World War, the Government had to decide how it was to be organised, funded and regulated. There were several choices.

1   The first was to follow the American route where the market determined who should broadcast, what they broadcast (within reason), and who listened. In Britain this was not seen as a good route to go down for various reasons: the 'chaos of the airwaves' that was seen to be happening in America, a distrust of commercialism and a distrust of American culture.
2   The second route was through a State-controlled broadcasting service where the State (in effect the Government) owned and controlled what was broadcast, who by and to whom. However, this was not thought to be 'democratic'. There was already a tradition of a free press – the fourth estate – after the monarchy, the government and the Church. State control of the dissemination of information could too easily lead to abuse of broadcasting for propaganda purposes, and this would interfere with the public's ability to make informed decisions in the democratic process.
3   A third way was therefore introduced: a non-commercial organisation that was politically independent of the Government but allowed the State to control who broadcast, and if not the content, then at least had some control over the services that were to be made avalible to a public 'licensed' to listen.

PSB was developed as a means of bringing the nation together in the 1920s and 1930s. The country had just emerged from the First World War; there had been a Communist revolution in Russia; there were possibilities of other socialist or Communist revolutions in countries like Germany; there was the General Strike in Britain in 1926; and eventually the Great Depression of 1929 set in, resulting in high unemployment and low morale. All of these events were seen to threaten the social and political stability of the country. Brodcasting was seen as one of the means of buoying the nation up despite adverse economic conditions and international political instability. Broadcasting was also seen as a way of educating people and making them responsible citizens. When broadcasting began in Britain, women still did not have the vote; universal suffreage was only granted in 1928. Because of the upheavals of the First World War and the Communist/socialist revolutions elsewhere in the world, democracy was seen as fragile and dependent upon ordinary people taking their responsibilities as citizens seriously.

In the beginning (and some would argue it remains so today) the BBC was very much part of the Establishment, the elite group that ran the country politically, economically and socially. As James Curran and Jean Seaton argue in *Power without Responsibility* (1997), the BBC was a 'public service for a social purpose'.

Today, however, broadcasters are no longer seen to be addressing a single national audience, but rather a diverse range of audiences representing a range of ethnic, social and religious groups. Increasingly, broadcast audiences also have access to specialist multi-channel and digital radio and television services. Broadcasting is now much more commercially competitive and people are increasingly seen as consumers, rather than citizens – as people who are able, and willing, to pay for what they perceive as extra services.

According to Curran and Seaton, during the 1980s, 'public service' became unfashionable. Margaret Thatcher said famously that there is no such thing as society – only individuals. During the Conservative rule of the 1980s and early 1990s, many of those organisations in Britain that had been set up for a social purpose, to help and support society, such as the Welfare State, the trade unions and nationalised industries like the railways and the Post Office were either dismantled, sold off or closely scrutinised by politicians and economists.

It is against this background that Rupert Murdoch made the speech below at the Edinburgh television festival in 1989. The News International newspapers, the *Sun* and *The Times*, were very critical of the BBC and supported calls for it to be 'broken up'. There were suggestions that Rupert Murdoch might buy parts of the BBC, for example those that appeared to be most popular and potentially most profitable, Radio 1 or BBC1.

> For 50 years British television has operated on the assumption that the people could not be trusted to watch what they wanted to watch, so that it had to be controlled by like-minded people who knew what was good for us. As one of those guardians, my distinguished friend Sir Denis Foreman, explained a few years ago, even so-called commercial television in Britain 'is only an alternative method of financing public broadcasting, and that method itself has depended on the creation of tightly held monopolies for the sale of advertising and programme production'. So even though the lure of filthy lucre was to become part of the British television system with the advent of ITV from the mid-1950s, it was done by subordinating commerce to so-called public service . . .
>
> I start from a very simple principle: in every area of economic activity in which competition is available, it is much to be preferred to monopoly. The reasons are set forth in every elementary economics text book, but the argument is best proved by experience rather than theory.
>
> Competition lets consumers decide what they want to buy: monopoly or duopoly forces them to take whatever the seller puts on offer. Competition forces

suppliers to innovate products, lest they lose business to rivals offering better; monopoly permits a seller to force outdated goods onto captive customers. Competition keeps prices low and quality high; monopoly does the opposite. Why should television be exempt from these laws of supply and demand?

The consensus among established broadcasters, however, is that a properly free and competitive television system will mean the end of 'quality' television and that multi-channel choice equals multi-channel drive – wall-to-wall *Dallas* is the sneering phrase most commonly trotted out to sum up this argument. Put aside the fact that the BBC is happy to run *Dallas* at prime time (and to repeat it as well); put aside the simple economic truth that if 15 channels were to run it wall-to-wall, 14 of them would quickly go bust. I want instead to concentrate on the assumption that is behind the establishment broadcasters' case: that only public service television can produce quality television.

There are real problems of definition and taste here. For a start I have never heard a convincing definition of what public service television really is . . . My own view is that anybody who . . . provides a service which the public wants at a price it can afford is providing a public service. So if in the years ahead we can make a success of Sky Television, that will be as much a public service as ITV . . . But quality is in the eye of the beholder, or in the current debate in Britain, the propagandist.

Much of what is claimed to be quality television here is no more than the parading of the prejudices and interests of the like-minded people who currently control British television. It may well be that at its very best, British television does produce what most viewers would regard as some of the world's best television. Examples have been given to prove the case, though the fact that the same examples are trotted out all the time, and they are all getting a bit long in the tooth, suggests to me that the case is weaker than generally believed.

Moreover, the price viewers have had to pay for these peaks in quality has been pretty high. The troughs of British television, such as much of the variety, situation comedies, sporting coverage, and other popular fare, are not particularly special by international standards . . . This public-service TV system has had, in my view, debilitating effects on British society, by producing a TV output which is so often obsessed with class, dominated by anti-commercial attitudes and with a tendency to hark back to the past . . .

People often say to me, however, that the current British system encourages creative risk taking, and that a market-led system would not fund all manner of excellent programming currently on show. 'Without public-service television, there would be no Dennis Potter plays on television' was how the argument was put at a recent seminar organised by the Broadcasting Standards Council . . . My argument, however, is not that television can be left entirely to the market . . . What I am arguing for is a move from the current system of public broadcasting,

CONTINUED

in which market considerations are marginal, to a market system in which public broadcasting would be part of the market mix but in no way dominate the output the way it does at present. I suspect that the market is able to provide much more variety, and risk taking, than many of you realise . . .

This brings me to my next point. Contrary to conventional wisdom in this country, there is much to admire about American television . . . because America provides the best example of a market-led television system and because it has been so disgracefully misrepresented by propagandists in this country . . . I watch television regularly on both sides of the Atlantic; when there were only four channels on this side, I was regularly frustrated by the lack of choice; and given the quality of much of the prime-time programming it was always difficult to believe that I was tuning in to a cultural citadel which had to be preserved at all costs.

At News International, we stand for choice. I say this aware of the fact that some of our critics accuse us of stifling choice in the media because we are supposed to own so much of it . . . in television; our role is that of a monopoly destroyer, not a monopolist. At present, we have less than 1 per cent of the TV audience. Our critics cannot make up their minds if Sky Television is a threat to the existing broadcasters or destined to be seen by fewer people than have seen the Loch Ness monster.

The truth is that, even by the time Sky is in several million British homes, it has no prospect of dominating the medium. For just as Wapping so lowered the cost of newspaper production as to enable the *Independent* and others to enter, so Sky has paved the way for non-Sky channels . . . in Britain cross-ownership of media is a force for diversity. Were it not for the strength of our newspaper group, we surely could not have afforded to have doubled the number of television channels available in Britain . . . We could not have created Sky News, which has become a third force in British television news alongside the BBC and ITN.

Public service broadcasters in this country have paid a price for their state-sponsored privileges. That price has been their freedom. British broadcasters depend on government for protection: when you depend on government for protection, there will come a time when that government, no matter its political complexion, will exact a price. The pressure can be overt or, more likely, covert. The result is the same either way: less than independent, neutered journalism. I cannot imagine a British Watergate, or a British Irangate, being pursued by the BBC or ITV with the vigour that the US networks did. British broadcasters are now constantly subject to inhibiting criticism and reporting restrictions . . . if, like the BBC, you're dependent on the government to set the licence fee, you think twice before offending powerful politicians . . .

Across the world there is a realisation that only market economies can deliver both political freedom and economic well-being, whether they be free market economies of the right or social market economics of the left. The freeing of broadcasting in this country is very much part of this democratic revolution and an essential step forward into the Information Age with its golden promise.

It means freeing television from the lie of spectrum scarcity; freeing it from the dominance of one narrow set of cultural values; freeing it for entry by any private or public enterprise which thinks it has something people might like to watch; freeing it to cater to mass and minority audiences; freeing it from the bureaucrats of television and placing It in the hands of those who should control it – the people.

Rupert Murdoch, 'Freedom in Broadcasting', MacTaggart Memorial Lecture,
Edinburgh International Film Festival, 25 August 1989

Murdoch's speech is critical of those who run British television, saying that they are a narrow 'elite' who produce television that is 'obessed with class, dominated by anti-commercial attitudes and with a tendency to hark back to the past'. Like the Conservative Government, Rupert Murdoch is critical of the licence fee, which is described as an 'indirect tax' that is especially unfair on those who did not use the BBC's radio and television services. Murdoch argues that public service broadcasting militates against consumer choice and that one of the key priciples of public service broadcasting has been that viewers and listeners are not allowed free choice but rather are given what is deemed 'good' for them. He also argues that the market-led American system generates much greater quality and choice of programming.

ACTIVITY

➤ Outline, in your own words, what Rupert Murdoch's main points are in the speech.

Why do you think he has this particualar view? To what extent do you agree with him about the quality and choice of American television? How would you counter his arguments?

OCCUPYING POWERS

Our television has been ripped apart and falteringly reassembled by politicians who believe that value is a monetary term only, and that a cost-accountant is thereby the most suitable adjudicator of what we can and cannot see on our screens. And these accountants or their near-clones are employed by new kinds

CONTINUED

of media owners who try to gobble up everything in their path. We must protect ourselves and our democracy, first by properly exercising the cross-ownership provisions currently in place, and then by erecting further checks and balances against dangerous concentrations of the media power which plays such a large part in our lives. No individual, group or company should be allowed to own more than one daily, one evening and one weekly newspaper. No newspaper should be allowed to own a television station, and vice versa. A simple act of public hygiene, tempering abuse, widening choice, and maybe even returning broadcasting to its makers.

The political pressures from market-obsessed radicals, and the huckster atmosphere that follows, have by degrees, and in confused self-defence, drawn the BBC so heavily into the dogma-coated discourses of so-called 'market efficiency' that in the end it might lose clear sight of why it, the BBC, is there in the first place. I fear the time is near when we must save not the BBC from itself but public service broadcasting from the BBC . . .

Thirty years ago, under the personal pressures of whatever guilt, whatever shame and whatever remaining shard of idealism, I found or I made up what I may unwisely have termed a sense of vocation. I have it still. It was born, of course, from the already aborted dream of a common culture which has long since been zapped into glistening fragments by those who are now the real, if not always recognised, occupying powers of our culture. Look in the pink pages and see their mesh of connections. Open the *Sun* and measure their aspirations. Put Rupert Murdoch on public trial and televise every single second of it. Show us who is abusing us, and why. Ask your public library – if there is one left – to file the television franchise applications on the shelf hitherto kept for Fantasy, Astrology and Crime bracket Bizarre bracket.

I was exceptionally fortunate to begin my career in television at a time when the BBC was so infuriatingly confident about what public service broadcasting meant that the question itself was not even on what would now be called the agenda. The then ITV companies shared much more of this ethos than they were then willing to acknowledge. Our profession was then mostly filled with men and women who mostly cared about the programmes rather than the dividend. And the venomous hostilities of the small minority who are the political right – before its ideological transformation into the type of venal, wet-mouthed radicalism which can even assert without a hint of shame that 'there is no such thing as society' – before those who had yet launched their poisoned arrows. Clunk! they go. Clunk! Clunk! And, lo and behold, we have in the fullness of such darkness sent unto us a Director-General who bares his chest to receive these arrows, a St Sebastian eager for their punishing stings.

The world has turned upside-down. The BBC is under Governors who seem incapable of performing the public trust invested in them, under a Chairman who seems to believe he is heading a private fiefdom, and under a Chief Executive who must somehow or other have swallowed whole and unsalted the kind of humbug-punctuated pre-privatization manual which is being forced on British Rail or British Coal. But I do not want to end on a malediction . . . I first saw television when I was in my late teens. It made my heart pound. Here was a medium of great power, of potentially wondrous delights, that could slice through all the tedious hierarchies of the printed word and help to emancipate us from many of the stifling tyrannies of class and status and gutter-press ignorance. We are privileged if we can work in this, the most entrancing of all the many palaces of varieties. Switch on, tune in and *grow*.

I hope it is clear by now that I happen to care very much about the medium that has both allowed and shaped the bulk of my life's work, and even my life's meaning. However, I do have the odd hour or two in each day in which to pretend to be a St George rather than a St Sebastian. I therefore hereby formally apply in front of witnesses of substance, here at the Edinburgh International Television Festival, for the post of Chairman of the Governors of the British Broadcasting Corporation.

Dennis Potter, 'Occupying Powers', MacTaggart
Memorial Lecture 1993, Edinburgh Film Festival

In 1993 the playwright Dennis Potter offered a defence of public service broadcasting which he thought was under attack from commercial media organisations like Rupert Murdoch's News International ('new kinds of media owners who try to gobble up everything in their path') and the policies of 'venal, wet-mouthed' right-wing politicians. He was particularly critical of the BBC Board of Governors and the then Director-General, John Birt, who had been appointed by the Conservative government. He argued that the people who were running the BBC could only judge 'value' in terms of money, that they were accountants rather than creative people with vision.

It is also interesting to note that when he gave this speech, Dennis Potter was critically ill with cancer and that he gave his cancer the name 'Rupert'.

ACTIVITIES

> What is Dennis Potter's idea of what television should be like? Do you think that this is realistic and would it prove popular? In which case, how should broadcasting be organised to ensure that this happens?
> Do you agree with Denis Potter that PSB is an important part of broadcasting? If so, what do you think are the best ways of ensuring its continuation?

In August 2000 Richard Eyre, the then Chief Executive of ITV, said that 'public service broadcasting will soon be dead'. However, according to Tessa Jowell, the Minister for Culture, Media and Sport, speaking at the 2001 Radio Festival, public service broadcasting will be important in the digital future as it is today: 'The BBC must be enabled to fulfil its remit in the future as it has in the past.' However, she also stated that 'Public service broadcasting needs to be restated and re-defined for the future that beckons.' Curran and Seaton too suggest there needs to be a new definition of PSB more suited to the realities of media production and consumption in the twenty-first century.

According to the current Director-General of the BBC, Greg Dyke, speaking at the 2001 Radio Festival, the BBC will have a continued national role across the whole of Britain. He claimed that the BBC is 'part of the glue which brings the whole of the nation together' at a time when there are many pressures forcing it apart. The year before he had also spoken at the Edinburgh Television Festival where he outlined his vision for a new BBC that balanced both the demands of PSB and the demands of the ditigal broadcasting market. Dyke described BBC1 as the 'gold standard' of mainstream televison but also outlined the BBC's plans for new digital radio and televison services. Dyke spoke of the dangers of creating a 'digital underclass' who could not afford or did not want digital broadcasting services and where 'some are information rich while others are information poor'. He talks of the 'principle of universality' where all 'our publicly funded services' are available in 'all homes'.

MAINTAINING THE 'GOLD STANDARD'

I believe the stark choice facing the BBC today is that we either change or we simply manage decline gracefully, and none of us joined the BBC to do that . . . I believe one of the problems of BBC television today is that too many of our services have been underfunded . . .

If we want to spend more money on our traditional services, and we do need to, there are certain consequences. First, we have to find the money, and second we have to limit our plans for new services to what we can afford.

I believe the potential for savings is significant. The BBC currently spends 24 per cent of its income on running the institution of the BBC. Our target is to reduce that figure to 15 per cent over the next three years which will give us an extra £200 million a year to spend on programmes and services . . .

I also believe we can increase our commercial income.

The second thing we have to do, if we want better-funded services, is to limit our ambitions for expansion. We cannot possibly afford to have a tank on every lawn, or compete in every area of the marketplace . . .

In the year 2002–2003 we will be spending £480 million a year more on our programmes and services than we spent last year . . . This amounts to the biggest increase in programme expenditure in BBC history.

So what are we planning to do with the money?

We believe that in the age of digital television it will not be sufficient for the BBC to offer only two mixed-genre channels which are somehow supposed to meet the needs of everyone. We need a more coherent portfolio of channels.

As we are inevitably constrained by money, this means we must limit the size of this portfolio. But there is another more important reason for limiting the number of channels we plan and that is the principle of universality. What universality means is making all our publicly funded services available in all homes.

We must avoid the emergence of a digital underclass, a world where some are information-rich while others are information-poor.

In order to achieve this principle of universality it means we are only going to offer a portfolio of channels now which, within a reasonable time will be available in every household in the land.

BBC1 and BBC2 will continue as the mainstays of BBC television for the foreseeable future. Getting these channels right for the future is the big challenge.

BBC1 needs to have a greater impact on people's lives. While this may mean that some of the old faithfuls disappear and others move from the fringe of BBC1 to peak time on BBC2, it does not mean we are banishing all current affairs, documentaries, religion and arts to other channels. Far from it. But programming in these genres, just as in drama and entertainment, needs to be more engaging, more exciting, more gripping if it is to be on BBC1.

Our aim is to make BBC1 the gold standard of mainstream television . . . More than half of the extra money to be spent on the BBC overall will go on improving and modernising BBC1 and BBC2 with most going to BBC1 . . .

In the long term we plan that BBC2 will increasingly focus on intelligent specialist programmes, our key leisure and lifestyle programmes, thoughtful analysis, creatively ambitious drama and comedy and specialist sports . . .

Now for the new channels. Imaginatively we've given them the working titles of BBC3 and BBC4. BBC3 will offer original British comedy, drama and music as well as providing arts, education and social action programmes delivered in a way likely to be attractive to the young audience . . . I suspect in developing BBC3 we will need to break a lot more rules before we're through. BBC3 will emerge out of BBC Choice but will have a significantly higher budget.

BBC4 will be very different. It will be unashamedly intellectual, a mixture of Radios 3 and 4 of television. It will be based around arts, challenging music, ideas and in-depth discussion. It will be serious in intent but unstuffy and contemporary . . . I am also very keen for us to deliver a rolling breakfast time business news on BBC4 . . . BBC4 will be developed out of BBC Knowledge. But

again it will have a significantly higher budget. In all we plan to spend £130 million a year on BBC3 and BBC4.

Our fifth new channel will be News 24. It seems obvious to me that the world's biggest news gatherer, the BBC, needs a 24-hour news service as part of its channel mix. We plan two new children's services to be played in the daytime on the channels occupied by BBC3 and BBC4 in the evenings. One will be for pre-school children and the second for children between 6 and 13 . . .

Together these channels will deliver the BBC's core aims. All will carry predominantly British original productions. All will make a contribution towards achieving our educational goals which I regard as one of the principal aims of my period as Director-General. All will include a broad news and current affairs agenda and all will carry challenging factual programmes. However, over time each channel will develop its own personality and will increasingly be aimed at particular target audiences.

In the digital era I believe the BBC's single most important role will be to make possible the production of great British programmes. Our channel strategy is a means of achieving this – a way of commissioning, producing and broadcasting original British programmes of all kinds on a mix of channels which will make sense to audiences in the digital age . . . This means creating inside the BBC an environment in which talented people can flourish.

Greg Dyke, MacTaggart Memorial Lecture delivered at the
Edinburgh International Film Festival, 25 August 2000

ACTIVITY

➤ To what extent do you think that the new digital services outlined by Greg Dyke fulfill the BBC's PSB remit? (You may wish to look at a recent copy of the BBC's schedules to gain an up-to-date idea of what the BBC is broadcasting.)
➤ The BBC is criticised because it is seen to be 'poaching' on the territory of commercial television companies like Sky One or Disney. Do you think this is true?
➤ Is it possible to come up with a clear definition of what is meant by 'public service' broadcasting in today's digital media environment?
➤ What forces are arguing over the future of public service broadcasting in Britain today and why?

Although it is hard to predict what the future is for public service broadcasting, especially now that we have digital radio and television, the BBC's involvement with the digital Freeview package can be seen as an attempt by the BBC to bring the idea of PSB into the digital age. Freeview is a service offered through a partnership of the BBC, BSkyB and Crown Castle International. The BBC has introduced a range of new free digital radio and television services that are a mixture of news and information as well as entertainment. They also target particular groups of people (children, particular ethnic groups and those interested in speech and culture) who are less well served by the more popular entertainment-led commercial broadcasters. These new BBC services include News 24 and Parliament channels, BBC3 for 'young people', UK History and BBC4, an arts and current affairs channel, as well as two new digital television services for children, CBBC and CBeebies . New BBC digital radio stations include 1Xtra, which specialises in new black music, 6Music, the Asian Network, Five Live Sports Extra and BBC7 that combines 'classic' comedy, children's programmes and speech-based programmes. Freeview seems to be popular with those people who do not wish to pay monthly subscriptions to a range of cable or satellite services such as BSkyB, but who seem to be confident about making a one-off payment to receive a package of mainly BBC channels. (For further discussion of Freeview, see the section that follows on 'New Technology'.)

ACTIVITIES

➤ Consider the leaflet below which outlines the new services offered by BBC4. Who do you think this channel is aimed at? As it is paid for out of the licence fee, is it important that this channel is popular and attracts large audiences?

THE LAUNCH OF BBC FOUR

Imagine you lived close to a new, world-class cultural centre – so close that you could go there whenever you liked.

Each evening you might drop in to enjoy the best in contemporary documentary, music, theatre or international cinema. It would bring you performances that you've read about and wanted to see, and create compelling productions of its own.

You could check out the day's news from a global viewpoint, or discover the engrossing new films about history, people, politics, culture and the arts.

Or you could seek out the pleasures of intelligent discussion, spending time with some of the world's most eloquent people – writers, thinkers, scientists, business leaders – offering the liveliest thinking on everything from philosophy to physics.

Naturally, entry to everything would be free.

This is the vision we aim to bring to life with BBC FOUR – a new television channel which we hope will surprise, delight and challenge, but above all offer something satisfyingly different from the mainstream.

BBC FOUR is the biggest innovation in cultural broadcasting for a generation, and it's available free to anyone with a digital television or receiver. Yours to visit for an enriching experience, every evening from 7pm.

The doors will be open from 2 March 2002. We look forward to welcoming you.

Roly Keating

Roly Keating
Controller of BBC FOUR

➤ The MacTaggart Memorial Lecture is given annually as part of the Edinburgh Television festival held every August. The Festival is attended by all of the industry 'bigwigs', and the MacTaggart Lecture is one of its main events. Who gave the MacTaggart Memorial lecture this year and what were they discussing?

FURTHER READING

Crisell, A. (1999) 'Broadcasting: Television and Radio' in J. Stokes and A. Reading (eds), *The Media in Britain: Current Debates and Developments*, Macmillan Press.
An overview of the development of broadcasting in UK with a discussion of Public Service Broadcasting past and future.

Curran, J. and Seaton, J., (1997) Power without Responsibility: the Press and Broadcasting in Britain, Routledge.
A comprehensive look at the development of broadcasting in Britain with specific chapters on public service broadcasting and its future.

Franklin, B. (ed.) (2002) *British Television Policy: A Reader*, Routledge.
A comprehensive compilation of policy statements from a wide range of sources.

Goodwin, P. (1999) 'The Role of the State', in J. Stokes and A. Reading (eds) *The Media in Britain: Current Debates and Developments*, MacMillan.
An analysis of the relationship between the State and broadcasters, looking specifically at the role of the Thatcher governments in the 1980s and early 1990s.

Ouelette, L. (2002) 'Public versus Private', in T. Miller (ed.), *Television Studies*, British Film Institute.
Looks at PSB from a wider international perspective.

Scannell, P. and Cardiff, D. (1991) *A Social History of British Broadcasting Vol.1*, Blackwell.
A detailed history and analysis of broadcasting in Britain, and particularly the BBC, from its inception up to the start of World War Two in 1939.

▼ **7 NEW TECHNOLOGY**

Technological development has often had a significant impact on the way in which media products are both produced and consumed. Technology has also had an important influence on the relationship between different media forms. For example, the advent of television clearly changed the attitude of audiences to listening to the radio. Alternative sources of news such as the Internet or rolling news channels on satellite and digital television channels have led to a decline in the readership of mass circulation newspapers, such as the *Sun* and the *Mirror*. Similarly, record companies have seen a reduction in sales, especially in the singles charts, as music fans find access to music through other means, such as Internet downloads or jukebox-style digital music channels.

The precise effect of technological innovation is not always easy to predict. The rapid take-up of domestic video recorders in UK homes in the 1980s was expected to lead to a rapid decline in cinema audiences. It was argued that people would rent the latest film on video rather than going to the cinema. The actual effect was the opposite: video rental stimulated interest in watching films and box office figures for cinemas were set to increase rather than decline.

At the beginning of the twenty-first century we are witnessing a rapid change in the way technology is used for both producing and consuming the media. So great are these changes that the term 'New Media', is used widely in both media production and academic circles to describe the products of this technological change. Precisely what can be identified as 'New Media', and what precisely is 'new' about it, is not easy to define. However, media that function 'digitally' is a convenient place to start. Digital media can be said to have certain defining characteristics. These include an increase in the choice available to audiences through, for example, the increase in channels available to television viewers able to receive and decode digital signals. An example of this is the channels available as part of the Freeview package broadcast to viewers with digital receivers. Freeview is a service offered through a partnership of the BBC, BSkyB and Crown Castle International. Viewers without a digital television, cable or satellite need to make a one-off payment to buy a set-top decoder which will enable them to receive the Freeview channels. Freeview is important to the BBC because it allows them entry to the digital market while still

WHAT'S IN THE FREEVIEW PACKAGE?

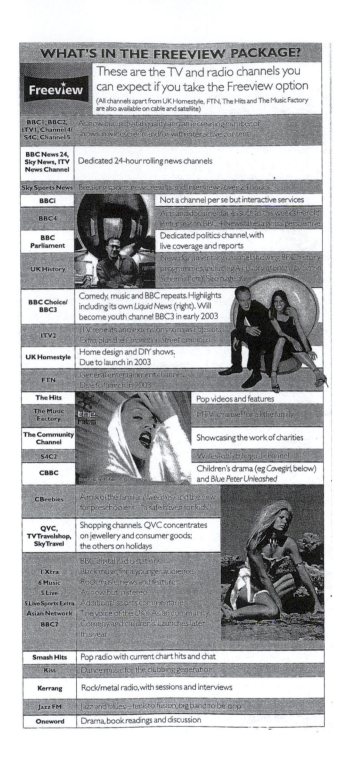

Freeview	These are the TV and radio channels you can expect if you take the Freeview option (All channels apart from UK Homestyle, FTN, The Hits and The Music Factory are also available on cable and satellite)
BBC1, BBC2, ITV1, Channel 4/ S4C, Channel 5	As now, but in digital quality and an increasing number of shows in widescreen and/or with interactive content
BBC News 24, Sky News, ITV News Channel	Dedicated 24-hour rolling news channels
Sky Sports News	Breaking sports news, results and interviews over 24 hours
BBCi	Not a channel per se but interactive services
BBC4	Arts and documentaries such as this week's Harold Pinter season. BBC 4 News takes a global perspective
BBC Parliament	Dedicated politics channel, with live coverage and reports
UK History	New documentary channel showing BBC history programmes, including *A History of Britain* by Simon Schama (left). See page 30
BBC Choice/ BBC3	Comedy, music and BBC repeats. Highlights including its own *Liquid News* (right). Will become youth channel BBC3 in early 2003
ITV2	ITV repeats and extensions such as *Popstars Extra*, plus the *Coronation Street* omnibus
UK Homestyle	Home design and DIY shows. Due to launch in 2003
FTN	General entertainment channel. Due to launch in 2003
The Hits	Pop videos and features
The Music Factory	MTV channel for all the family
The Community Channel	Showcasing the work of charities
S4C2	Wales-only bilingual channel
CBBC	Children's drama (eg *Cavegirl*, below) and *Blue Peter Unleashed*
CBeebies	A mix of the familiar (Tweenies) and the new for preschoolers – "a safe haven for kids"
QVC, TV Travelshop, Sky Travel	Shopping channels. QVC concentrates on jewellery and consumer goods; the others on holidays
1 Xtra **6 Music** **5 Live** **5 Live Sports Extra** **Asian Network** **BBC7**	BBC digital radio stations: Black music for a younger audience Rock music news and features As now but in stereo Additional sports commentaries The voice of the UK's Asian community Comedy and children's. Launches later this year
Smash Hits	Pop radio with current chart hits and chat
Kiss	Dance music for the clubbing generation
Kerrang	Rock/metal radio, with sessions and interviews
Jazz FM	Jazz and blues – funk to fusion, big band to be-pop
Oneword	Drama, book readings and discussion

MEDIA STUDIES: THE ESSENTIAL RESOURCE

maintaining their public service broadcasting remit by dedicating several channels to minority audiences.

The cost of Freeview, a one-off payment of £99 as opposed to the ongoing monthly subscription required for BSkyB, makes it a more attractive proposition to many viewers. The issue of cost is always important in terms of new technology. It raises the question of the extent to which a public body funded through licence payers' money should be allowed to invest in digital technology which may only be available to those who are able to afford it. We may be in danger of creating a new underclass of the digitally poor, unable to access the entertainment and information available to those who can afford digital technology.

ACTIVITY

➤ Conduct a survey of the possible benefits of the Freeview package. What services does it offer? What is missing from Freeview in comparison with other digital packages? If possible, talk to people who have taken up Freeview to see why they prefer this package to others such as BSkyB.

The Freeview package includes a new channel, BBC3, launched in February 2003. As the following article from *Metro* demonstrates, this digital channel is aimed at a specific market: the young adult.

WHAT MAKES AUNTIE'S NEW DIGITAL TV CHANNEL, BBC THREE, SO DIFFERENT?

BBC Three, launched last night, has been a long time coming. The first set of plans for the digital channel were submitted to Tessa Jowell in 2001, and it's a channel that has already been through a lot of changes. Controller Stuart Murphy believes that this has only made BBC Three better. It has certainly made it more balanced: from 7pm until close there's a hugely varied schedule (from fantasy pensions to the Appleton sisters via Swiss Toni), all aimed squarely at that elusive beast: the young adult.

Murphy (at 31, himself one of the BBC's youngest executives) and his team want you: a 25- to 34-year-old, employed and in the first throes of responsibility. The approach is not to dismiss the audience as a mass of tasteless yoof. 'They are a savvy, sharp, intelligent audience. Our average viewer has responsibilities but still wants to have a laugh and go out,' says Murphy. In return for a few hours of your time, he's promising a channel that's 'radical, imaginative, funny and very different'.

Other digital and satellite channels are after the same viewers, but BBC Three comes with a public service remit and guidelines that will keep a lid on the worst excesses of repeats and shoddy buy-ins. Rules are rules, and BBC Three's state that 90 per cent of its output will be made in the UK; independent production companies must get a fair crack of the whip and repeats can make up only 20 per cent of the output. That should mean lots of lovely new stuff, including fresh animation and specially made drama that chimes in with British sensibilities and humour and feels like a treat.

BBC Three's opening schedule displays enthusiasm on a grand scale. Every effort has been made to tick all the necessary boxes, resulting in a solid spread of programmes covering drama, entertainment, celebs, science, news and current affairs, music, arts and animation. Murphy is keen to emphasise the channel's responsibility to 'bring on the next generation of talent'. 'Other broadcasters will benefit; it helps everyone,' he adds. That means new on-screen faces backed by experienced producers and directors, and taking risks with programmes (especially animation) that will not be to everyone's taste.

Views of BBC Choice, BBC Three's predecessor, will recognise familiar young adult-pleasing faces, including Dermot O'Leary and Johnny Vaughan, but much is new and has been saved for the long-awaited launch. Matt Greenhalgh's late-coming-of-age drama Burn It; a six-episode outing for Charlie Higson's lady-loving Swiss Toni; Underground 2003, BBC Three's awards for young talent, and Body Hits, a look at the science of excess.

A real curiosity is Appleton On Appleton, a one-off 'at home with Nat'n'Nic' affair. The domestic behaviour of the Appleton beaus – Liam Howlett and Liam Gallagher – will be of most interest, with highlights including Gallagher's admission that he 'prepares' his hair.

'What makes Auntie's new digital TV channel, BBC Three, so different?'
Metro, 10 February 2003, p. 23

Digital media represent significant changes to analogue technology; one of these is interactivity. Interactivity means that the audience can exercise a degree of control over what is available on the television screen. For example, a sports fan is able to select particular camera shots or angles during a match rather than simply having to accept those chosen by the director or vision mixer in the studio. In addition it allows access to a host of on-screen background information which viewers can access through their remote control. By including a modem in a satellite receiver, viewers are able to order films and other products online, send and receive text messages, and vote on important issues such as reality TV shows.

The television in the corner of our lounge is beginning to take on many of the properties of a computer. Technically, this bringing together of the television set, the computer and the telephone is called 'convergence'. As this convergence gathers pace, especially through the use of broadband technology (which allows large amounts of information to be transmitted at high speeds down telephone lines and via satellite signals), the way in which audiences consume the media is also likely to undergo radical change. One such change is the ability of individual members of the audience to determine their personal patterns of media consumption rather than being at the mercy of schedules determined by television broadcasters. Just as the VCR in the 1980s allowed people to time shift programmes to fit with their own lifestyles, so digital and broadband technologies should enable audiences to call up programmes, films or information on demand.

In their book *New Media: A Critical Introduction*, Martin Lister and colleagues examine the phenomenon of 'dispersal' as a distinguishing feature of New Media.

DISPERSAL

. . . In order to understand new media we will have to develop a framework that recognises the way in which both the production and distribution of new media have become decentralised, highly individuated and woven ever more closely into the fabric of everyday life.

This dispersal is the product of shifts in our relationships with both the consumption and production of media texts.

Consumption

Through the period 1980–2000 our consumption of media texts has been marked by a shift from a limited number of standardised texts to a very large number of highly differentiated texts. The media audience has fragmented and differentiated as the number of media texts available to us has proliferated. From an era of a limited number of network TV stations, no VCRs or DVD players, very limited use of computers as communication devices and no mobile media at all, we find ourselves confronted by an unprecedented penetration of media texts into everyday life. 'National' newspapers are produced as geographically specific editions, network and terrestrial TV stations are surrounded by independent satellite and cable channels, the networked PC in the home offers a vast array of communication and media consumption opportunities, mobile telephony and ubiquitous computing offer a future in which there are *no* 'media free' zones in everyday life.

In sum, the new media determine a segmented, differentiated audience that, although massive in terms of numbers, is no longer a mass audience in terms of simultaneity and uniformity of the message it receives. The new media are no longer mass media in the traditional sense of sending a limited number of messages to a homogeneous mass audience. Because of the multiplicity

of messages and sources, the audience itself becomes more selective. The targeted audience tends to choose its messages, so deepening its segmentation, enhancing the individual relationship between sender and receiver.

(Sabbah 1985: 219; quoted in Castells 1996: 339)

Traditional mass media were the products of the communicative needs of the first half of the twentieth century in the industrialised world. As such they had certain characteristics. They were centralised, content was produced in highly capitalised industrial locations like newspaper printworks or Hollywood film studios. In broadcast media, press and cinema, distribution was tied to production, studios owned cinema chains, newspapers owned fleets of distribution vans, the BBC owned its own transmission stations and masts. Consumption is here characterised by uniformity: cinema audiences all over the world see the same movie, all readers read the same text in a national newspaper, we all hear the same radio programme. Twentieth-century mass media can be characterised by standardisation of content, distribution and production process. These tendencies toward centralisation and standardisation in turn reflect and create the possibility for control and regulation of media systems, for professionalisation of communicative and creative processes, and for very clear distinctions between consumers and producers.

A useful way to conceptualise the difference between centralised and dispersed media distribution systems might be to think about the differences between radio and television broadcast networks and computer networks. The technology at the heart of the original radio and TV broadcast systems is radio wave transmission; here transmission suites require high investment in capital, plant, buildings, masts, etc. Airwave transmission is supplemented by systems of coaxial cable transmission, again where massive investments throughout the twentieth century have established a global network of cable systems. The technology of transmission has the idea of 'one to many' at its core – one input signal can be relayed to many points of consumption. The radio transmitter works on a centralised model.

The computer server is the technology at the heart of the dispersed systems of new media. A server, by contrast to a transmission mast, is a multiple input/ output device, capable of receiving large amounts of data as input as well as making equally large quantities available for downloading to PC. The server is a networked device. It has many input connections and many output connections, and exists as a node in a web rather than as the centre of a circle.

A radio transmitter capable of handling broadcast radio and TV signals is an expensive capital investment way beyond the reach of most enterprises or individuals. The server, on the other hand, is cheap, being commonplace in medium or large enterprises of all kinds. Access to server space is commonly domestically available as part of online subscription packages.

However, this simple opposition between the centralised and the dispersed prompts as many questions as it answers. Most interestingly, this points up how there is no radical and complete break between 'old' and 'new' media. Networked media distribution *could not exist* without the technological spine provided by existing media routes of transmission, from telephone networks to radio transmission and satellite communications. 'Old' media systems of distribution are not about to disappear – they are essential to new media. However, new media, multimedia, and CMC networks have, as it were, been able to reconfigure themselves around this core to facilitate new kinds of distribution that are not necessarily centrally controlled and directed but are subject to a far higher degree of audience differentiation and discrimination. Many different users can access many different kinds of media at many different times around the globe using network-based distribution. Consumers and users are increasingly able to customise their own media use to design highly individualised menus that serve very particular and specific needs.

This market segmentation and fragmentation should not be confused with a general democratisation of media – as Steemers, Robins and Castells have argued, the multiplication of possible media choices has been accompanied by an intensification of merger activities amongst media corporations: 'we are not living in a global village, but in customised cottages globally produced and locally distributed' (Castells 1996: 341).

Lister, M., Dovey, J., Giddings, S., Grant, I. and Kelly, K., *New Media: A Critical Introduction*, Routledge, 2003, pp. 30–1

Another area of technological advance is technology on the move. The mobile phone industry has just about saturated the market in the western world for mobile phones. In order to continue making profits, the industry needs to introduce new technologies in order to be able to market new and more advanced products that will make the hardware currently used by consumers obsolete. If you look at mobile phone advertising, for example, much of it preys on people being so embarrassed by large, clumsy, out-of-date handsets that they feel obliged immediately to upgrade to the latest, more stylish, lightweight model. The type of convergence that is taking place in the living room with television/computer/telephone is mirrored with mobile phones. Broadband technology makes it possible to access the Internet or watch a film using a mobile phone. The question is: to what extent do people want these things? No matter how advanced the technology, there has to be an audience demand for the product. In the article that follows, Brian Winston looks at consumer resistance to one of the latest technological innovations, picture messaging via mobile phone.

WHY PICTURE MESSAGING WON'T TAKE OFF

The bubble may have long since burst but that hasn't stopped manufacturers from putting all their hopes into the next big thing: phones that can be turned into cameras. And the good news doesn't stop there. Beyond taking and trans-mitting pictures, these mini wonders are also old-fashioned dictation machines and pocket PCs with calendars, contact lists and all the rest. They are games consoles. They can do emails, access the web, and let you make calls at the same time. And all this can be yours for a mere £180 and up.

The industry is pinning its hopes on the new generation of mobiles because Vodafone and its rivals are floating on a sea of debt. Over the last year sales of phones which merely allow for talk and text messaging have slumped alarmingly. How could it be otherwise? Seventy per cent of us in the UK already have one and the suspicion must be that the remaining 30% are resolute non-users. It is therefore crucial that we start throwing these fossils away. To make sure we do, Vodafone is spending £158m to advertise its new services, while Orange is forking out more that £13m advertising the wonders of their SPV (for sound, pictures, video) 'Smartphone'.

There's a lot at stake in these campaigns. The companies incurred their debts buying grossly overpriced licences from governments to let them build the new infrastructure, due to be rolled out next year, which would allow them to offer more advanced services. The industry, gripped as it is by the profound faith in the attraction of new gizmos, sees picture-messaging and advanced web access as the answer to all its problems. In Japan, Vodafone has already noted that photo-messaging subscribers spend around 20% more with the company than do ordinary mobile users. How can the rest of us resist?

Given that images over the phone were first introduced in 1927 but went nowhere, the answer has be to that we will probably resist it rather well. In that year, Dr Herbert Ives, head of the television research team at the Bell Labs, introduced a videophone with a 2in × 2.5in [5cm × 6.5cm] screen with an (extremely) low definition image of 72 lines. By 1929 Ives had produced a colour version and a videophone circuit was installed in Manhattan. In 1938 the Germans linked Berlin and Nuremburg using phones which produced a 180-line picture. After the Second World War, at various times videophone gadgets attached to conven-tional phone wires were offered to an uninterested public. And now we are being tempted yet again.

The question of the success or failure of any given technology is never actually a matter of machines alone. Today's mobile phone is essentially a two-way radio, a device dating from 1906, made possible by digital signal processing, a technique first demonstrated in 1938. Diffusing this technology, as is always the case, has depended at least as much on social factors as technological capabilities.

The current talk-and-text mobile phone 'fits' the way we live now. It allows us flexibility in making social and business arrangements. It permits ever-greater exploitation of our labour. It enables us to monitor the kids. It gets the teenagers off the home phone. And, if we live in a country unsaturated by conventional telephones, it provides the means of leaping a whole generation of landline networking. 'Hello, I'm on the train,' is not an infuriatingly redundant communication but a genuine expression of how well mobiles mesh with our lifestyles. That's why by the turn of the century, worldwide, there were already more than 470 million of them.

Dr Ives was asked by a visitor in 1931 whether he thought the videophone had a future. He admitted 'frankly that he has not the remotest idea whether the public want to see the fellow at the other end of the telephone line badly enough to pay a high price for the privilege'. In the event, we the public did not and, probably, still don't. 'Hello, I'm still in the office . . . What did you say? . . . You can see a barmaid behind me?' (My daughter pointed out to me that you couldn't call your boyfriend unless you had your make-up on.) Private corporate video conferencing systems have not stopped people travelling to meetings, because tele-conferencing tends to avoid making really contentious decisions. For serious business, we humans need to speak face to face . . .

Picture text messaging simply doesn't 'fit'. The only people in our culture who take photographs all the time are professional photographers or amateurs of a peculiarly obsessive kind. The only spheres that demand instant transmission of pictures are journalism, certain sorts of 'distributed' film production (where images are electronically transmitted from location to editing facility), or highly specialised uses within tele-medicine.

Why should the rest of us need this capacity? Instead of the postcard of the holiday hotel with the Biro-ed X indicating your room, you can send loved ones back home instant 'wish you were here' images. Absent family can get little Janice blowing out her birthday candles within seconds of her doing it. (Of course, if they are really absent in Australia or America, they might well be asleep.) Teenagers can flash each other images of their dirty bits. But even these minor excitements can be short-lived. While Vodafone points to its 20% increase in revenues, a Japanese survey found that only one in three camera/phone owners ever uses the facility and even that third gives up sending pictures within the year.

As with pictures, so with the other services. The hand-holdable camera-telephone-games-console-recording-computer might be a wonder but it is essentially redundant since all its functions already exist in other handy, widely used forms. Being a little phone adds nothing but portability to the laptop and palm computer (both capable of playing games). And even the miniature size is not an obvious advantage.

Texting, like the Qwerty keyboard, may well suggest there is no limit to the human capability to overcome inappropriately designed features. Nevertheless the lack of alphanumeric keyboard and a minuscule 12-line by 30-character phone screen cannot match the ergonomics of the discrete machines. (The phones do not have the touch-screens and styluses of the pocket PCs.)

Moreover, despite the enthusiasm of the technophiles, putting disparate functions together doesn't necessarily attract buyers. We still insist on acquiring separate televisions and video/DVD machines, for example, when common sense suggests they should be together in one box. Given the different circumstances in which we use the various facilities the new phones offer, what's the real advantage in having all these together in one package, however small?

New technologies appear in our lives for a variety of reasons. Some are grounded in the needs of those selling the technology. Others are smart technological responses to what we call public need. In the nature of the cases, these advances, being based on social demand, 'fit'.

This is by no means the case if engineering or entrepreneurship is the driver. Being able to rearrange the TV schedule, for example, ensured that the comparatively unsung home VCR achieved a penetration rate greater than that of almost any other recent technology including the much-hyped home computer. We needed VCRs. They 'fitted'. On the other hand, the only people who needed 16rpm records or Polaroid instant movie film, to take two random examples, were the manufacturers. We left them twisting in the wind.

Of course, the new phones might not turn out this way, but it does seem likely that we won't need a camera-telephone-games console-recording-computer just yet . . . In fact, bet you that if there is a camera/phone in your life, you won't be sending pictures with it this time next year. You'll have nobody to transmit to, for one thing.

B. Winston, 'Why Picture Messaging Won't Take Off', New Humanist, 4 January 2003

Another issue that may make consumers cautious about embracing new technology is that of compatibility. When domestic videos were introduced in the 1980s, there were initially three formats. Only after these three incompatible systems had been marketed alongside for several years did it become apparent that the VHS would outlast the other two. Ironically, one of the 'losers' was Betamax, developed by Sony, which was considered technically far superior to VHS.

Currently a similar doubt hangs over the DVD recorder formats. A reduction in the price of hardware and the availability of films on DVD have ensured the popularity of DVD players. Although DVD recorders have fallen significantly in price, the 'format war' identified in the following article from *Satellite TV Europe* is likely to present something of a gamble to anyone thinking of purchasing a machine.

PHILIPS DVDR880

With breathtaking speed DVD recorders have plummeted down to the £500 price barrier where the extra quality, capacity and convenience might just be enough to push out the grainy old VHS for good.

But there's a war on. Not those pesky terrorists, but a format war the like of which hasn't been seen since VHS out-sold the superior Betamax.

In the red corner is Philips, with DVD+R and DVD+RW, in the blue corner stands just about everyone else with DVD-R and DVD-RAM. Just about every player can cope with either +R or –R (although –R discs are cheaper), but it's those rewritable formats which cause trouble, and because most people will just want to re-use the same few discs the way they do videotapes, they're at the heart of the battle.

In simple terms, DVD-RAM is more like having a portable hard disc drive which you can edit on the fly, and read and write simultaneously, but it uses an impractical caddy and isn't compatible with many players. DVD+RW is just an erasable recording format, but there's no caddy and the discs are compatible with most players produced in the last couple of years.

Catching on quick

Enter the DVDR880, officially priced at £500 but already retailing as low as £400, and a sure sign of things to come. Even with VCRs at £80 this has got to be tempting.

It looks nicer than a VCR to start with, especially the sexy rounded corners and slim chrome strip of buttons which leads the eye. The remote has a lot of new buttons, and indeed there are a few new concepts to master in creating recordable DVDs, but it's well laid out to help you learn.

There's an analogue TV tuner, although integrating a digital tuner has got to be on someone's list of enhancements now anyone can get the 30 Freeview channels. You do get an RGB-compatible Scart input for recording at the best possible quality from a Digibox, and the RGB output Scart ensures playback will look its best on TV. There's also a coaxial digital audio output, composite and S-video outputs on the back, plus stereo audio inputs.

The auto-setup effortlessly tunes your five channels and sets the clock, so now you can record using the six-event one-month timer with Videoplus and PDC. All of your recordings are shown as thumbnails on a separate Disc menu, which is carried on each disc created, so you'll see the same handy contents menu when you put the disc in any DVD player. Basic editing is on tap for DVD+RW discs – you can edit unwanted sections or rename recordings.

The five recording levels give between one hour and four hours per 4.7GB disc (DVD+R or +RW), with quality from near perfect to VHS. The HQ level (1hr) rivals the best professional discs, SP (2hr) is on a par with good digital satellite.

Sound recording is on a par with the HQ video level, using the built-in hiss-free Dolby Digital 2.0, and playback is beautiful whether it's multi-channel DVD audio or CD music.

Good features and with excellent picture quality, the DVDR880 makes it tempting to leave the age of tape behind completely, and though it's too soon to call on who will win the DVD format war, you'll feel like a winner for catching on to recordable discs so early.

'Sound & Vision-Digital Equipment', *Satellite TV Europe*, January 2003, p. 214

Finally it is interesting to look at the impact of digital technology from the viewpoint of the media producer. Digital production techniques are much trumpeted by the film industry especially in the field of animation and special effects. The latest *Star Wars* film 'Attack of the Clones' is an example of this new production technique. In the article that follows, film director Alex Cox questions the value of this technological revolution and argues the case for 35mm, 'one of the last of the truly international media forms'.

WHY WE SHOULD JOIN IN AN ATTACK ON THE DIGITAL CLONES

Film studios and distributors are exerting intense pressure on cinemas, pushing them in the direction of digital production – the way *Attack of the Clones*, the new *Star Wars* film, was made.

In 'Digital Star Wars Heralds New Dawn' (*Debate*, May 20), Keith Randle and Nigel Culkin said the new format would bring about a 'technological revolution'. But why are the studios so keen on the idea, and what does it mean for audiences, and for directors and producers of independent, and non-English language film?

'Job titles such as clapper loader and focus puller will vanish from the credits,' Culkin and Randle say, and 'the cinemas will lose their projectionists.' That sounds like studio and technology company hype: buy our new gear and you can sack your workforce. And by now, we all know where that fantasy leads.

I recently experimented with a Sony 24p high definition digital camera, and a focus puller was most definitely required. So was a clapper loader. And projectionists will always be needed, because someone must be responsible for maintaining and monitoring the sound system and the projectors; and digital projectors (with three lenses rather than one) are more apt to go kerflooey than 35mm ones.

The unspoken, but insistent, assumption of all the digital hype is that 'it all looks the same', and that audiences cannot tell the difference. In fact, the aesthetic issues of digital production and protection versus celluloid are far from being resolved.

Over the past 20 years I have attended a number of 'demonstrations' of digital video technology. Often the video images produced are of outstanding quality. But, in spite of all the speeches, the brochures, the white wine and canapes, I have never seen a video projection, analogue or digital, which looked like projected film.

In the case of *Attack of the Clones*, quality may not matter much since (a) almost all the shots are special effects shots done mainly by computer, and (b) the film is shite.

But try to imagine *Citizen Kane* shot on digital video (in colour, naturally), or *Amélie* or *Moulin Rouge*. If its promoters are serious about the quality of their technology, let them put it to the test against the best work of contemporary and classic cinematographers – not against the worst.

I suspect this isn't going to happen. 35mm film – like the vinyl record – is one of the last truly international media forms. A 35mm print (especially one with a mono soundtrack) can play in any cinema, anywhere in the world. The technology is already in place, everywhere.

All that is needed to show a 35mm movie well is a bright bulb, a clean screen, and decent speakers. More recent forms of media distribution – videos, DVDs, CDs – have been ghetto-ised by corporate-led copyright law, 'regionalism', anti-recording protection, and the incompatible television standards of PAL, NTSC and Secam.

Why are there six non-compatible DVD 'regions'? Not for the benefit of the consumer.

Any centralised satellite or cable-delivered video system is likely to be affected by similar political economics.

If cinema owners do get rid of 35mm, what becomes of all the 35mm prints? And what happens to the work of third-world, or independent, film-makers who prefer film on economic or aesthetic grounds?

Finally, if cinema owners do convert to video, what will they get for it? Put yourself in the place of the owner of a multiplex, with – say – *Captain Corelli's Mandolin* on screen one (the big screen) and *Bend It Like Beckham* on screen two. Both films opened on Friday. By Sunday, it's obvious that *Corelli* has tanked, and

MEDIA INSTITUTIONS

that *Beckham* is a hit. Naturally you yank *Corelli* from the larger cinema and put *Beckham* in there. The studios hate this, but can do nothing about it. However, once the new technology is installed, *Corelli* will be beamed direct to screen one for the duration of its scheduled run, and will play to empty houses. You, the cinema owner, can do nothing except lose money on *Corelli*, and turn customers away from screen two.

Bad technology sometimes beats out good. Consider the triumph of VHS over Beta, of CDs over vinyl, of the Microsoft operating system over the Mac. In each case, inferior technology triumphed because of huge corporate pressure. George Lucas may be the visible guilty party right now, but, for all his wealth, he is merely a small front man for multinationals like Sony, Universal/Vivendi, 20th Century Fox, and AOL Time Warner.

These are big-time, corporate control freaks. They are not interested in freedom, in democracy, in art, or in diversity. They want to dictate not only what we see, but where and how we see it. Whether we see *Clones* in 35mm or on video, indeed whether we see it at all, will be watched closely by our corporate masters.

The film may be silly, but the issue is serious, since it concerns the future of our one modern art form, film.

Alex Cox, 'Debate', *Guardian*, 5 October 2002, p. 22

ACTIVITIES

➤ One potential use for interactive technology is online shopping. Imagine a situation whereby with the click of a remote control button it is possible to order an item displayed on the screen. This need not necessarily be from an advertisement, but might include, say, an item of clothing or furniture, or even food that takes the viewer's fancy during a programme such as a soap. What do you think will be the implications of this for:

■ programme-makers
■ audiences
■ regulators?

➤ How easy did you find it to understand the technical details in the review of the Philips DVDR880? What does this tell you?
➤ One criticism levelled at the so-called digital revolution in television broadcasting is that it is still the same old players, such as the BBC and BSkyB, deciding what audiences should view. Do you think it would be appropriate for the Government to pass legislation that would encourage new programme

FURTHER READING

Probably the best way to keep up to date with new media technology is through the trade and special interest press and the media section of the broadsheets such as the *Media Guardian* on Monday.

The following recently published books should also prove useful as should the websites.

Gauntlett, D. (2000), *Web. studies: Rewiring Media Studies for the Digital Age*. Arnold.

Lister, M., Dovey, J., Giddings, S., and Grant, I. (2003) *New Media: A Critical Introduction*, Routledge.

www.radiotimes.beeb.com/content/features/guidetodigital/
www.newmediastudies.com/
www.nmk.co.uk/industry_trends/default.cfm

▼ 8 OWNERSHIP AND THE MUSIC INDUSTRY

Media companies, both public and commercial, figure prominently in almost all studies of the media – though it can often be difficult to get hold of detailed and up-to-date information as both the technical and financial circumstances of companies can change very rapidly.

As media technology changes almost overnight, so too are media institutions constantly changing their shape and structure in an attempt to remain one step ahead of their competitors. Generally speaking, most media institutions are aware that to concentrate on one area of the media is risky and that in order to survive, control of the media product, or media text, is important. Thus, for example, many of the major Hollywood studios do everything they can to control every aspect of a film from production through to distribution to exhibition. Wherever possible, record companies aspire to maintain this sort of control as well, and often the same companies that produce films also produce records.

In the first chapter of his book Producing Pop, Keith Negus quotes Tony Powell, the managing director of MCA Records in 1991: 'Record companies don't see themselves as record companies anymore. They see themselves as entertainment companies.' He adds:

'Since the latter part of the 1980s, these companies have been explicitly defining themselves as 'global organisations'. However, what needs to be ascertained is whether they have been successful.

Audiences are unpredictable, and what draws an audience in one year will not necessarily work in the next. This is true across all media forms. There are no guarantees of success, although there are some reliable formulas. For example, James Bond films have maintained their popularity over a period of over 30 years, although there was a time when there were a few doubts about how much longer the franchise could last, and the formula had to be overhauled and updated.

The music business is much more difficult to predict. Few recording artists can expect to maintain that same level of longevity as James Bond films, and the popular music business is characterised by one-hit wonders and occasional financial failures. But while records that fail to sell mean the loss of huge financial investments, a record that sells massively worldwide can mean tremendous profits for a record company. The UK domestic market is small – the USA domestic market larger – but each represents a relatively small percentage of the overall sales potential if a record/CD should become a worldwide hit.

ROBBIE'S £80M DEAL PUTS EMI ON NEW PATH

The music industry is notorious for signing artists to enormous deals that embarrassingly fail to recoup their multi-million pound advances. But once bitten, twice shy does not apply to recording giant EMI.

Despite paying Mariah Carey $20m to leave the label nine months ago when her deal collapsed after poor CD sales, EMI announced this week it had signed Robbie Williams to a 'truly ground-breaking' £80m contract.

It makes the one-time Stoke dustman, who has sold 20m albums, the highest paid British artist in recording history, second only to Michael Jackson. After an EMI press conference to announce the deal, with an understandably cheerful Williams shouting 'I'm rich beyond my wildest dreams!' EMI's share price fell 1½p.

The price could drop further with the news last night that Williams is likely to split from Guy Chambers, who wrote the music for hits such as 'Angels' and 'Millennium'. Chambers is thought to be keen to work with other performers, while Williams's management would prefer Chambers to work exclusively for the star.

The EMI deal is not the average, obscenely large pact between an avaricious label and a greedy star. Industry veterans say it is unprecedented, and could change the way the business works.

EMI will not only release Williams's next six CDs, it also gets a cut of his lucrative merchandising, publishing and touring rights. IT becomes a multi-interest entertainment business, rather than a mere record label. The result could be more control for artists, for long a sore point with stars of Williams's stature, and greater financial security for labels. EMI's president, Tony Wadsworth, said: 'It means record companies and artists are much more clearly on the same agenda. It may signal a change in the business, as investments we make in artists are realised in a greater range of potential income streams instead of solely recorded music sales.'

An industry source said: 'Labels have financial problems with enormous overheads and staffing levels, so they have to reinvent themselves. It's no longer about manufacturing records out in Hayes (EMI's factory in Middlesex) and sending them to shops in Oxford Street. They need to evolve into entertainment companies.'

Sales of singled dropped by 10 per cent to 60m in 2001. Album sales rose 4 per cent to 226m, but dance music compilations accounted for much of that, and the dance genre is rapidly losing popularity. Album sales for the first six months of 2002 were down by 10 per cent, and the vexed question of internet piracy and its threat to revenue is top of label agendas.

According to Tim Shepard, of independent label Underground Sounds, which makes its products freely available on the net: 'The Robbie deal will be the basis of future company business models. They know that, eventually, most music will be free on the Internet, so they're going to make money from peripherals like touring and merchandising.'

Clearly, EMI is not about to make Williams's music available quite as generously as that, but it is farsighted in acquiring fresh income streams. Jon Webster, founder of the Mercury Music Prize, said that a deal such as Williams's was EMI's insurance against the day he no longer sold so many records. Older acts shift negligible amounts of records yet make millions touring – as proved by the Rolling Stones.

'In 10 or 15 years, Robbie could be selling concert tickets till the cows come home but not selling records, so this will work for both sides.'

Other artists such as George Michael have campaigned for control over their careers. He produces his CDs and licenses them to Polydor Records on a single-by-single basis. U2 own their masters (the studio recordings).

'The underlying assets belong to U2, it's unique in the music business,' said manager Paul McGuinness.

Williams's arrangement offers similar control, with his recordings on licence to EMI. Furthermore, he received a promise to break him in America, a major undertaking when success has eluded most UK acts. 'One point Americans find

hard to grasp is irony, so most British bands don't do well there,' said the *Daily Express* showbusiness correspondent, Mark Jagasia.

'Williams's sensibility is very British, but he's also got charisma; so, if they can package that right, they might be able to sell him there.'

If Williams did do well in the US, other companies would redouble their efforts. There is only one English act in this week's US top 75 singles, Londoner Daniel Bedingfield at 72. A 'break America' clause could end up as a part of deals.

Caroline Sullivan, 'Robbie's £80m Deal Puts EMI on New Path',
Guardian, 5 October 2002

This is why the news about the £80 million deal with EMI and Robbie Williams is so interesting. Caroline Sullivan's report points out that EMI will not only release Williams's next six CDs, it also gets a cut of his lucrative merchandising, publishing and touring rights. It becomes a multi-interest entertainment business, rather than a mere record label.

What EMI have done is to consider every aspect of the artist's career as a commodity over which they have control in a process called 'synergy' whereby they sell or promote similar products across more than one medium. While Robbie Williams is reaping the financial benefits of this arrangement, there are bound to be other kinds of drawbacks. As their investment in him is so large, EMI are bound to want a considerable amount of control over his career and output. What will happen if their investment fails? How do they estimate what is an adequate return? To gain a return on £80 million, EMI are without doubt counting on global sales. To appeal to a worldwide market often involves projecting an inoffensive, conservative image and product. The instant that a large media audience feels it is being taken for granted or cynically catered to by an artist, the artist's integrity is called into question and the audience may lose interest. Ultimately many consumers do not like to be patronised and also want to be thought of as individuals – not as a homogeneous mass.

ACTIVITY

➤ Go to the Robbie Williams website at www.robbiewilliams.co.uk/ and consider how Robbie Williams is being presented as a commodity. Look at the range of products on sale that are not specifically items of music, for example, the clothes, mobile telephone covers, and Robbie Williams's autobiography. There is also a DVD EP that is 'exclusive' to members of the fan club. How do these items relate to the concept of synergy and in what ways does the website offer the 'fans' something special?

As was noted above, there is no guarantee of success in any area of the media. There are a number of reasons why audiences are fickle and volatile, particularly when looking at the music industry. One major reason is that music is very much wrapped up in things other than the music itself. Unlike most other media (though this may well be changing as technology rushes forward), music can be consumed in many different formats and there are few places where that consumption cannot take place. Music is available live in concert or on the radio – which means at home, in the car, in shops, or on a personal stereo. Channels exist on TV that are devoted solely to music, and with the increase in their popularity there are now different channels for different types of music (Kiss for R&B, Kerrang for Metal, Classic FMTV for classical). It exists on CDs, tapes, mini-discs, MP3s. It is played in bars and pubs, supermarkets, on trains and planes. It is an integral part of any TV programme we watch, any film we watch (at home or at the cinema) – and now more than ever with the burgeoning of advertising it has become a vital ingredient in the sale of products – from bread to insurance. (There are even compilation CDs exclusively featuring music from adverts seen on British TV.) So when an audience consumes music, it is frequently not so much of a positive choice as when they consume some other media. It is increasingly rare that one sits down just to listen to music except at a live concert– and live concerts are nowadays predominantly a chance to hear music *with which we are already familiar* being played in a different manner, where the emphasis is usually on the show as much as the music.

ACTIVITIES

➤ Over a short period of time keep a record of what music you listen to, either deliberately or by chance (such as the soundtrack to a film or music used in an advert). What percentage of the music you listen to is through deliberate choice? Why do you think adverts and films increasingly have pop music soundtracks? Where else might you hear music (for example whilst on 'hold' when phoning an organisation)? How ubiquitous is music in our society?

➤ If you have access to digital radio and/or television, make a list of all the music channels that are available. How do they 'segment' the audiences for different types of music? How are these different audiences addressed? How is the music used to promote other goods and in what ways are these other goods related to the music featured on the radio or television channel?

➤ Consider your own music collection: What are the formats of the music (LP, cassette, CD, mini-disc, MP3 etc.)? How much of the music is contemporary and how much is made up of old favourites? Do you have copies of the same pieces of music on different formats? If yes, have you bought the same product more than once? If yes, why? Are there particular pieces of music that you have listened to again and again? Is there any music in your collection that you do not listen to any more? If yes, why do you think some music retains its popularity with you while other pieces do not?

The conditions of consumption therefore are very different. And our ability to listen to the same piece of music over and over again also ensures that music is in fact a very different commodity to most other media. Many people collect music, and play it over again frequently for years after it was originally released; remember that classical music was the popular music of its time. Most contemporary popular music has a very short shelf life, and reflects all that was going on at the time it was made quite deliberately. Keith Negus (1992) again:

> Unlike the manufacturers of products like baked beans or toothpaste where a tried and tested product can be sold over and over again, the music industry is continually introducing new artists and simultaneously having to identify and construct an audience for their recordings.

And:

> A real artist is going to have a lot more than a good record. Being a pop star is not just about making records. Popular culture is about media manipulation. It's about how you present yourself. It's about utilising the avenues at your disposal to create an image, a lifestyle, a point of identification for people. And a genuine artist may well have a real understanding of that. David Bowie is the master manipulator of the media.

METAL AND RAP PUT VIVENDI UNIVERSAL AT TOP OF THE POPS

When EMI outlines the grand vision for its struggling recorded music division tomorrow, Britain's biggest music group will be trying to achieve a delicate balance between much-needed restructuring and the need for greater creative output.

Up to 1,000 job cuts are expected to be announced by Alain Levy, EMI's new head of recorded music as back office functions are merged. Regional offices will also be brought together and the overlaps between certain labels, such as Virgin and EMI, reduced.

What Mr Levy will be aiming for is a lean, mean fighting machine that is still capable of pumping up the volume with hit after hit. In short, he will be trying to do what one of EMI's competitors among the 'Big Five' music majors has already managed. Universal Music, the largest of the majors and home to artists such as US, Shaggy and Limp Bizkit, has been outperforming the industry to such an extent that it has set itself an extraordinary target. It expects to make more profit that Warner Music, Sony Music, EMI and BMG put together within two to three years.

'We think we have a good chance of getting there,' says Jorgen Larsen, the chief executive of Universal Music International, a division that includes all world markets apart from the United States. 'We know what we have coming up this year. It should be our strongest ever with two albums from Eminem and others from Limp Bizkit, U2, Shania Twain and some new signings from competitors.'

Universal, part of the Vivendi Universal conglomerate that also includes Universal Pictures, Canal Plus and a large utilities business, has already proved a resilient performer in a difficult market. Earlier this month it reported flat profits before interest, tax and depreciation of 1.2bn euros (£740m). This is in a global music market estimated to have declined by around 5 per cent. It also compares with the paltry figure of just £150m, which EMI is expected to achieve for the past year (or an estimated loss of £3m after exceptional items, according to some analysts).

Vivendi's results announcement this month stated that Universal accounted for one in four albums sold worldwide last year. And despite a falling music market, the business achieved unit sales just 1 per cent lower than the previous 12 months.

How is Universal managing to buck the trends? There are a combination of factors such as leading market share and strong positions in growing musical genres such as hip-hop and metal. There is also the avoidance, so far, of artist contract cock-ups such as the Mariah Carey deal at EMI, which cost the company £19.6m to sever.

One senior music executive says: 'It's down to management. They really concentrate on their successes. Once something happens they really go for it in a big way. The way they've helped U2 is an example.'

But for City analysts the most important factor is merger synergies. They say Universal's success in completing a major deal before the regulatory authorities clamped down on further industry consolidations has given the group a huge advantage. The mega-merger of Universal and PolyGram in 1998 brought together two companies that had already snapped up several other labels. Universal had acquired MCA, while PolyGram had picked up Island, A&M, Motown and Def Jam. All this preceded Vivendi's takeover of Seagram, which owned the Universal business as well as the drinks division which was later sold.

While Jean-Marie Messier's reinvention of Vivendi as a media giant has been widely criticised, the music business has certainly been a success.

The Universal-PolyGram deal therefore created a global giant with scope for significant cost-savings. Lorna Tilbian, media analyst at Numis Securities, says; 'They [Universal] were early in the consolidation when the regulators allowed the number of music majors to go down from six to five. Since then, they've shut the door.'

Simon Baker, at SG Securities, agrees. 'Whether they were lucky or had great foresight I don't know but getting that deal through has meant they are still enjoying significant synergies.'

Since that deal EMI has tried to catch up by holding merger talks with Warner Music and BMG, the music division of the German media group Bertelsmann, but failed to agree a structure capable of satisfying the competition authorities.

At Universal, Mr Larsen declines to comment on the costs-saving boost. 'You don't expect me to answer that, do you?' But he points to Universal's apparent efficiencies compared with rivals. 'As a result of that merger, we went through an intense period of restructuring and we got through that before the market declined. EMI and Warner have about 12,000 staff each. Universal has less than 12,000 [despite being much bigger]. That makes a big difference.'

Mr Larsen says Alain Levy will shake-up EMI but make it a better business. 'I've know Alain for 30 years and he'll operate with common sense. I think he'll combine the back office of Virgin and EMI. But I'm surprised that took so long.' Commenting further on EMI he says: 'It is a strong company with a good cata-logue but it has suffered for two reasons: an inability to break into the United States and internal paralysis as a result of these failed mergers.'

The second factor driving Universal's growth is its market share. According to SG Securities, Universal has 22.3 per cent of the global music market. This is way ahead of its nearest competitor, Sony, with 18.3 per cent while EMI is only fourth largest with 12.8 per cent. This kind of scale gives it major advantages in terms of distribution and marketing clout. Universal is particularly strong in the United States, the world's largest music market where it has a 27 per cent share. 'Why are we different? We are market leader in a third of the markets where we operate,' Mr Larsen says. 'In December we had 55.5 per cent of the music market in France and we have 41 per cent of the world market in classical music.' Though classical sales only account for 6 per cent of global music sales, this gives Universal a stable flow of earnings year after year that is relatively unaffected by musical trends and 'hits'.

The third factor is Universal's success in positioning itself within growing musical styles. Its Def Jam label has Eminem and Shaggy with Dr Dre also signed to a Universal label. Eminem's *Stan* was the world's bestselling single last year and Shaggy's album *Hotshot* was the fourth best-selling album.

The group's metal acts include not just Limp Bizkit but Blink 182, Sum 41 and Weezer. With the heavy metal magazine *Kerrang!* now selling more copies than NME, there is no doubt that metal is a growing market. EMI's list of best-sellers last year looks rather staid by comparison. Its biggest artists were Janet Jackson and Pink Floyd, followed by Robbie Williams, Gorillaz and the Beatles. To make matters worse Robbie Williams is out of contract and is said to be unhappy about EMI's failure to help him break into America.

He has been talking to other labels about a possible £20m deal. One of those wooing him is Universal.

Nigel Cope, 'Metal and Rap Put Vivendi Universal at Top of the Pops', *Independent*, 19 February 2002

The article by Nigel Cope from the *Independent* looks more closely at the major record companies and their shares of the global music market:

	%
Universal	22.3
Sony Music	18.3
Warner Music	13.0
EMI	12.8
BMG	11.8
Others	21.8

78.2 per cent of the global music market is controlled by what amounts to five companies – and the likelihood is that we all recognise the names of at least the top three of those companies.

There is little point in printing a list of the ownership pattern of these five big companies because no sooner is it printed than it is out of date. However, it is a worthwhile exercise doing the research on a regular basis just to see who and what they own. There is little doubt that when you buy a record or CD that comes from the Universal/Vivendi stable, the information identifying it as a Universal product will be featured on the label some-where – but it will be very hard to find. Much more prominent will be a more familiar name connected with the record business such as Decca. The same is true of virtually all the records now being released. Each major company has many different labels under the same umbrella, and this information tends to be tucked away in the small print on the CD sleeve.

There are exceptions. For example, it is interesting to note that the place where these major names are more prominent tends to be in classical music catalogues, though even there the smaller labels prevail. Thus Warner tend to release their avant-garde catalogue under the Nonesuch label.

> ➤ Classical music is increasingly being marketed in similar ways to pop music. Visit a local music store and look at the images used to market classical music and the ways in which the performers are presented. In what ways are they similar to the ways in which pop stars are marketed? What merchandising (if any) is associated with classical music?
>
> ➤ If you are able, look at Classic FMTV, a new digital television music channel run by Classic FM, and consider how it represents classical music, its artists and its audiences. Who do you think the channel is aimed at? What products are advertised around the music clips?

This is very much about brand equity – while these smaller labels have been absorbed by the larger parent companies, it has nonetheless been decided that the branding should remain with the original smaller label. Is this because as a record-buying public we are wary of multinationals? To what extent do we notice what label a record/CD is on? Is this simply a method employed by multinationals to allow each subsidiary label some degree of business autonomy, so that the empire does not stretch too far and become unwieldy?

To return to the Robbie Williams deal. At the same time that we read about this deal, we also read that there is a crisis in the record industry (see extract below). Yet is the problem simply one of easier access to music on the Internet?

PIRACY BLAMED FOR CD SLIDE

CD sales fell sharply in the US in the first 6 months of this year, while seizures of 'pirated' discs rose, according to new industry figures. American record industry bosses say the figures further cement their case that copied CDs and online file sharing are undermining legitimate sales.

There was a drop of 7 per cent in CD shipments and a 69.9 per cent rise in seizures, according to the figures released by the Recording Industry Association of America (RIAA). Last year CD shipments dropped 5.3 per cent, and the RIAA also pointed to a survey which suggested Internet users who download music buy fewer CDs. They say this is hitting sales across the board as well as reducing the number of big-selling records.

At the same point in 2001, 37 releases had more than one million sales, but after 6 months of 2002, only 20 titles have sold more than one million copies. In all, total US music shipments dropped 10.1 per cent from 442.8 million units in the first half of 2001 to 398.1 million units in the first half of 2002.

Downturn effect

This meant sales dropped 6.7 percent in the US, from US$5.93bn (£3.89bn) in the first half of 2001 to US$5.53bn (£3.63bn) in the first half of 2002. Record company bosses are adamant this drop can be explained by music 'piracy', despite the correlation with the downturn in America.

Researchers interviewed 860 Internet-connected music consumers and found that 41 per cent of those who said they downloaded more music revealed they were buying less. File-sharing sites have argued the downloading of music could help boost sales, but only 19 per cent of those questioned said they were downloading more and buying more music.

RIAA president Cary Sherman said that illegal music downloading was the main culprit in the drop in sales. 'Cumulatively, this data should dispel any notion that illegal file sharing helps the music industry,' he said. 'In fact, there are numerous red flags and warning bells that illustrate conclusively the harmful impact of illegal downloading on today's music industry . . . This industry must continue to combat piracy in new and innovative ways – commercial disc piracy continues to harm the industry.'

The survey found more than a third of young Internet-connected music buyers said the first thing they do after hearing a song they like by an unfamiliar artist was to download the song for free from a file-sharing service. But only 10 per cent of those questioned would go out and buy the album instead.

'Piracy Blamed for CD Slide', BBC *Online*, News 27 August 2002

When vinyl album sales started to prosper in the 1960s, the concern was that the invention of the cassette tape would mean that pirating of music would take place and sales would suffer accordingly. Indeed, there was a stage when all inside sleeves on 12-inch albums contained the slogan: 'Home taping is killing music'. Yet music did not die. In fact quite the reverse happened. The Internet and the downloading of music files is virtually impossible to stop. Record companies claim that this is piracy and that they are losing millions. The legal case against Napster is not the end of the affair. Nor is the creation of sites where consumers can download music that are owned by the record companies. In retrospect, we can suggest that home taping actually increased the sales of records since it is yet another method of playing music to a varied audience (friends, family, etc.) who may go out and buy the album if they like it. Is it not the same with downloaded music?

If, at the time of writing, the music industry sees itself in the middle of a 'crisis', the fact remains that our ability to listen to and watch music being performed has never been simpler. The number of music channels on cable and satellite bear testament to this. What will be fascinating is watching how the record companies react over the next few years.

FURTHER READING

Denselow, R. (1989) *When the Music's Over: the story of Political pop*, Faber.
Examines the history of postwar political pop from the McCarthy era to Live Aid and from Ewan MacColl to Red Wedge.

McDonald, P. (1999) 'The Music Industry' in J. Stokes and A. Reading (eds), *The Media in Britain: Current Debates and Developments,* Macmillan.
A short and accessible article that looks at the relationship between British and American music industries as well as focusing on issues around the copying of music.

Negus, K. (1992) *Producing Pop*, Arnold.
A very detailed and interesting look at the industrial side of the music business — perhaps slightly dated by now but still very useful.

O'Sullivan, T., Dutton, B. and Rayner, P. (1998) 'Media Institutions and Production' in *Studying the Media*, Arnold.
This chapter contains a case study involving the role of independent music labels in the music industry.

Much useful information is to be found on the Net — either in the many news sites that are available or on the sites produced by the record labels themselves. Judicious scanning of the financial pages of the major daily and Sunday broadsheet press is also useful.

▼ 9 GLOBALISATION AND CULTURAL IMPERIALISM

Globalisation is a highly politicised issue, as can be seen from the anti-capitalist riots that have routinely accompanied meetings of world leaders in recent years. For many people, globalisation is symbolic of the power of capitalism to dominate the world. This is especially true since the decline of communism in the Eastern bloc towards the end of the last century. The power of the western world, most specifically the United States, to dominate the world economically and culturally is one of the hallmarks of the beginning of the twenty-first century in the period which has become known as late capitalism.

In Media Studies terms, globalisation is often identified through the concept of 'media imperialism'. Imperialism is synonymous with the conquest and control of other countries through military might. For example, the Roman Empire was a great imperial power that dominated the world through military conquest. Media imperialism is the domination of other countries through the export of media products and their attendant ideologies to other countries. This export process is often in the hands of a small number of 'multinational' companies that operate across national boundaries. Such multinationals, or conglomerates, are able to operate outside, and in some cases above, the control of national governments.

The power of these companies to export their products across the globe has been bolstered by technological advances. Satellite technology, for example, permits the dissemination of media products across national boundaries. It is no longer possible to regulate the entry of media products into a country by carefully patrolling its borders; satellite signals can be beamed into a country directly, making it much harder for governments to determine the media products that their people are able to consume.

Globalisation is seen by many as a negative force that will ultimately destroy the cultural identity of individual countries by bombarding them with American media output. Even highly developed and affluent European countries are susceptible to this process, sometimes known as 'McDonaldisation'. In France, for example, there have been concerted attempts by the government to fight this process in order to preserve native French cultural production. Perhaps the best-known example of this initiative is the imposition of a limit on the number of English language pop songs that French music stations are allowed to play.

The countries most vulnerable to globalisation are of course the poorest, which may not be able to afford to fight off the invasion of western culture wholesale. However, there is evidence of resistance, for example through the rise in the power of Islam. Islamic fundamentalism can be seen as form of resistance to cultural imperialism by developing countries. In fact, some Islamic commentators would argue that there is a danger that the voice of the west is so powerful that western nations have been able to define the very nature of Islam itself.

In the extract that follows, Sean Redmond provides a brief but insightful overview of the nature of media imperialism by offering us a definition of it. He also looks at a typical American television export *Baywatch* and considers how such a programme might impact upon national identities.

DEFINING MEDIA IMPERIALISM

Media imperialism can be defined in the following four ways:

1. Media imperialism involves the global domination of media production by a small number of western, transnational media conglomerates. These conglomerates own and control much of the technical and research expertise, the technologies involved in transmitting media texts, and the production and distribution networks that wire the world.

A UNESCO compiled table (1989) of the complete turnover of the 78 largest multimedia companies gives a sense of this. The table showed that not one of these companies came from the so-called 'third world', and that many of the company's revenues outstripped the gross national product (GNP) of third world countries. Clear evidence of economic scale and monopoly power.

2. Media imperialism involves the global imposition of commodified western media products onto/over what are seen as the fragile and vulnerable traditional

cultures of, in particular, third world countries. This has also been referred to as the 'core–periphery model' where information, news and entertainment are seen to flow from the west to the 'the rest' (poorer, developing countries) who are unable to resist or reply to this domination because of power and resource inequalities.

Such power and resource inequalities are played out in the international television syndication market. The (amended) table below gives the average rates paid by international broadcasters for rights to broadcast US TV movies, dramas and situation comedies:

Country	Movies	Dramas	Sitcoms
	$	$	$
Germany	300,000	20,000	60,000
Canada	100,000	50,000	35,000
Mexico	18,000–20,000	9,000	1,500–4,000
New Zealand	12,000–18,000	4,500–5,000	2,500
Russia	5,000	4,000	3,000
Brazil	4,000	2,000	1,000
Egypt	3,000	1,500	650
India	2,000	1,000	500–750

Source: *Variety*, 28 Sept.–4 Oct. 1998

What this table shows, it can be argued, is that generally the poorer a country, the less they are asked to pay for US television products, to the extent, finally, where the fee is nominal (see India's charges). American companies can afford to do this because production costs have already been paid for 'in country'. Poorer countries syndicate the shows because there is often a waiting and expectant domestic market for the programmes, and the production budgets that they have are often not big enough to produce original local programming and so buying American is cost effective or, in fact, the only real choice available to them.

But this 'buying American' also actually contributes to a vicious loop. Poorer countries do not have enough money to invest in their own programming and they buy American, so technical, creative and production resources are laid to waste; the domestic market becomes flooded with American product; and the local audiences become ever more familiar with these products and demand them as part of their television experience. And so, as the loop turns again, poorer countries syndicate the shows because buying American is cost effective or the only real choice available . . . and so on and so on until, with demand high and broadcasters reliant on this programming, American producers control the supply and demand of their products, raising prices, or 'bundling' programme packages together.

3. Media imperialism involves the global transmission of what is argued to be a homogenised and low quality western culture: a mass culture broadcasting wall-to-wall *Baywatch* which threatens to flatten out all cultural distinctions, the very existence of what are argued to be rich and culturally diverse world/national/regional cultures. If we draw again on Marie Gillespie's research on Asian teenagers in Southall we find:

> it is perhaps no wonder that they turn to a third, alternative space of fantasy and identification: they draw on utopian images of America to construct a position of 'world teenagers' which transcends those available in British or Indian cultures.

4. Media imperialism involves the global transmission of a dominant, western ideology that both naturalises the western way of life as the only life worth having, and fetishises its democratic structures, social relationships and lifestyles.

The globally syndicated *Baywatch* perpetuated a whole set of western cultural myths about individualism and individuality; morality and community; love and bonding. The sex and surf lifestyles, the free and easy behaviour are far removed, for example, from traditional Indian/Hindu culture where duty and honour and religious faith are sacrosanct. What happens, therefore, to Indian identity (or any national identity) when *Baywatch* goes global? The answer, for some critics, is that the local gets to be annihilated in the face of the onslaught of the global.

Another consequence, arguably, is that the push to 'go global' affects the content and the organisation of the media in host nation states. In terms of Britain, the form and content of television news, it is argued, have been 'dumbed down', while public service broadcasting has been said to have been decimated as British television has adopted the commercial imperatives and new technologies of much of the global media.

Sean Redmond, 'Defining Media Imperialism', *Interpreting Institutions*, Auteur, 2001

Globalisation and cultural imperialism are readily seen as a one-way process moving from west to east. This movement is symbolised by the power of American multinational media companies, such as AOL/Time Warner or Disney, (see www.cjr.org/owners/ for details of what the large multinational media companies own) to dominate the markets of third world countries with their exports. In his book, *Television, Globalization, and Cultural Identities* (1999), Chris Barker argues that there are certain problems inherent in seeing globalisation as cultural imperialism:

It is not necessarily the case that the global flows of cultural discourse are any longer constituted as one-way traffic from 'west to east'. In so far as the predominant flow of cultural discourse is from west to east and north to south, this is not necessarily to be understood as a form of domination. It is unclear that globalization is simply a process of homogenization since the forces of fragmentation and hybridity are equally as strong.

He supports this argument by looking at South African culture. Not only is English the main language in a country that has many languages, but European culture is evident throughout South Africa in 'architecture, music, food, painting, film [and] television'. However, in terms of music, Barker highlights two examples which, he argues, complicate the idea of simple cultural imperialism:

1   A quartet from Soweto that plays European chamber music underpinned by African rhythms
2   A group called 'Prophets of Da City' who take American hip hop and rap music and give it an African slant.

'Both take non-African musical forms and give them an African twist to create a form of hybridisation which is now being exported back to the west.' Barker also points out that rap, which we think of as an American musical genre, can be traced back to West African music and the impact of slavery.

ACTIVITY

➤   Can you think of any further examples of how countries such as South Africa have taken the products of western culture and then exported them back in a hybrid form? One recent example might be 'Mundian to Bach Ke' by Panjabi MC, a bhangra tune featuring the bass line from 'Knight Rider'.

Barker takes a detailed look at the way in which the television market has been globalised. He points out that in 1995 there were in excess of 850 million television sets in more than 160 countries watched by a global audience of 2.5 billion people. In the previous decade it was in the developing world where the number of sets grew most quickly with a threefold increase in Africa and Asia.

GLOBALIZING THE TELEVISION MARKET

. . . The globalization of the institutions of television is an aspect of the dynamic logic of capitalism, which stems from the pursuit of profit as the primary goal. This requires the constant production of new commodities and new markets so that capitalism is inherently expansionist and dynamic. While there is money to be made from the production and sale of television programmes these are also a means to sell the technological hardware of television, from satellites to sets, and to deliver audiences to advertisers so that television stands at the core of wider commercial activities and is central to the expansion of consumer capitalism. Thus, to understand the globalization of television, we need to grasp the changing character of its economic and organizational facets.

The changing economies of world television

The British Broadcasting Corporation (BBC) is one of the world's oldest and largest vertically integrated television organizations and, as such, makes, sells and transmits programmes. Funded primarily from a licence fee, the BBC has stood like a colossus across the British television landscape, both technically and artistically, making it one of the most famous and respected television companies in the world. In contrast, BSkyB is a relatively recent satellite channel manager transmitting from the Luxembourg-registered Astra satellite; it takes between 5 and 8 per cent of the UK television audience with its mix of sport, news, movies and archive programmes. Sky makes few programmes other than news, preferring to buy them in, and relies heavily on its coverage of football to secure itself a foothold in the market. On the face of it, one would not rush to buy shares in Sky nor imagine it is going to give the executives of the BBC much in the way of sleepless nights.

However, appearances can be deceptive and, in comparative terms, it is not the BBC which is the colossus but Sky; or rather, it is a segment of a colossus, the gigantic News Corporation owned by the ubiquitous Rupert Murdoch. Indeed, during 1996 Murdoch removed the BBC from his Asian satellite system Star TV, apparently because BBC news was irksome to the Chinese government. Further, the BBC supplies programmes for UK Gold, a satellite channel which operates under the Sky umbrella, is dependent on a deal with Sky for its football coverage and looks set to play second fiddle to Murdoch's digital television plans. Given that Murdoch has already dented the American networks by establishing the cable system Fox-TV as a virtual fourth network, one would not bet against the success of his projected satellite venture in the US market either.

In the mid-1980s, such a scenario was unthinkable, except perhaps by Murdoch himself, which prompts the question, how is it that the television order could be turned upside down? Explanations for such changes in world television require attention to a number of interrelated factors which include ownership, technology, political decision-making and social/cultural contexts.

Ownership matters

The significance of television ownership lies with issues of constraint and independence related to diversity or monopoly control so that, it is argued, diversity of programmes is related to diversity of ownership and control. Murdock and Golding (1977) have argued that the ownership of communications by private capital is subject to a *general* process of concentration via conglomeration. This produces multimedia and multi-industry corporations who are part of a wider process of capital conglomeration. Thus, many commercial television companies have investment interests in both media and non-media activities or are part of organizations who do. On the basis of their core activities, Murdock (1990) distinguishes three basic kinds of conglomerates operating in the global communications field:

- industrial conglomerates
- service conglomerates
- communications conglomerates.

Any contemporary exploration of television technology and ownership needs to be placed in the context of wider changes in the global communications industries. Radical changes in telecommunications have been constituted by a combination of technological developments and market change which has contributed both to the creation of global communications giants and to the convergence (or erosion of boundaries) between sectors. Thus, technological developments such as the unfolding of fibre-optic cable, satellite technology and digital switching technology have opened up commercial possibilities that have led telecommunications to be hailed by corporation and state alike as *the* industry of the future. Of particular significance are the processes of synergy, convergence and deregulation (or re-regulation).

Synergy and convergence in global television

From the mid-1980s onwards there has been a good deal of diversification by financial, computer and data processing companies into telecommunications, creating multimedia giants dominating sectors of the market. Companies need the financial power that can come from mergers to undertake the massive investment needed to be a player in the global market. For example, the 1989 merger of Time and Warner created the largest media group in the world with a market capitalization of $25 billion. This was followed in 1995 by Time-Warner's acquisition of Turner Broadcasting (CNN). In late 1993 the merger of Paramount communications and Viacom, owner of MTV, saw the emergence of a $17 billion company, making it the fifth largest media group behind Time-Warner, News Corporation, Bertelsmann and Walt Disney.

One of the prime reasons for these developments is the search for synergy. In effect, synergy means the bringing together of the various elements of television and other media at the levels of both production and distribution so that they fit together and complement each other to produce lower costs and higher profits. No communications organization represents that synergy better than Rupert Murdoch's News Corporation.

News Corporation

The acquisition by News Corporation of the Hong Kong based Star TV for $525 million has given Murdoch a satellite television footprint over Asia and the Middle East with a potential audience of 45 billion viewers. When allied to his other television interests – BSkyB (UK) and Fox-TV (USA and Australia) – his organization's television interests alone have a global reach of some two-thirds of the planet. What is significant in looking at the News Corporation dominion is not just the spatial breadth of ownership but the potential link-ups between its various elements. In Twentieth Century Fox and Star TV, Murdoch acquired a huge library of film and television products which he can channel through his network of distribution outlets. He clearly hopes to create a lucrative global advertising market. At the same time, Murdoch can use his newspapers to promote his television interests by giving space in his press holdings to the sporting activities covered by his television channels. Thus does News Corporation make the gains accruing to synergy whose intertextual link-ups are paralleled by technological and organizational convergence.

Television and computers

It is estimated that by the year 2005 there will be 25 million interactive cable households in the USA and some 22 million in Europe (*Screen Digest*, October 1994). This expansion of the Internet and interactive cable is said to be laying the foundations for a 'super information highway', that is, television with built-in personal computers (PCs) linked to cable which allow us to order and pay for shopping, transfer e-money, keep an eye on our bank account, call up a selection of films, and search the world-wide web for information. The idea of PC-TV highlights the issue of technological *convergence*, that is, technologies which had been produced and used separately are beginning to merge into one. Thus, convergence refers to the breakdown of boundaries between technologies, which is paralleled by organizational convergence, as documented above, so that synergy is sought through mergers and take-overs giving rise to multimedia corporations.

Digital technology

To a considerable degree such technological convergence is enabled by digital technology, which enables information to be electronically organized into bytes, or discrete bundles of information, which can be compressed during

transmission and decompressed on arrival. This allows a good deal more information to travel down any given conduit, be that cable, satellite or terrestrial signals (it also opens up previously unusable zones of the spectrum to use) and at greater speed over larger distances. Indeed, the impact of new technologies in general, and digital processes in particular, can be summed up in terms of speed, volume and distance, that, is more information at greater speed over larger distances. Alongside the development of digital television, it is becoming apparent that the technologies having the most impact are those concerned with distribution – cable and satellite. Organizations which control the distribution mechanisms are eclipsing the power of producers because no one wants to commit expensive resources to a project which has not secured a distribution agreement.

Satellites

Satellites are able to offer a much increased number of TV signals, either directly or via head stations of cable systems and, despite high start-up costs, have the potential to offer high-quality picture and sound on a much increased scale. Of course, the impact of satellite technology has been distinct in different parts of the world. In India, the development of commercial satellite television threatens state-owned television's (Doordarshan) dominance (forcing the government to entertain commercial broadcasting) whereas in Britain, though the satellite channels of BSkyB have had some success in creating a niche for themselves, especially in relation to sport, the audience share of 8 per cent has some way to go before it can be seen to dislodge the BBC or Independent Television (ITV) channels. A similar contrast be can be made between the Netherlands, where the Luxembourg based Radio Télévision Luxembourg 4 (RTL4) satellite station has made decisive inroads into the Dutch market, and the USA, where Direct Broadcasting by Satellite (DBS) has had little impact having been eclipsed by cable (though News Corporation's intervention in the market may change this).

Cable systems

Most of the present cable systems are based on the copper coaxial specification. However, its future will lie with the use of fibre-optic cable with its far greater capabilities in terms of channel capacity and the potential for interactive programmes. Unsurprisingly, there is still extremely unequal development of cable across the globe with, for example, nearly 70 per cent of television households having access to cable in North America, some 23 per cent in the European Union, 20 per cent in Asia and only 7 per cent in South America. World levels of cable penetration of television households stands at about 23 per cent, which represents about 189 million households (*Screen Digest*, April 1995).

In the USA, cable expanded at a considerable rate during the early 1980s (indeed Fox-TV is effectively a fourth network) though the latter part of the decade saw a considerable slowing of penetration rates. In contrast, cable struggled in the UK, which has one of the lowest cable density rates in Europe despite the government's attempts to encourage its development. However, during the 1990s a new wave of American investment in British cable, combined with its use as a carrier for satellite programmes, has prompted a gradual expansion of cable though it is a long way from the 95 per cent penetration level enjoyed by the Netherlands – the most densely cabled country in Europe.

Industry and government

The kinds of *synergy* and *convergence* described above have been made to happen by the captains of industry and allowed to happen by politicians. For, though multimedia conglomerates have existed for many years, the scope of their activities has been permitted to widen by governments who have relaxed the regulations that restricted cross-media ownership and the entry of new players. That is, the media have been undergoing a period of deregulation.

Deregulation and re-regulation in global television

The mid-1980s and early 1990s witnessed a significant period of deregulation in television or, to be more accurate, re-regulation. These new regulations, which are considerably less stringent than their predecessors, have been occasioned by a number of factors including

- the growth of 'new' communication technologies which have invalidated the natural monopoly argument since digital technology allows frequencies to be split and alternative delivery systems employed
- the establishment by court rulings in various countries of the legal right to communicate and the adoption of diversity as a key public principle
- governmental enthusiasm (particularly in the USA and UK) for the market, including a preference for the funding of television by commercial means rather than through taxation.

Thus, it was the relaxation of television and newspaper ownership rules that allowed Murdoch to launch Fox cable TV in the USA and to own newspapers and television companies in the UK. Similarly, deregulation has allowed AT&T, the biggest telephone operator in the USA, to participate in the television market from which it had previously been excluded by law. In the UK, the privatization of British Telecom (BT) and the deregulation of the telecommunications industries has led BT, best known for its telephone business, to seek new global partners, which will let it into the cable television market and allied services.

New European tele-landscapes

Deregulation and commercial expansion have prompted widespread discussion about the emerging shape of the new tele-landscapes. In Europe, the 'old order' was marked by the subordination of broadcasting to public service goals set in the context of a broadly political process of regulation. Television was of a largely national character and was generally non-commercial in principle. The 'new order' in television is marked by the coexistence of public and commercial broadcasting, the deregulation of commercial television, the increasing emergence of multimedia transnational companies and pressure on public service television to operate with a commercial logic.

Public television viewing figures

Data . . . certainly suggest a decline, though not as yet a terminal one, in the viewing figures for public television in Europe. For example, in France and Germany, public television which in 1975 accounted for 100 per cent of viewers took only 33 and 60 per cent respectively in 1990. The decline was somewhat less dramatic in the UK where the percentage move was from 52 (1975) to 48 per cent (1990). Nevertheless, public service broadcasting has proved surprisingly resilient in the face of competition. For example, in Australia the nationally funded Australian Broadcasting Commission (ABC) has achieved its highest ratings for decades, in Italy the public Radiotelevisione Italiana (RAI) channels rate better than their combined commercial rivals, in India the state owned Doordarshan is fighting back against commercial opposition and in Britain the BBC looks set to remain a major player for the foreseeable future. However, though they have survived, public service organizations are now simply *one* player, instead of being *the* player, in the more plural and fragmented global television landscape which has sedimented itself in the 1990s and looks set to grow into a new century.

Globalization and technology

Overall, the technologies of cable, satellite, digital technology and international computer networks enable media organizations to operate on a global scale by assisting in the process of internal organizational communication and in allowing media products to be distributed across the world. Both functions of new technology are intimately bound up with the globalization of media in general and television in particular which, it can be argued, are laying the foundations of a global electronic culture.

Chris Barker, 'Global Television and Global Culture', in *Television, Globalization and Cultural Identities*, Open University Press, 1999, pp. 45–51

➤ Collect examples of American media products that have played an important role in British media consumption. What do you think is the underlying ideological 'message' of these texts?

FURTHER READING

Curran, J. and Park, M. (2000) *De-westernizing Media Studies,* Routledge.
A collection of essays exploring the media throughout the world. The introduction is a source of useful examples of current thinking on the issue of globalisation.

Sreberny, A. (2002) 'Media Imperialism', in T. Miller (ed.), *Television Studies,* British Film Institute.
A short but useful overview of the debates surrounding media imperialism.

▼ CONCLUSION: MEDIA STUDIES AND POSTMODERNISM

As we noted in the Introduction to this book, many of the ideas and theories that have been used to underpin Media Studies during its growth in the second half of the twentieth century are now being reassessed or questioned as we move into the new millennium.

For many commentators in the fields of Cultural and Media Studies, postmodernism is one of the key concepts in understanding our changing relationship with media texts and cultural products. Postmodernism, however, is a word that can be seen to pose more questions than it can answer. This is not least because it is a word that is asked to do so much work. One reason that the word has become overworked is that it is applied to so many disciplines, as well as being used to sum up much of what is seen both to excite and disappoint people about culture in western societies in the early twenty-first century. Often 'postmodern' is an adjective applied to any facet of our cultural life that we find baffling, confusing, or irritating, or which simply cannot be explained by any earlier theory or model.

In his essay on postmodernism, John Storey quotes Dick Hebdige, who in 1988 suggested some of the current meanings of the word.

> When it becomes possible for people to describe as 'postmodern' the decor of a room, the design of a building, the diegesis of a film, the construction of a record, or a 'scratch' video, a television commercial, or an arts documentary, or the 'intertextual' relations between them, the layout of a page in a fashion magazine or critical journal, an anti-teleological tendency within epistemology, the attack on the 'metaphysics of presence', a general attenuation of feeling, the collective chagrin and morbid projections of a post-War generation of baby boomers confronting disillusioned middle age, the 'predicament' of reflexivity, a group of rhetorical tropes, a proliferation of surfaces, a new phase in commodity fetishism, a fascination for images, codes and styles, a process of cultural, political, or existential fragmentation and/or crisis, the 'de-centring' of the subject, an 'incredulity towards metanarratives', the replacement of unitary power axes by a plurality of power/discourse formations, the 'implosion of meaning', the collapse

of cultural hierarchies, the dread engendered by the threat of nuclear self-destruction, the decline of the university, the functioning and effects of the new miniaturised technologies, broad societal and economic shifts into a 'media', 'consumer' or 'multinational' phase, a sense (depending on who you read) of 'placelessness' or the abandonment of placelessness ('critical regionalism') or (even) a generalised substitution of spatial for temporal co-ordinates – when it becomes possible to describe all these things as 'postmodern' (or more simply, using a current abbreviation, as 'post' or 'very post') then it's clear we are in the presence of a buzzword.

D. Hebdige, *Hiding in the Light: On Images and Things*, Comedia, 1988, pp. 181–2.

ACTIVITY

➤ Choose one of Hebdige's suggested meanings and explain how it might relate to the concept of postmodernism as you understand it.

One of the fundamentals of postmodernism is its rejection of the divide between high and low culture. This means that popular or mass culture has to be reconsidered and re-evaluated. In the work of a 1960s pop artist such as Andy Warhol, for example, we see the merging of high and popular culture. Warhol takes his inspiration from popular cultural forms, such as Marilyn Monroe, and produces an art that plays with her image and becomes in itself much valued as a high art form and worth huge sums of money on international art markets. In 1999, as part of the Turner Prize, visitors to the Tate Britain Art Gallery in London walked into an exhibition space to study a work of art called 'My Bed'. This piece, an unmade bed by Tracey Emin, was supposed to be a reflection of her ordinary, daily life, and included soiled underwear, used condoms, remains of food and drink, and other examples of daily human existence. Paradoxes such as this, a piece of 'ordinary' life exhibited in a world-class gallery as a piece of 'high' art, lie at the heart of postmodernism.

Some commentators argue that postmodernism is itself a transitory force. They suggest that it exists only as a bridge between one type of modernism and a new modernism that is yet to emerge. Whatever the truth of the matter, it is clear that postmodernism is an important concept for Media Studies. Creators of texts choose to refer to people like Myra Hindley or Diana Princess of Wales in their work because of their celebrity status and the way in which their images, histories and reputations become part of our daily lives and popular culture. This status is achieved through the media itself: television programmes that repeatedly tell and retell their stories, their images occurring and recurring in magazines and the scandals and details about their private lives reported, often salaciously, in the press. This is therefore a complex relationship where the (popular) media will create personalities or celebrities who then become part of the iconography of (high) art which is in turn reported and commented on in the (popular) media.

In the extract that follows, Dominic Strinati attempts to pin down some of the key features of postmodernism. An important aspect of postmodernism for Strinati is the fact that it represents an attempt come to terms with the predominance of mass media in our society. As Strinati points out, 'The world has come to consist of media screens and cultural surfaces.' This insistence on the importance of surfaces is for many people the essence of postmodernism, a world of superficial transitory images.

The complete essay, 'Postmodernism and Popular Culture' in *An Introduction to Theories of Popular Culture*, is worth tracking down and reading as it goes on to exemplify the concept across a range of media and cultural forms.

WHAT IS POSTMODERNISM?

In order to identify postmodernism, the following – by no means exhaustive – set of points summarises some of the most salient features which writers about the phenomenon have chosen to emphasise. . . .

The breakdown of the distinction between culture and society

First, postmodernism is said to describe the emergence of a social order in which the importance and power of the mass media and popular culture mean that they govern and shape all other forms of social relationships. The idea is that popular cultural signs and media images increasingly dominate our sense of reality, and the way we define ourselves and the world around us. It tries to come to terms with, and understand, a media-saturated society. The mass media, for example, were once thought of as holding up a mirror to, and thereby reflecting, a wider social reality. Now reality can only be defined by the surface reflections of this mirror. Society has become subsumed within the mass media. It is no longer even a question of distortion, since the term implies that there is a reality, outside the surface simulations of the media, which can be distorted, and this is precisely what is at issue according to postmodern theory.

This idea, in part, seems to emerge out of one of the directions taken by media and cultural theory. To put it simply, the liberal view argued that the media held up a mirror to, and thereby reflected in a fairly accurate manner, a wider social reality. The radical rejoinder to this insisted that this mirror distorted rather than reflected reality. Subsequently, a more abstract and conceptual media and cultural theory suggested that the media played some part in constructing our sense of social reality, and our sense of being a part of this reality . . . It is a relatively short step from this (and one which need not be taken) to the proposition that only the media can constitute our sense of reality. To return to the original metaphor, it is claimed that this mirror is now the only reality we have.

Moreover, linked to this is the notion that in the postmodern condition it becomes more difficult to distinguish the economy from popular culture. The realm of consumption – what we buy and what determines what we buy – is increasingly influenced by popular culture. Consumption is increasingly bound up with popular culture because popular culture increasingly determines consumption. For example, we watch more films because of the extended ownership of VCRs, while advertising, which makes increasing use of popular cultural references, plays a more important role in deciding what we will buy.

An emphasis on style at the expense of substance

A crucial implication of the first point is that in a postmodern world, surfaces and style become more important, and evoke in their turn a kind of 'designer ideology'. Or as Harvey puts it: 'images dominate narrative' (1989: 347–8). The argument is that we increasingly consume images and signs for their own sake rather than for their 'usefulness' or for the deeper values they may symbolise. We consume images and signs precisely because they are images and signs, and disregard questions of utility and value. This is evident in popular culture itself where surface and style, what things look like, and playfulness and jokes, are said to predominate at the expense of content, substance and meaning. As a result, qualities like artistic merit, integrity, seriousness, authenticity, realism, intellectual depth and strong narratives tend to be undermined. Moreover, virtual reality computer graphics can allow people to experience various forms of reality at second hand. These surface simulations can therefore potentially replace their real-life counterparts

The breakdown of the distinction between art and popular culture

If the first two points are accepted, it follows that for postmodern culture anything can be turned into a joke, reference or quotation in its eclectic play of styles, simulations and surfaces. If popular cultural signs and media images are taking over in defining our sense of reality for us, and if this means that style takes precedence over content, then it becomes more difficult to maintain a meaningful distinction between art and popular culture. There are no longer any agreed and inviolable criteria which can serve to differentiate art from popular culture. Compare this with the fears of the mass culture critics that mass culture would eventually subvert high culture. The only difference seems to be that these critics were pessimistic about these developments, whereas some, but not all, postmodern theorists are by contrast optimistic.

A good example of what posmodernist theory is getting at is provided by Andy Warhol's multi-imaged print of Leonardo da Vinci's famous painting 'The Mona Lisa'. The print shows that the uniqueness, the artistic aura, of the 'Mona Lisa' is destroyed by its infinite reproducibility through the silk-screen printing technique employed by Warhol. Instead, it is turned into a joke – the print's title is 'Thirty are better than One'. This point is underlined by the fact that Warhol was renowned for his prints of famous popular cultural icons like Marilyn Monroe and Elvis Presley as well as of everyday consumer items like tins of Campbell's soup, Coca-Cola bottles and dollar bills.

One aspect of this process is that art becomes increasingly integrated into the economy both because it is used to encourage people to consume through the expanded role it plays in advertising, and because it becomes a commercial good in its own right. Another aspect is that postmodern popular culture refuses to respect the pretensions and distinctiveness of art. Therefore, the breakdown of the distinction between art and popular culture, as well as crossovers between the two, become more prevalent.

Confusions over time and space

It is argued here that contemporary and future compressions and focusing of time and space have led to increasing confusion and incoherence in our sense of space and time, in our maps of the places where we live, and our ideas about the times in terms of which we organise our lives. The title and the narratives of the *Back to the Future* films capture this point fairly well. The growing immediacy of global space and time resulting from the dominance of the mass media means that our previously unified and coherent ideas about space and time begin to be undermined, and become distorted and confused. Rapid international flows of capital, money, information and culture disrupt the linear unities of time, and the established distances of geographical space. Because of the speed and scope of modern mass communications, and the relative ease and rapidity with which people and information can travel, time and space become less stable and comprehensible, and more confused and incoherent (Harvey: 1989, part 3).

Postmodern popular culture is seen to express these confusions and distortions. As such, it is less likely to reflect coherent senses of space or time. Some idea of this argument can be obtained by trying to identify the locations used in some pop videos, the linear narratives of some recent films or the times and spaces crossed in a typical evening of television viewing. In short, postmodern popular culture is a culture *sans frontières*, outside history.

The decline of metanarratives

The loss of a sense of history as a continuous, linear 'narrative', a clear sequence of events, is indicative of the argument that, in the postmodern world, meta-narratives are in decline. This point about the decline of metanarratives arises out of the previous arguments we have noted. Metanarratives, examples of which

include religion, science, art, modernism and Marxism, make absolute, universal and all-embracing claims to knowledge and truth. Postmodernist theory is highly sceptical about these metanarratives, and argues that they are increasingly open to criticism. In the postmodern world they are disintegrating, their validity and legitimacy are in decline. It is becoming increasingly difficult for people to organise and interpret their lives in the light of metanarratives of whatever kind. This argument would therefore include, for example, the declining significance of religion as a metanarrative in postmodern societies. Postmodernism has been particularly critical of the metanarrative of Marxism and its claim to absolute truth, as it has been of any theory which tries to read a pattern of progress into history.

The consequence of this is that postmodernism rejects the claims of any theory to absolute knowledge, or of any social practice to universal validity. So, for example, on the one hand there are movements in the natural or hard sciences away from deterministic and absolute metanarratives towards more contingent and probabilistic claims to the truth, while on the other hand people appear to be moving away from the metanarrative of lifelong, monogamous marriage towards a series of discrete if still monogamous 'relationships' . . . The diverse, iconoclastic, referential and collage-like character of postmodern popular culture clearly draws inspiration from the decline of metanarratives.

D. Strinati, 'Postmodernism and Popular Culture', An Introduction to Theories of Popular Culture, Routledge, 1995, pp. 223–8

Part of the difficulty facing Media Studies as a discipline is this omnipresence of media images in our lives. Jean Baudrillard (1983) argues that the media, and in particular television, stand at the centre of postmodern culture as they produce an explosion of signs, images and texts that are consumed across a variety of genres, channels and media. Baudrillard uses the notion of the 'hyperreal' to describe the way in which the media have created a reality that is in many ways more real than 'everyday reality'. By selecting and editing information and images, the media are able to produce a constant stream of heightened reality which is continually delivered into our homes 24/7, to use a term typical of postmodernism. This heightened reality Baudrillard calls the *simulacra*, or culture of simulation, where the media's version of reality becomes more important than, and/or indistinguishable from, social reality.

In the 1991 film *Slacker*, directed by Richard Linklater, we are introduced to a character (video backpacker, Kalman Spellitich) who lives in a room filled with televisions, including one which he wears on his back. His explanation of his delight in the video image is clearly based on Baudrillard's notion of the hyperreal. For this character, the video experience is preferable to real life, as he explains:

To me, my thing is, a video image is much more powerful and useful than an actual event. Like back when I used to go out, when I was last out, I was walking down the street and this guy, that came barreling out of a bar, fell right in front of me, and he had a knife right in his back, landed right on the ground and . . . Well, I have no reference to it now. I can't put it on pause. I can't put it on slow mo and see all the little details. And the blood, it was all wrong. It didn't look like blood. The hue was off. I couldn't adjust the hue. I was seeing it for real, but it just wasn't right. And I didn't even see the knife impact on the body. I missed that part.

Baudrillard also sees contemporary society as homogenized by a movement towards mass consumerism and increased commodification, where every experience can be separated from its 'reality' and instead be packaged and sold as part of a consumer culture. Eating sushi in a UK-owned fast food chain with a jokey French name, *Pret-A-Manger*, is an example where the immediate consumption of a certain type of food is separated from the reality of the culture that originally produced the food or the culture that originally created the term *prêt-à-porter* (ready to wear) from the fashion world.

ACTIVITY

> ➤ Go to www.pret.com/philosophy/ to see how a fast-food company presents itself, its philosophy and how it tries to turn buying sandwiches into a special shopping experience. Consider, in particular, the image that the company tries to create for itself by claiming that its staff are highly talented and that they have 'chosen' to work for the company, or the way in which the company highlights the fact that 'Whatever we haven't sold by the time we close, we prefer to give to local charities to help feed those who would otherwise go hungry'. In what ways do you think Pret-A-Manger could be considered postmodern?

In section 8 on 'Ideology and Advertising' in Part 1, we examined the ways in which brands are advertised as something more than just products, jeans, coffee, sandwiches or whatever. Instead these goods are sold to us as part of a lifestyle. Advertisers try to suggest to us that by buying these particular brands our lives will somehow be better, that we will become better people living in a better world. Thus shopping promises to make us somehow complete. It is interesting to note that in 1940 Winston Churchill extolled the British to fight 'on the beaches . . .' whereas in America post 9/11 George Bush exhorted the Americans to go shop so that the economy would not falter or be damaged.

The media play a central part in this increasing commodification of experience whether it is through films like *Rabbit-Proof Fence*, which tries to capture the experience of kidnapped Aborigine children in Australia for paying cinema audiences, or the television programmes on wildlife, natural history or exotic destinations on subscription channels like Discovery or National Geographic. Celebrities like Geri Halliwell or Kylie Minogue also become commodities who then use their images as brands to sell more commodities, their keep-fit videos or CDs and concerts. As Gauntlett notes, the media are increasingly packaging and repackaging their products, trying to sell them to us again and again, for example the reissue of No.1 singles by Elvis Presley or the Beatles in special

compilations or the recycling of television's own history through programmes like *Auntie's Bloomers* or the *One Hundred Greatest* . . . series.

Compounding this increased blurring of the boundaries between the hyperreal and the real, between high and low culture, we must add the proliferation of media outlets. As we noted in section 5 on 'Audience Segmentation' in Part 2, in recent years the expansion of digital technology has resulted in increasing access to the Internet, digital radio stations and television channels as well as the development of increasingly sophisticated mobile-phone services. Alongside this is the convergence of the 'lean-back' technologies of entertainment such as television, video or DVD and hi-fi music and radio and the 'lean-forward' technologies of work and communication associated with PCs. Increasingly the distinction between these two areas of domestic consumption is also blurring. We use hard disks to store and access television programmes and music files and use television services to email and access the Internet. MP3 files may be downloaded from a PC but can be played through a hi-fi system. Eventually we may have one piece of domestic hardware that will provide telephone, email, fax and audio webcasts and stored files as well as television broadcasts both broadcast and stored on hard disk. All this could be linked together and equipped with a sound system that provides a 'cinema-like' experience.

In the face of this expansion of domestic consumption of the media, it is increasingly problematic to apply traditional ways of thinking about the media. It is no longer appropriate to consider the production and consumption of media texts in narrow and particular ways.

As the range of media outlets available to us increases, so too does the demand for content. It is expensive to make original high-quality television programmes and so the need to recycle old material becomes greater. Reality television and chat shows are cheap to produce and so become more widespread in the schedules. The 'Who are You?' campaign below is an opportunity for us, the audience, to become both the producers and subject of the programmes and to construct, or reconstruct, ourselves in particular ways; in effect to be part of our own process of mediation of our identities. As with Tracey Emin's unmade bed, these portraits will become 'art' and be exhibited in one of London's main art galleries, the National Portrait Gallery. As Storey (1993: 179) notes, these postmodern trends raise many questions 'not least the role of the student of popular culture: that is, what is our relationship to our object of study? With what authority, and for whom, do we speak?'

The flyer text reads:

challenging the nation's image and our notions of 'Britishness'

self portrait uk

Who are you?

Do you want to be part of a national self-portrait project and see your own self-portrait on primetime TV and displayed at exhibition sites across the UK?

Can you reveal the real you?

Self Portrait UK invites us all - young and old - to make our own self-portrait.

You can use any medium to make an image or statement about yourself, from a quick sketch, cartoon or snapshot to a digital image, video, painting, drawing, poem, piece of writing, photograph or animation. Your self-portrait can be funny, thoughtful, serious, abstract or realistic and you don't have to be an artist to take part. It's your chance to be bold and imaginative and to present yourself as you really want to be seen!

Self-portraits which best reveal the unique imagination, individuality and diversity of modern Britain will be featured in a primetime slot on Channel 4, displayed at the National Portrait Gallery and toured to key arts venues across the UK.

Do you want to find out more?

At www.channel4.com/selfportraituk you can find further information about Self Portrait UK, together with ideas on how to start making a self-portrait and details of how to take part.

You can also call 0845 6023635 (calls are charged at local rates) or write for further information to:

SELF PORTRAIT UK
MEDIA 19
PO BOX 83
GATESHEAD
NE9 5WZ

The closing date for submitting self-portraits is February 14th 2003

www.channel4.com/selfportraituk

Self-Portrait UK is a Media 19 initiative supported by Channel 4, Northern Arts and the National Portrait Gallery.

Who are you?
www.channel4.com/selfportraituk

And finally

ACTIVITY

➤ Consider the flyer for the 'Who are You?' campaign. In what ways is this similar to Tracey Emin exhibiting her unmade bed at the Tate Modern? What does it say about the ways in which personal identity are constructed, mediated and distributed? How useful are the key concepts of Media Studies in understanding and explaining this text? It is not clear what genre it belongs to nor what the narrative of the text may be. Who do you think will be the audience for these programmes? What do you think will be the appeal of these programmes for audiences? In what ways could this campaign be considered a postmodern activity?

▼ REFERENCES

Abercrombie, N. (1996) *Television and Society*, Polity.

Allen, S. (2000) *News Culture*, Open University.

Ang, I. (1985) *Watching Dallas*, Routledge.

Barker, C. (1999), *Television, Globalization and Cultural Identities*, Open University.

Barker, M. (1998) 'Critique: Audiences 'R' Us', in R. Dickinson, R. Harindranath and O. Linné (eds), *Approaches to Audiences: A Reader*, Arnold.

Barker, M. and Petley, J. (eds) (2001) *Ill Effects: The Media/Violence Debate*, 2nd edn Routledge.

Barthes, R. (1973) *Mythologies*, Paladin.

—— (1977) *Images–Music–Text*, Fontana.

Baudrillard, J. (1983) *Simulations*, trans. P. Foss, P. Patton and P. Beitchman, Semiotext(e).

Bazalgette, P. (2000) 'It's only a Gameshow', *Guardian*, 6 September 2000.

Bell, A., Joyce, M. and Rivers, D. (1999) *Advanced Media Studies*, Hodder & Stoughton.

Bignell, J. (1997) *Media Semiotics: An Introduction*, Manchester University Press.

Blaikie, A. (1999) *Ageing and Popular Culture*, Cambridge University Press.

Bordwell, D. and Thompson, K. (1990) *Film Art: An Introduction*, McGraw Hill.

Branston, G. and Stafford, R. (1999) *The Media Student's Book*, 2nd edn, Routledge.

Burton, G., (2000) *Talking Television: An Introduction to the Study of Television*, Arnold.

Casey, B., Casey, N., Calvert, B., French, L. and Lewis, J. (2002) *Television Studies: The Key Concepts*, Routledge.

Castells, M. (1996) *The Rise of the Network Society*, Blackwell.

Chippendale, P. and Horrie, C. (1990) *Stick it up Your Punter: The Rise and Fall of the* Sun, Heinemann.

Cohen, S. (2002) *Folk Devils and Moral Panics*, Routledge.

Collins, J. (1993) 'Genericity in the Nineties: Eclectic Irony and the New Sincerity', in J. Collins *et al.* (eds), *Film Theory Goes to the Movies*, Routledge.

Cottle, S. (1999) 'Ethnic Minorities and the British News Media: Explaining (Mis)Representation' in J. Stokes and A. Reading (eds), *The Media in Britain: Current Debates and Developments*, Macmillan.

Cramer, J. (1993) 'A Woman's Place is on the Air', in P. Creedon (ed.), *Women in Mass Communication*, 2nd edn, Sage.

Crisell, A. (1986) *Understanding Radio*, Methuen.

Crisell, A. (1999) 'Broadcasting: Television and Radio' in J. Stokes and A. Reading (eds), *The Media in Britain: Current Debates and Developments*, Macmillan.

Curran, J. and Seaton, J. (1997) *Power Without Responsibility: The Press and Broadcasting in Britain*, 3rd edn, Routledge.

Davies, S. (2002) 'A Semiotic Analysis of Teenage Magazine Covers' www.aber.ac.uk/media/Students/Sid9901.

Denselow, R. (1989) *When The Music's Over*, Faber.

Dickinson, R., Harindranath, R. and Linné, O. (eds) (1998) *Approaches to Audiences*, Arnold.

Dovey, J. (2000) *Freakshow: First Person Media and Factual Television*, Pluto Press.

Dyer, G. (1989) *Advertising as Communication*, Routledge.

—— (2000) *Maintaining the 'Gold Standard'*, MacTaggart Memorial Lecture 2000.

Eldridge, J.E.T. (1995) *News Content, Language and Visuals: Glasgow Media Reader*, Routledge.

Eliot, M. (1989) *Rockonomics: The Money behind the Music*, Omnibus Press.

Engel, M. (1996) *Tickle the Public. One Hundred Years of the Popular Press*, Gollancz.

Fiske, J. (1990) *Introduction to Communication Studies*, 2nd edn, Routledge.

—— (1991) *Understanding Popular Culture*, Routledge.

Franklin, B. (ed.) (2002) *British Television Policy: A Reader*, Routledge.

Frith, S. (1996) *Performing Rites: On the Value of Popular Music*, Oxford University Press.

Frith, S. and Goodwin, A. (eds) (1990) *On Record: Rock, Pop and the Written Word*, Routledge.

Gabb, J. (1999) 'Consuming The Garden: Locating A Feminine Narrative within Popular Cultural Texts and Gendered Genres', in J. Stokes and A. Reading (eds), *The Media in Britain: Current Debates and Developments*, Macmillan.

Gallagher, M. (1995) *An Unfinished Story: Gender Patterns in Media Employment*, UNESCO Reprints on Mass Communications, 110.

Gauntlett, D. (1995) *Moving Experiences: Understanding Television's Influences and Effects*, John Libbey.

—— (1997) *Video Critical: Children, the Environment and Media Power*, John Libbey Media.

—— '10 Things Wrong with the Effects Model', in R. Dickinson, R. Harindranath, and O. Linné (eds), *Approaches to Audiences*, Arnold. Available online at: www.theory.org.uk/effects.htm.

—— (ed.) (2000) *Web.studies: Rewiring Media Studies for the Digital Age*, Arnold.

Geraghty, C. (1991) *Women and Soap Opera*, Polity Press.

—— (1998) '*Audiences and Ethnography: Questions of Practice*' in C. Geraghty and D. Lusted (eds), *The Television Studies Book*, Arnold.

—— (2000) *British Cinema in the Fifties: Gender, Genre and the 'New Look'*, Routledge.

Gerbner, G. (1994) 'The Politics of Media Violence: Some Reflections', in O. Linné and C.J. Hamelink (eds), *Mass Communication Research: On Problems and Policies*, Ablex Publishing.

Gerbner, G., Gross, L. and Melody, T. (eds) (1973) *Communication Technology and Social Policy*, Wiley Interscience.

Gerbner, G., Gross, L., Morgan, M. and Signorelli, N. (1986 'Living with Television: the Dynamics of the Cultivation Process' in J. Bryant and D. Zillman (eds), *Perspectives in Media Effects*, Lawrence Erlbaum.

Gill, R. (1993) 'Justifying Injustice: Broadcasters' Accounts of Inequality in a Radio Station', in E. Burman and J. Parker (eds), *Discourse Analytic Research*, Routledge.

Glaessner, V. (1990) 'Gendered Fictions' in A. Goodwin and G. Whannel (eds) *Understanding Television*, Routledge.

Glasgow University Media Group (1985) *War and Peace News*, Routledge.

Goodwin, P. (1999) 'The Role of the State' in J. Stokes and A. Reading (eds), *The Media in Britain: Current Debates and Developments*, Macmillan.

Gray, A. (1991) *Video Playtime*, Routledge.

Greeber, G. (2001) *The Television Genre Book*, British Film Institute.

Greer, G. (2001) 'Watch with Brother', *Observer*, 24 June 2001.

Griffin, C. (1993) *Representations of Youth: the Study of Youth and Adolescence in Britain and America*, Polity Press.

Gunter, B. (2000) *Media Research Methods*, Sage.

Gunter, B., Sancho-Aldridge, J. and Winstone, P. (1994) *Television: The Public's View 1993*, Independent Television Commission Research Monographs series, John Libbey.

Hagell, A. and Newburn, T. (1994) *Young Offenders and the Media: Viewing Habits and Preferences*, Policy Studies Institute, London.

Hall, S. (1980) 'Encoding, Decoding', in S. Hall *et al.* (eds), *Culture, Media, Language: Working Papers in Cultural Studies*, Hutchinson.

Hall, S. (ed) (1997) *Representation: Cultural Representations and Signifying Practices*, Sage.

Hanks, R. (2002) 'Deconstructing *Buffy*', *Independent*, 1 July 2002.

Harcup, T. and O'Neill, D. (2001) 'What is News? Galtung and Ruge Revisited', *Journalism Studies*, vol. 2, no. 2, Routledge.

Hartley, J. (1982) *Understanding News*, Routledge.

Harvey, D. (1989) *The Condition of Postmodernity*, Blackwell.

Hill, A. and Calcutt, I. (2001) 'Vampire Hunters: the Scheduling and Reception of *Buffy the Vampire Slayer* and *Angel* in the UK', *Intensities: The Journal of Cult Media* online at www.cult-media.com, issue 1 Spring/Summer 2001.

Hobson, D. (1982) *Crossroads: The Drama of a Soap Opera*, Methuen.

Hollows, J. and Jancovich, M. (1995) *Approaches to Popular Film*, Manchester University Press.

Jenkins, H. (1992) *Textual Poachers: Television Fans and Participatory Everyday Life*, Routledge.

Jordan, M. (1981) 'Realisms and Convention' in R. Dyer *et al.* (eds), *Coronation Street*, British Film Institute.

Kaveney, R. (ed.) (2002) *Reading the Vampire Slayer: An Unofficial Critical Companion to Buffy and Angel*, Tauris Parke Paperbacks.

Klein, N. (2000) *No Logo*, Flamingo.

Lister, D. (2002) 'Why We Should be Complaining about the PCC', *Independent*, 5 February 2002.

Lister, M., Dovey, J., Giddings, S. and Grant, I. (2003) *New Media: A Critical Introduction*, Routledge.

Livingstone, S. (1990) *Making Sense of Televsion*, Routledge.

Lull, J. (1990) 'How Families Select Programs', in J. Lull, *Inside Family Viewing*, Routledge.

MacCabe, C. (1981a) 'Realism in the Cinema', in T. Bennett *et al.* (eds), *Popular Television and Film*, British Film Institute/Open University Press.

—— (1981b) 'Days of Hope: A Response to Colin MacArthur', in T. Bennett *et al.* (eds), *Popular Television and Film*, British Film Institute/Open University Press.

McDonald, P. (1999) 'The Music Industry' ,in J. Stokes and A. Reading (eds), *The Media in Britain: Current Debates and Developments*, Macmillan.

McRobbie, A. (1996) '*More!* New Sexualities in Girls' and Women's Magazines' in J. Curran, D. Morley and V. Walkerdine (eds), *Cultural Studies and Communications*, Arnold.

—— (2000) *Feminism and Youth Culture: from* Jackie *to Just Seventeen*, 2nd edn, Macmillan.

Miller, T. (ed) (2002) *Television Studies*, British Film Institute.

Mitchell, C. (ed) (2000) *Women and Radio: Airing Differences*, Routledge.

Modleski, T. (1982) *Loving with a Vengence: Mass-produced Fantasies for Women*, Archon Books.

Monaco, J. (1981) *How to Read a Film*, Oxford University Press.

Moores, S. (1993) *Interpreting Audiences: The Ethnography of Media Consumption*, Sage.

Morley, D. (1992) *Television, Audiences and Cultural Studies*, Routledge.

Morrow, F. (2000) 'Dumb and Dumber' MediaWatch 2000, *BFI/Sight & Sound*.

Morse, M. (1986) 'The Television News Personality and Credibility', in T. Modleski (ed.) *Studies in Entertainment*, Indiana University Press.

Morse, M. (1988) *Virtualities*, Indiana University Press.

Mulvey, L. (1975) 'Visual Pleasure and Narrative Cinema', *Screen*, vol. 16, no. 3.

Murdoch, R. (1989) *Freedom in Broadcasting*, MacTaggart Memorial Lecture 1989.

Murdock, G. (1990) 'Redrawing the Map of the Communications Industries', in M. Ferguson (ed.) *Public Communication: the News Imperatives*, Sage.

Murdock, G. and Golding, P. (1997) 'Capitalism, Communications and Class Realations', in J. Curran, M. Gurevitch and J. Woollacott (eds), *Mass Communications and Society*, Edward Arnold for the Open University Press.

Negus, K. (1992) *Producing Pop*, Arnold.

O'Rorke, I. (1999) 'Who Do You Fancy for Breakfast?', *Guardian*, 1 November 1999.

O'Sullivan, T., Dutton, B. & Rayner, P. (2003) *Studying the Media*, 3rd edn, Arnold.

Petley, J. (1999) 'The Regulation of Media Content' in J. Stokes and A. Reading (eds), *The Media in Britain: Current Debates and Developments*, Macmillan.

Plunkett, J. (2002) 'Reality TV Shows Scoop Viewers', *Guardian*, 16 October 2002.

Potter, D. (1993) *Defending Public Service Broadcasting from 'Occupying Powers'*, MacTaggart Memorial Lecture 1993.

Pullen, K. 'I-love-Xena.com: Creating Online Fan Communities', in D. Gauntlett (ed.) *Web.studies: Rewiring Media Studies*, Arnold.

Radway, J. (1991) *Reading the Romance: Women, Patriarchy and Popular Literature*, University of Carolina Press.

Rayner, P., Wall, P. and Kruger, S. (2001) *Media Studies: The Essential Introduction*, Routledge.

Roscoe, J. and Hight, C. (2001) *Faking It: Mock-documentary and the Subversion of Factuality*, Manchester University Press.

Ronson, J. (2002) 'The Egos Have Landed', *Sight and Sound BFI*. Online at: www.bfi.org.uk/sightandsound/2002_11/feature01_egos_have_landed.

Rushdie, S. (2001) 'Reality TV: a Dearth of Talent and the Death of Morality', *Guardian*, 9 June 2001.

Scannell, P. (1999) 'The Phenomenology of *Blind Date* in J. Stokes and A. Reading (eds), *The Media in Britain: Current Debates and Developments*, Macmillan.

Seiter, E. (1992) 'Semiotics, Structuralism and Television', in R. Allen (ed.) *Channels of Discourse Reassembled*, Routledge.

Stam, R. (1983) 'Television News and its Spectator', in E.A. Kaplan (ed.) *Regarding Television*, University Publications of America.

Stevenson, N. (1997) 'Critical Perspectives with Audience Research', in T. O'Sullivan and Y. Jewkes (eds) *The Media Studies Reader*, Arnold.

Stokes, J. (2003) *How to do Media and Cultural Studies*, Sage.

Storey, J. (1993) *An Introductory Guide to Cultural Theory and Popular Culture*, Harvester Wheatsheaf.

Strinati, D. (1995) *An Introduction to Theories of Popular Culture*, Routledge.

Shuker, R. (1998) *Popular Music: The Key Concepts*, Routledge.

Tasker, Y. (1993) *Spectacular Bodies: Gender, Genre And The Action Cinema*, Routledge.

Taylor, L. and Willis, A. (1999) *Media Studies: Texts, Institutions and Audiences*, Blackwell.

Tilley, A. (1991) 'Narrative', in D. Lusted (ed.) *The Media Studies Book: A Guide for Teachers*, Routledge.

Tunstall, J. (1977) *The Media are American*, Constable.

Van Zoonen, L. (1998) 'One of the Girls? The Changing Gender of Journalism', in C. Carter, G. Branston and S. Allan (eds) *News, Gender and Power*, Routledge.

Vestergaard, T. and Schrøder, K. (1992) *The Language of Advertising*, Blackwell.

Wells, M. (2002) 'TV Watchdog Attacks News Budget Cuts', *Guardian*, 6 March 2002.

Whitehorn, K. (2000) 'Same Old Story', *Guardian*, 1 December.

Williams, R. (1980) 'Advertising: Magic System', in R. Williams, *Problems in Materialism and Culture*, Verso.

Williamson, J. (1978) *Decoding Advertisements: Ideology and Meaning in Advertisements*, Marion Boyars.

Winston, B. (1995) *Claiming the Real: The Documentary Film Revisited*, British Film Institute.

WEB RESOURCES

Media organisations/companies

www.bbc.co.uk

www.bfi.org.uk (British Film Institute)

www.carlton.co.uk

www.channel4.co.uk

www.channel5.co.uk

www.cjr.org/owners (US journalism site detailing who owns what)

www.cnn.com

www.commedia.org.uk (Community Media Association)

www.cpbf.org.uk (Campaign for Press and Broadcasting Freedom)

www.dailyexpress.co.uk

www.dggb.co.uk (Director's Guild of Great Britain)

www.disneychannel.co.uk

www.equity.org.uk (Equity, the actors' union)

www.europemedia.net (latest news on European media)

www.filmeducation.org (resources for GCSE/A level film students)

www.freepress.org.uk (newsletter from CPBF)

www.ft.com (Financial Times)

www.granadatv.co.uk

www.htv.co.uk

www.imdb.com (Internet Movie Database – wealth of information on films)

www.independent.co.uk

www.indymedia.org (website for various alternative and independent media organisations)

www.itn.co.uk

www.itv.co.uk

www.media.guardian.co.uk

www.nuj.org.uk (National Union of Journalists)

www.radiotimes.beeb.com

www.reuters.com

www.s4c.co.uk (Welsh media site)

www.sky.co.uk

www.telegraph.co.uk

www.theherald.co.uk

www.timesonline.co.uk

www.vlv.org.uk (Voice of the Listener and Viewer)

Regulatory and audience research bodies

www.abc.org.uk (Audit Bureau of Circulations – provides data on ABC publications)

www.adassoc.org.uk (Advertising Association)

www.asa.co.uk (Advertising Standards Association)

www.bacc.org.uk (the BACC checks TV advertisements for compliance with various regulations)

www.barb.co.uk (Broadcasters Audience Research Board – provides TV viewing figures))

www.bbfc.co.uk (British Board of Film Classification)

www.bsc.org.uk (Broadcasting Standards Commission)

www.itc.org.uk (Independant Television Commission)

www.mediawatch.com

www.nmk.co.uk/industry_trends/default.cfm (Industry Trends: information about UK's new media industry)

www.ofcom.gov.uk/ (Office of Communications)

www.pcc.org.uk (Press Complaints Commission)

www.rab.co.uk (Radio Advertising Bureau)

www.radioauthority.org.uk

www.radio-now.co.uk/index2.htm (industry news on UK radio)

www.rajar.co.uk (Radio Joint Audience Research – provides radio listening figures)

Academic websites

www.aber.ac.uk/media/index.html (University of Wales, Communication and Media Studies website)

www.cf.ac.uk/jomec/vieira/index.html (doctoral research by Gabriela Vieira into children's use of media)

www.cult-media.com (online journal *Intensities: the journal of cult media*, hosted by the School of Journalism, Media and Cultural Studies, Cardiff University)

www.marxists.org/glossary/about/index.htm (Encyclopedia of Marxism with useful definitions of terms)

www.newmediastudies.com/ (UK University site exploring new media)

www.theory.org.uk/main.htm (UK website devoted by David Gauntlett devoted to Media and Cultural Studies)

▼ INDEX

Note: page numbers in italics denote illustrations

INDEX